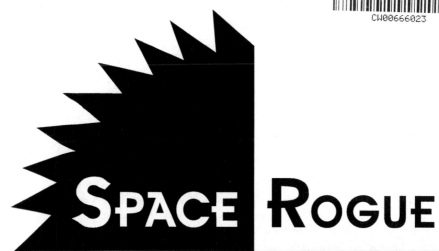

SPACE ROGUE

**HOW THE HACKERS
KNOWN AS
LØPHT CHANGED
THE WORLD**

CRIS THOMAS

SPACE ROGUE
How the Hackers Known as L0pht Changed the World

Copyright © 2023 Cris Thomas

ISBN 979-8-98-703240-4 (hardcover)
ISBN 979-8-98-703241-1 (paperback)
ISBN 979-8-98-703242-8 (eBook)

Library of Congress Control Number: 2022918006

Publisher's Cataloging-in-Publication data

Names: Thomas, Cris, author.
Title: Space rogue : how the hackers known as L0pht changed the world / Cris Thomas
Description: Includes bibliographical references. | Jenkintown, PA: Cris Thomas, 2023.
Identifiers: LCCN: 2022918006 | ISBN: ISBN 979-8-9870324-0-4 (hardcover) | 979-8-9870324-1-1 (paperback) | 979-8-9870324-2-8 (eBook)
Subjects: LCSH Hackers. | L0pht Heavy Industries. | Cyber intelligence (Computer security)--History. | Cyberspace--Security measures. | Computer crimes--Prevention. | BISAC COMPUTERS / Security / General | BIOGRAPHY & AUTOBIOGRAPHY / Personal Memoirs | BIOGRAPHY & AUTOBIOGRAPHY / Science & Technology | BUSINESS & ECONOMICS / Industries / Computers & Information Technology
Classification: LCC HV6773 .T46 2023 | DDC 364.16/8--dc23

This book is memoir. This work depicts actual events in the life of the author as truthfully as recollection permits and/or can be verified by research. It reflects the author's present recollections of experiences over time. Occasionally, dialogue consistent with the character or nature of the person speaking has been supplemented. Some events have been compressed, and some dialogue has been recreated.

Cover font (Ambient) used with permission copyright © 1993 by Eric Oehler.
Book and cover design by Shelby Gates.

First Edition: January 2023

www.spacerogue.net | @spacerog@mastodon.social | @spacerog

All my love to my wife, Maureen, without whose love, encouragement, and compliments this book would not have been written.

Thanks to Javaman for the motivation to start this book. It was his poignant words that made me realize the importance of this history and the significance of recording my own version of events.

CONTENTS

ACKNOWLEDGEMENTS

Writing a book is never a singular endeavor, and this one is no exception. Many thanks to Jen Ellis and Trey Ford for motivating me enough to finally write more than a few pages. My deepest thanks to Gabriella Coleman, Brian Martin, Robert Ferrell, and Richard Thieme for beta reading the manuscript, offering criticism, helping me fact-check, offering advice, and being a voice of reason on what to include and what was irrelevant. My developmental editor, Cathy Suter, helped to build the flow of the story and really turned this book into something worth reading. My wife, Maureen, deserves more thanks than I can write on these few pages. This is a much better book because of the time they spent reading and editing, as well as their full candor in providing feedback and ongoing support. Thank you.

INTRODUCTION

There have been a few efforts to capture small bits of L0pht stories over the years—a chapter in a book here or a long news article there. These attempts provided brief glimpses behind the curtain of the L0pht inner workings. Some of these efforts were fairly accurate and others—not so much. This version of the stories will bring some cohesiveness to the previously published material.

The L0pht began as a storage area, evolved into a clubhouse, transformed into a full-on hacker collective that testified before Congress and became a rising star of the dot-com era, and, finally, evolved into an almost mythical part of history. Along the way it inspired generations of hackers, helped birth the entire cyber security industry, and set the stage for ethical debates that are still raging. The L0pht has become more than just a sum of its parts. From people who only read the L0pht's early web pages or used the L0phtCrack password auditing tool, to those who visited the L0pht's physical location, L0pht Heavy Industries had a profound impact that still resonates nearly thirty years later.

Several years ago, I found myself in a nearly empty Congressional hearing room in one of the House or Senate office buildings, setting up a hacking training session for some Hill staffers with Jen Ellis and Trey Ford[1]. We spent a few hours configuring laptops and installing some basic hacking tools to allow the staffers to get hands-on keyboard time through a few basic hacker training sessions. The idea was to give the staffers a feel for just how easy hacking, or in this case, subverting cyber security measures actually was. We wanted to remove a bit of the mystery and mystique that often surrounds hacking.

Being in a congressional hearing room with its wood paneling, raised dais, and stately iconography lead me to tell stories of an earlier time when I was in a similar room along with some high-profile senators, numerous CSPAN cameras, and a packed audience during the L0pht's (in)famous Senate testimony in 1998. Soon I was the only one telling stories, and they were asking questions. By the time we finished setting up the laptops, Jen asked me why I hadn't written a book. I said I'd tried several times but always hit a wall. She encouraged me to keep trying.

I did, but I never got very far—a few pages at most. The story just felt so big, and it was hard to know where to start or what to include. Then a few months later, I had a brief text exchange with an old friend, who used the handle Javaman, that finally motivated me to write my version of the L0pht story. That time, over several weeks of nights and weekends, words came pouring out. Before I knew it, I had written 30,000 words and the trickle of memories had become a flood. Most of that flood occurred chronologically, but when putting the book together for publication, it made sense to move a few things around and group some other things together. I did my best to make note of parts of the story that are presented out of order, and I hope my choices make sense.

This book is the culmination of memory-mining, some deep web searches, and a lot of work. It is just one version of a complex story. My version of the L0pht story is no more important or accurate than any other. The L0pht happened and had an immense impact—but everyone involved will remember that impact differently. I sincerely hope that other versions of 'the L0pht book' get written. I would love to see this story from different perspectives—from those who were part of the L0pht and participated in it as well as those whose lives and experiences were impacted by the L0pht.

There are a few books that try to tell hackers stories from this same time period. One person from that time period, Kevin Mitnick, now a well-known hacker, has at least four books that attempt to tell his story, including one he wrote himself. Which is most accurate? Which tells the actual truth? I think the real truth is in the mix. The L0pht story is similar. No single person knows the complete story. As other versions of the story are told, we will get closer to the complex history of how the hackers known as the L0pht changed the world.

EARLY YEARS

I could hear the footsteps coming down the hallway. Quickly I released my finger from the light bulb to extinguish the light. I put my book down and laid my head on the pillow but kept it under the covers. I could hear the doorknob slowly turn. The hinge made that tiny creak, once as the door opened, then a pause, then again as the door closed. I waited a few seconds and then lifted my head and put my finger back on the light bulb to complete the circuit and turn the light back on. I continued reading with the blanket still pulled over my head.

###

I grew up in a mobile home on a seed farm in Winthrop, Maine, a small town in the middle of the state nestled between the capital of Augusta and the Lewiston-Auburn area. Our John Deere tractor, gleaming in its hand-painted, not-quite-the-right-shade green, was usually parked right out front alongside whichever Ford station wagon we had at the time.

Our mobile home wasn't mobile any longer, as it was up on blocks and my father had hand-built an entire second half of the house, technically making it a double-wide. We also had two long greenhouses. The first was an A-Frame nailed together out of two-by-fours, covered in plastic that my father had built by hand and was probably fifty feet long. The second was much longer, maybe 150 feet. While the frame was commercially built in the traditional half-circle style, it had been assembled and covered with plastic by hand. The entrance to both greenhouses faced our dirt driveway with the mobile home and its customized second half at the end.

There wasn't much in the way of technology in rural Maine in the seventies, pretty much just a television, a radio, and a telephone. Our television was an old large-console TV, black and white of course, with the stereotypical coat hanger covered in aluminum foil sticking out of the back, which allowed us to receive all four stations. Channel 8 WMTW, which carried ABC, was always a bit grainy, especially when it rained, since the transmitter was on top of Mount Washington way over in New Hampshire.

My father had a transistor radio which he had somehow permanently attached and wired into the electric pole next to the short greenhouse. It was exposed to the rain and snow, but every spring, when it was time to set the seedlings in the greenhouse, it would always work and would always be tuned to WPOR, the country music station out of Portland. In March, when there was usually still a foot or more of snow still on the ground, my brother and I would work in the 80-degree greenhouse listening to Waylon Jennings, Johnny Cash, Linda Ronstadt, John Denver, Dolly Parton, and the other greats of the mid-seventies country music scene.

Starting when we were probably six or seven years old, my brother and I would mix up "the soup," a mixture of water, peat moss, and commercial planting soil, and then fill seedling trays for my father to add seeds to. Tomatoes, marigolds, cucumbers, petunias, squash, pansies, lettuce, anything that needed to get an early start in the short Maine growing season would get planted in those trays of soup in the greenhouse.

We had a traditional Western Electric model 500 telephone. You may know the one—solid black plastic with a rotary dial. This phone was hooked to a party line that, although less expensive than individual service, forced you to share a phone line with your neighbor. As the name implies, both parties could listen in to the other parties' phone calls. This was pretty common in rural areas at the time, less so in more populated places.

The only other technology we had was a second transistor radio that my father would take with him on the tractor. This one was not as robust as the one on the pole next to the greenhouse, as it got replaced every couple of years. Carrying the radio on the tractor with him meant he couldn't jack it into the electric pole and instead had to use C and D cell alkaline batteries. These batteries would get depleted rather quickly. I would take these mostly depleted alkaline batteries and make flashlights out of them so I could read under the covers at night.

The batteries were easy for me to come by because my father would burn through a set in his portable radio about once a week.

Especially during spring planting or fall harvesting when he was on the tractor all day long. The batteries would be weak and almost used up but still had plenty of life left to light up one small bulb.

Light bulbs were a different matter. These I had to scavenge by taking apart sealed alkaline flashlights. They were simple flashlights but had no way to open to replace the batteries. My father always bought these things because they tended to last longer, were cheaper than normal batteries. Unfortunately, since the flashlight was completely sealed when the batteries were depleted, they were useless.

One day when I was very young, maybe four or five years old, I found one of these old flashlights, and as kids do, started banging on it with a hammer. Probably not the safest thing for a five-year-old to do, but once I got it apart, what I found inside was fascinating. I know, it was just a light bulb, a battery, and a switch, but I sat there for what seemed like hours just flicking the switch and watching as the metal contacts came together, essentially teaching myself the basics of an electric circuit. However, the battery was dead, and the light would not come on.

It may have been another year after I smashed that first flashlight open before I built my first flashlight. I had my father's old C and D cell batteries that he had cast aside after using up most of the charge in his radio and a light bulb from one of the sealed alkaline flashlights that I had smashed. For wire, I used garbage bag twist ties. Back in the seventies, each box of plastic garbage bags came with a bunch of twist ties to close the bags up with. These were not plastic but small thin pieces of wire usually covered with paper. My family tied a knot with the corners of the trash bag, so we ended up with a kitchen junk drawer full of these twist ties which were, for my purposes, three-inch-long insulated wires.

I would use two or three garbage bag twist tie wires and tape one exposed end of the wire to the negative end of one battery, then stack two or three batteries on top of the first one and tape them all together. Next, I would twist the other end of the wire around the bottom of the flashlight light bulb. Holding the batteries in my hand, I could use my thumb to touch the light bulb to the top of the batteries. Voilà, flashlight! With the added benefit of a sort of dead man's switch: if I fell asleep while reading at night, my hand would slide off the light bulb, not only preserving the battery but preventing my mother's discovery of me staying up past my bedtime.

This is pretty much how I spent my childhood. In between filling seedling trays, pulling weeds out of rows of corn, beans, and potatoes, and watering the tomato plants in the greenhouse, I was reading school library books under the covers at night with my homemade flashlight.

When I was eight or nine years old, we visited my Uncle Dale, who lived even deeper in the backwoods of rural Maine than we did. My uncle worked in the forestry business and years later would invent and sell a portable sawmill. He lived in a big house that he had built by hand with his wife, my Aunt Bea, and their four kids.

At some point my uncle had purchased a Pong video game. Pong was one of the first home video games, originally sold by Sears and then later by Atari. It was basically a really simple version of video tennis. The game worked by attaching the console to the external antennae terminals on your TV. You could then turn a knob on the console to make your racket or paddle move up and down to hit a white dot or "ball" that moved across the screen. The controllers were attached to the console and the game only worked in black and white. Its simplicity is so far removed from any sort of video game available today that I find it hard to even call it a video game. But I sat there on the floor in front of the TV playing Pong for hours while my parents visited my aunt and uncle. The game was completely enthralling. To watch something on the screen that I could control by turning a dial in my hand was like magic. My father had to pick me up and carry me out to the car screaming when it was time to go home.

When I was thirteen, my parents split. My mother took me and my brother, who is two years younger, and we moved to Auburn, Maine, about a half hour away. Compared to where we had been living, Auburn was a big city with all of twenty-three thousand people. We ended up on the outskirts of town on top of a hill in the middle of a huge apple orchard. The transition of having my parents split and moving to a new town was disruptive, as it is to all kids from broken homes. Like most kids in similar situations, I've struggled with that pain most of my life.

One day during the summer of 1981, a friend of the family whose name I have forgotten told us he was going to start selling a new item and wanted to bring it over to show us. It was the age of Tupperware,

Avon, Mary Kay, and Amway, all items people sold to friends and neighbors or door to door. At the time, it was a successful business model (for the businesses anyway, not always so great for the people doing the selling). When my mother told me he was coming over with his new products he was going to sell, I didn't really think much of it.

I watched as he walked up the driveway carrying this huge and obviously heavy suitcase. He brought it inside and tried to set it gently on the kitchen table, but it landed with a light thud. I was curious as to what was in the case, but to the extent as a teenager who thinks the suitcase might contain beauty products or vitamin supplements or, what I was really hoping for, chocolate bars. However, he dropped the front panel and revealed what looked to me like the inside of a spaceship. I stood there and stared while he got the power cord, looked for an outlet, and hooked up the front panel (which was actually the keyboard).

In the center of the device was a small five-inch glass square. On both sides were horizontal slots with latches and below that was a row of... things. At the time, I didn't know what they were. Each one was labeled in white lettering printed directly on the case. I would learn later that the device was called Osborne 1.

The Osborne 1 was the first commercially successful portable microcomputer, released in 1981. Despite reaching sales of 10,000 units per month, the company declared bankruptcy by late 1983.[2]

Our friend reached into his bag and pulled out this square flat plastic object in a paper holder. It was about five inches square, and when he removed the paper holder, you could see a large circular hole in the center. He inserted the plastic object into the horizontal slot and closed the latch. Then he reached around the side and flipped the power switch. The machine came to life. It started whirring, and weird grinding noises emanated from the horizontal slot. It was louder than I expected. Then the glass square in the center displayed glowing white words.

Over the next half hour he introduced me to BASIC, an early computer programing language[3]. He showed me simple PRINT and GOTO statements and how to make the screen fill up with the repeating words that said "Hello World." It fascinated me. This wasn't some dumb TV screen that had only had a few channels, which if you didn't like them, tough. Nor was it a simple video game that only had two or three variations on a theme. This was something you controlled, that you told what to do. Even if you told it the wrong way, it would try to do that too. When our friend told me it cost around two thousand dollars, I realized my mother could never afford one. It crushed me. It was amazing that he carried this very expensive machine around in the backseat of his car.

Within a few years, other personal computers became available and were sold at stores like RadioShack and Sears. Of course, whenever we went to the mall, I would head straight to any store that had computers on display. I quickly learned to escape whatever self-running demos the store had installed and then try to quickly type something in BASIC that would display something on the screen. Depending on how observant the salesperson was, I would have anywhere from a few seconds to a few minutes. Often, I only had time to write simple GOTO statements.

```
10 PRINT "TRS-80s are the best computers. You
should buy one!"
20 GOTO 10

RUN
```

My goal was always to make sure the print statement had over forty characters. Forty-character statements were as wide as the screen, so if the text was longer than that, it would wrap around and make a cool diagonal-looking pattern as the message scrolled down.

A couple of years later I started high school at the Walton High School in Auburn Maine. At the time, it was a freshman-only school on a hilltop on the other side of town. The student population was too large at the time to fit in the general high school, so they bused all the freshman to a completely different school. I think it is an elementary school today. One of the extracurricular activities offered was a computer club that met once a week in the mornings before school started. The "club" description was really a stretch, as the school only had one computer, a Commodore PET 4032. The 4032 was an integrated all-in-one computer with a small black-and-green screen that predated the more powerful Commodore 64 by two years. It was stuck in the corner of a classroom, and none of the teachers knew how to use it. There were probably seven or eight of us who showed up on the first day of the club. It was clear that most of us didn't know how to use the computer either. Two of the kids said they had computers at home, so the student advisor to the group, a math teacher, told one of those two kids, "You're in charge," and then left us alone. He sat on the other side of the room, graded papers all morning, and occasionally yelled at us to keep quiet.

The two kids who knew how to use the system weren't really interested in teaching the rest of us at all. In fact, they pretty much hogged the machine and didn't let anyone else touch it, so we got to stand behind them and just watch. The two of them would alternate between playing games they had brought with them from home and attempting to use BASIC to write their own game, but they weren't very good at that. I wasn't really interested in standing there watching someone else play games for forty-five minutes. So, after a few weeks, I stopped going to the club.

I have encountered that sort of superior attitude many times over the years. Each time I am reminded of sitting there in that classroom, watching someone else act like the aristocracy simply because they had a small amount of knowledge you lacked and access to expensive resources.

It wasn't until my junior year at the Edward Little High School that I was finally allowed take an actual computer class. The first semester was History of Computers, and the second semester was Practical Application. The only thing I really remember learning about from the first semester is Charles Babbage, who invented a weaving loom that could be programed with pieces of hole-punched paper (what would later be known as punch cards). He is considered the father of computers. I only remember that because the teacher made up this terrible rhyme "Charles Babbage, his head was full of cabbage." It was silly, but she said we would never forget it, and sure enough, I never have. I got an A+ in that class, and yet on my report card's note section, the teacher wrote "could do better." I remember going up to her after and pointing it out, saying, "How could I do better, I got the best possible grade?" And she said, "Yes, but you didn't apply yourself." I just stood there like, "What?" Looking back now, she was absolutely right; I hardly did anything in that class.

The second semester of the class included hands on the computers, finally! We were given an assignment to write a program that had some sort of animation. We were required to write the program out on paper first, then get it approved by the teacher before you could start typing it. I, of course, created a gigantic project. It was basically a graphic of a huge white Nike sneaker—with the characteristic Nike swoop logo in bright red—walking across the screen. I had it all drawn out on graph paper. It took me weeks to type it in via the keyboard, character by character. We didn't have floppy disks for the computers to save our work on; we only had tape drives, which used standard audio cassettes. At the conclusion of one class near the end of the semester, when I had almost finished typing the whole thing in, I entered the command to save my progress back to the cassette.

```
SAVE "SNEAKER",1
```

But I was in a hurry. I was late for my next class, and I didn't wait for the tape drive to finish saving. Instead, I hit eject before my work finished copying. I grabbed the cassette and ran to my next class. When I got back to the computer class the next day and tried to load my program, I realized what had happened. I was devastated. Somehow, I still got a B in the class. I asked the teacher how. She said even though I hadn't finished the project, I had written the program down on paper, so she had given me my grade based on that. I considered myself lucky.

I really had no idea what I was going to do after high school. We were just barely scraping by as it was; there was definitely no money to go to college. With my parents split and my home in the big city, high school was a rough time for me and my grades suffered. My poor grades meant scholarships were pretty much out. I was working the drive-through at Burger King after school with nothing to look forward to. The future was scary. I didn't want to be stuck asking people if they wanted fries with that for the rest of my life but didn't see many other options. During my early junior year, a military recruiter came to school. You got to get out of study hall if you listened to them, so I did. He talked about the ROTC program and college scholarships; he really sold it. They signed everyone up for the ASVAB (Armed Services Vocational Aptitude Battery) test that weekend. When the scores came back, he told me how well I had done. I thought, well, that's great, but my school grades are nowhere near good enough for an ROTC scholarship. But that got me thinking, and at some point in my junior year, I went down to the recruiting station across the river in Lewiston and signed up to for the Army Reserve.

Despite joining the Army Reserve, I quickly found out there still wasn't much in Maine for me. Although I pretty much knew that beforehand, the stark reality was a bit of a shock. I was doing my Reserve drills once a month, and I got a job working at the fish counter at the Stop & Shop supermarket. But I still had no money and no plan. It wasn't long before I returned to the recruiter and reenlisted for active duty. The GI Bill was my only option to get away from dead-end, no-skill jobs, and not to mention nowheresville, Maine.[3]

For the next three years, I carried around a fifty-pound ruck and an M16 rifle all over the back yard of Fort Ord in California. My unit, the 9th Infantry Regiment, deployed to Utah, Arkansas, Honduras, and Panama, yes, *that* Panama. I was mostly focused on my ETS (Estimated Time of Separation) date and counted down the number of days remaining until that last wake up. That, and figuring out how to get into college.

As I got close to the end of my enlistment, and I began to think more and more about college, I knew I would need a computer. One weekend I went to downtown Monterey, just outside the base, and started computer shopping. Unfortunately, over the previous three years I hadn't really saved any money. Every computer store I walked into I would look at the computers for a minute and then ask the salesperson if I could buy the computer on credit. They all said no. All the stores had mainly PC-XTs, or IBM PC compatibles based on the Intel 8088 chip. These machines were some of the very early personal computers with names like Compaq, Epson, Comtex and AST. The PC-AT computer, based on the Intel 286 chip, was still new and way out of my price range (Although at the time I had no idea what the computers' differences were other than the prices.) After taking the bus all around Monterey and visiting four or five different stores, I eventually wandered into ComputerLand on West Franklin Street and flat out asked, "Can I get a computer on credit?" The salesperson stunned me by saying "sure!"

I walked out with a Macintosh SE with 1 megabyte of RAM (Random Access Memory); two 800K, 3.5-inch floppy drives; and a copy of Microsoft Write (no, not Microsoft Word, MS Write). The SE was a successor to the Mac Plus and had just been released a few months earlier. I carried the large white box over to the bus stop, got on the bus, and got off at the barracks back on post.

I spent all my free time in the barracks seated in front of my new computer. While my Mac SE did not come with the famous MacWrite or MacPaint, it did come with a scripting language called HyperCard. I started buying *MacUser* magazine and reading every issue from cover to cover, including the ads. I often learned more from the ads than from the magazine articles. There were ads for scanners, modems, and networking gear—things I had never actually seen, but there they were in a magazine with descriptions of what they did. One of those ads was for MacWarehouse, a mail order computer supply company. I ordered their catalog, which had pictures of an attractive saleswoman in the bottom corner of most pages (I found out years later that it wasn't a stock photo and that she actually worked there; her name was Kerry.) I would read the description of each product and try to figure out from that description exactly what it would do. It was non-stop information ingestion for me. I bought a HyperCard book, I even found a local HyperCard user group. The group was all the way over in Carmel, about forty-five minutes by bus, and with my unit's deployment schedule I only had time to take the bus to a couple of meetings.

Eventually I tired of feeding 800K floppy disks into the two front slots of the machine. I spent $500 (a considerable amount of money in the late eighties) and ordered a 20-megabyte SCSI hard drive (that's megabytes, not gigabytes or terabytes). You can get about eighteen terabytes for the same amount of money today. The only problem was I couldn't figure out how to install the drive. I paid for the long-distance phone call to the hard drive company from the pay phone in the barracks hallway for tech support. They said to try a new cable and hung up. So I got on the bus, again, and made rounds of the computer shops. At one shop, I showed the salesperson the cable that came with the hard drive. He looked at me and then at the cable and said, "I don't know what this is, but it isn't a hard drive cable." He then grabbed a different cable and said, "This is a hard drive cable." I said, "No, this cable fits my drive; it just doesn't work. I need a new cable that looks just like this." He shrugged and said, "Sorry, can't help you." He had only ever worked on PCs and had never seen the fifty-pin internal SCSI hard drive cable used in Macs. The next store on the other side of town let me rummage through an old box of cables they had lying around, and I was able to find one SCSI ribbon cable that had to be three feet long. They charged me fifty dollars for it.

When I got back to the barracks and again tried to get the hard drive to work, I realized my crucial mistake. I had been so excited and in such a rush to get the hard drive working, I had plugged in the fifty-pin data cable but had completely forgotten to plug in the four-pin Molex power cable. It worked just fine after that. I never laugh at "is it plugged in?" jokes.

I finally ETS'd (was discharged) in December of '89 and headed back to Maine. I got a small apartment and a job at one of the local shoe factories across the river in Lewiston. I worked second shift, moving supplies around the hot factory floor from one rubber sole manufacturing machine to another. To the laughter of my coworkers in the break room, I gave myself the haughty title of Internal Product Transportation Specialist.

There really weren't many other opportunities available. The Lewiston-Auburn area has a population of maybe fifty thousand people, and if you didn't work in healthcare, there really wasn't much else to do (especially as unskilled labor) other than work in the few remaining shoe factories in town.

My apartment came with its own phone line, and I could finally get something I had only read about up until then: a modem. A modem allowed you to connect your computer to your telephone line so it could call other computers. Having my computer "talk" to another computer sounded really exciting to me. I spent two hundred dollars on a 2400-baud Hayes-compatible modem, which opened a new and priceless world. In early nineties Maine, you could only call your local town and each neighboring town without incurring a long-distance toll charge, but even with that limited calling area, I still had a half dozen local bulletin board systems (BBSs) I could dial into.

A BBS was a computer configured with a modem and special software that allowed other computers with a modem and special software to call each other. The person doing the calling could then read messages left by other people and leave messages in response. They could also trade software programs, transfer files, or even play text-based online games. Unlike today where dozens or even thousands of people can chat constantly online in real time, most BBSs were limited by the number of phone lines they had, usually one. The slowness of the data transfer and the relatively low power of the computers compared to today's meant everything was only in text—no movies and no pictures. You were lucky if you could even get the text displayed in color.

There were several BBSs in my local calling area. There was the L/A PC Forum (the L/A meaning Lewiston and Auburn) and The Kobayashi Alternative in Greene, Maine. The biggest BBS in the local calling area was Amig-Comm, a huge two-line BBS with lots of Amiga software. The Amiga was an early personal computer that was completely incompatible with other computers. Which of course, because I was using a Macintosh, meant all the Amiga software was useless to me.

There was also a very small board called the IMF Message Base. It was so small that no one really ever called it. The board wasn't listed on Jason Scott's BBS List archive at textfiles.com[4] when I recently checked, and I can't even find a listing for it on my own BBS phone number lists from back then. It had no files or games, just messages. I never found out what IMF was supposed to stand for,[5] so I would occasionally retype newspaper articles about the International Monetary Fund into the BBS. No one ever complained or even responded to my posts. I would check the call logs on the BBS, and I could tell a few people were calling, but almost no one left any messages. I couldn't figure out why the SYSOP, or owner of the BBS, kept it online, but it intrigued me. I kept calling, checking to see if anyone else had called and left a message. (I never watched the Mission Impossible TV show so I never made the connection between IMF and Impossible Mission Force.)

Various flame wars, or passionate arguments about nothing of consequence, erupted on the message bases of busier systems. A perennial favorite argument was who had the better computer. There was a long-standing argument between Mac and Amiga owners. I was heavily in the Mac camp and wrote many vitriolic posts extolling the greater performance and capabilities of the Macintosh while the Amiga users constantly told me I was wrong. Until, one day, one of the Amiga users challenged me, saying he could prove that the Amiga was better. That I should go over to his house so he could demonstrate the superiority of his Amiga. I walked a few blocks away from my apartment and met this kid, who was probably only thirteen years old. He led me, then twenty-two years old, into his basement to show me his exceptional Amiga.

He was right. The Amiga could run circles around my Mac SE. Multiple windows opened at once with color graphics running in the background, all while playing music and dialing into a BBS. My Mac SE under System 6 was still black and white. It did not yet have preemptive multitasking and wouldn't until the introduction of the MultiFinder with System 7 a few years later. My Mac couldn't do half of what the Amiga could do. Even after System 8 was released in 1997, a Macintosh would struggle to do as much as that Amiga did that afternoon.

It took me many years to recognize it, maybe decades, but that humbling fifteen-minute basement meeting where a young kid's computer showed funky animated graphics and multitasked significantly influenced how my online persona developed over the years. I became much less prone to flame someone or get involved in so-called religious wars online. In fact, I would often watch from the sidelines and recognize some of the same arguments I had made when trying to extol the virtues of one computing platform over another. I also realized that while I still enjoyed using my Mac and thought it was the best for me, no one single platform was the best at all things; something that would become apparent to me years later when Windows 3.1 became more popular. I also realized then that there were vast worlds of computing that I knew absolutely nothing about. Years later, as I became exposed to other micro computer platforms, mainframes, different operating systems, etc., I would think back to that one meeting with that kid and his Amiga and remind myself that I really knew nothing.

Eventually I tired of calling Amiga-based bulletin boards or the local teacher's educational board. I wanted to call some Macintosh BBSs, maybe even set up my own BBS. I made a few calls to long distance systems, but I kept them short, as I could not afford the long-distance charges on a minimum-wage salary. However, I eventually heard about Hermes BBS software, which would run on my Mac. I just had to have a copy. I found a BBS that claimed to have it available, but it was so big it kept the software offline. I pestered the SYSOP of the board to put the software online so I could download it. I called the board every day for about a week, checked to see whether the file was online, and then left increasingly angry messages for the SYSOP. I was the classic asshole user.

With my own copy of the BBS software, I set about partitioning, or dividing via software, my tiny 20 MB hard drive into two 10 MB chunks and setup the BBS on one side. I kept the BBS online for maybe a month and received a few dozen calls at most. It didn't help that the software would often crash while I was at work or sleeping, or that I would take the system down myself anytime I wanted to use the computer or dial out to other BBSs. I was lucky to get the few calls I did.

###

One reason I had joined in the Army in the first place was to find a way to college and get away from dead-end jobs in shoe factories and supermarkets. During the summer of 1989 while I was walking around the barracks, or standing in line at the mess hall, or anywhere there was downtime, I would pull out a stack of homemade vocabulary word flashcards in preparation to take the SATs.

The library at Fort Ord was small, but I started using it to research different colleges. I ended up applying to about a half dozen schools, including MIT. MIT was unusual because it required an in-person interview with an alumnus. I called the alumna assigned to me and set up an interview time and realized they were all the way on the other side of town and about a mile from the nearest bus stop. As I walked up to her house a little tired and a bit sweaty, I found out her house had just been robbed a few hours earlier, as in, the police car was leaving the driveway. Unsurprisingly, the interview did not go that well, and I was not accepted into MIT.

Every other school I applied to accepted my application, and I eventually decided on Boston University. I think I chose BU based solely on its perceived reputation and not based on which school I thought would be the best fit for me. As it turns out, it was not a good fit. I had been away from formalized education for a few years, but I quickly remembered how much I disliked that environment.

Boston University was also an expensive school. I hadn't bothered to figure out the cost of school prior to arriving. I had received no guidance or advice from the financial aid office, but naively assumed my GI Bill would magically cover everything. After enrolling and arriving on campus, I discovered that the GI Bill was only going to cover three hundred dollars a month. So I sought additional assistance from the financial aid office. After listing out my assets and income, the financial aid officer subtracted three hundred dollars from the financial aid package. I questioned his actions. He said that since I had that three-hundred-dollars-a-month income, I didn't need that amount in aid, so it was removed from the package. I just sat there dumbfounded. Three years of crunching gravel in the US Army for zero practical benefit.

Of course, I took a computer class: Introduction to C, or maybe it was Programming 101, but I remember on that first day there were easily one hundred people in one of those huge auditorium classrooms. The instructor spent most of the class ranting at everyone about making sure that assignments were turned in on time and that there would be no acceptable excuses for late assignments—especially the school's network being down, which evidently it was, a lot. That was a lesson I always took to heart. Having just gotten out of the military, I knew that the maximum effective range of an excuse was zero meters, so not blaming the computers for missing an assignment was something I could relate to.

For the rest of that first class, the instructor went over rudimentary things, such as the location of the terminal labs on campus and how to dial into the school's modem pool. He then covered a brief introduction of some basic unix commands like "cd" and "ls" to navigate the file system. At the end of the class, he told everyone to read the first three chapters of the assigned book and handed out a C program printed out on a sheet of paper. That week's assignment was to retype the program while fixing all the bugs, and then drop the completed, working program file in a directory on one of the school's main computers. He did not instruct us on actual computer coding at all.

I went straight from that class to the North side of Commonwealth Ave, across the street and behind the School of Communications building to what was at the time the dark alley of Cummington Street. There, tucked into the mildew-scented basement, were several rows of dumb terminals set up on cheap folding conference tables. The terminals were simple screens and keyboards connected by wire to the larger mainframe computer in another room. There were maybe four or five terminals on each row of tables with metal folding chairs in front of them. The neon green-and-orange screens were vainly trying to make a dent in the wash of off-white fluorescent light from the ceiling.

I immediately sat down on one of the wobbly folding chairs, cracked open the assigned book, logged into the terminal, and started to not only teach myself how to use unix but attempted to debug the program from the handout. It was a pretty simple birthday program. You would enter your birthday, and it would tell you how many days old you were. About three hours later, I had not only completely debugged the program but added numerous features, like days until your next birthday and a little ASCII birthday cake. I also added a ton of comments and banners, making it the most over-the-top birthday program you could create. With nothing else to do when I was done, I set about exploring.

My newly learned unix computer commands of `cat`, `finger`, `cd`, `ls`, and a few others were great to poke around with, even though I had no idea what I was looking at. The talk command was interesting, but no one else on the system was interested in chatting with a freshman;

they were all busy doing whatever it was you did in September on a college computer system. Besides, the talk command took over your terminal, and you couldn't chat or do other stuff at the same time. But seeing the split screen of the talk command and watching words someone else was typing appear in real time, even if that person was only in the room next door, or even the next table over, was amazing. With enough poking around I also found NetHack. NetHack is a text-based adventure game where you are likely to be eaten by a gru.

I vaguely remember stumbling out of the terminal lab that night barely able to stay awake and somehow navigating my way across campus to Bay State Road and my dorm room. The next day, I tried dialing from my Mac to the modem pool. It worked okay, but the black-on-white text of the Mac SE screen didn't have the same effect as the green-on-black terminal screen (I still use green on black as my favorite terminal colors today.) While the modem in my dorm worked fine, I had three other roommates who shared the one phone line, so spending long hours online connected with my dorm computer would not work. Instead, I spent many long hours in a dank basement on the other side of campus.

Adjusting to college life and formal education wasn't working for me. It didn't help that I had taken three years off from school; that the class sizes were gargantuan and fast-paced; that I was in a large, strange city; that I was feeling isolated; or that I spent way too much time in a dank basement staring at a CRT. It wasn't long before I stopped going to classes all together, including the computer class. It was frustrating that the instructor expected you to know the stuff he wanted you to know—not the stuff you wanted to know—and seemed to have no interest in actually teaching you anything. So, while I kept going to the terminal lab in the basement, kept poking around the BU computer network, and kept absorbing new information at an amazing rate, I wasn't receiving any grades.

Everything came to a head after Christmas break when I didn't have any money to pay for the next semester and still owed thousands for the previous semester. After a few weeks, BU evicted me from the dorms. I ended up sharing an apartment in Allston near the old Stockyard restaurant with a couple of guys who had advertised for a roommate in the *Boston Phoenix* newspaper. Soon after I moved in, I discovered they were heavy into their marijuana smoking, but I didn't mind. I'd told them I would need my own phone line, so I stayed in my room and logged on to BBSs when I wasn't working while they stayed in the living room and got high.

The first job I got after leaving Boston University was with Bayview Security, a physical security company (basically rent-a-cop). You wear a shirt with a funny-looking badge on it and try to look tough and intimidating with a Motorola radio in your hand. The first place they stuck me was the LaFayette Place Mall. The mall was located a few blocks from the old Boston Combat Zone in one direction and Downtown Crossing in the other direction. The shopping center was pretty much in decline from the day it opened, and by the time I started working there, it was fast on its way to the bottom. Many of the stores were empty and foot traffic was minimal, but it gave me a paycheck.

I had little to do other than work; I needed money, and I didn't enjoy hanging out with my pothead roommates very much, so I volunteered for every work shift I could. This often meant working one shift in the afternoon, where I would walk around the ghost town of that mall, which at that point had maybe six or seven stores open, and then work an overnight shift. The overnight shift meant either watching the security camera monitors in the control room upstairs or babysitting the fire alarms down in the basement. Evidently, the building owners wanted someone in the fire alarm room. The fire department had access to all of the necessary equipment already, so I had no idea what I was supposed to do in case of a fire other than sit there and maybe chat with the firefighters when they showed up. But if they wanted to pay me to sit there, then I would sit there.

The basement fire alarm room was barren. There was a small desk and a chair in a brightly lit room and a selection of old dog-eared, worn-out magazines. On one side of the room were huge six- and eight-inch pipes painted white with large red hand-crank valves. On the other wall was nothing but panel after panel of fire alarm boxes with blinky red lights.

After a couple of hours staring at them on my first night, I explored exactly what systems were there on the walls. I didn't know the first thing about fire alarm systems, but it was amazing what you could learn just by looking. Looking at where the wires were going, looking at which lights were lit and which ones weren't, looking at the small labels and icons next to switches. It turns out that fire alarm systems are actually pretty simple. And then, there between the panels, I saw what looked like an unused telephone jack.

I thought there was no chance it would work, but I still couldn't wait until my next shift. I brought a cheap telephone I had lying around with me to work the next night, plugged it into the phone jack, and picked up the receiver. The telltale buzz of a dial tone emanated from the speaker. I immediately hung up. I couldn't believe it. I picked up the receiver again, and this time dialed the local automatic time announcing number.

"US Naval Observatory master clock, at the tone, Eastern Daylight Time, eleven hours, three minutes, fifty seconds." Beeeep.

Unbelievable. My supervisor checked up on me that night. He didn't usually; he had several sites to monitor, and there was nothing going on in the fire control room in the basement of a mall.

When he came in, I asked, "Hey, any problem if I bring my computer in here and get some schoolwork done?" Most of the other employees who worked the night shift were in college, and he had no idea I wasn't in school anymore.

He said, "Sure, as long as you don't fall asleep, I don't really care what you do in here."

I lugged my nearly twenty-pound Mac SE onto the Green Line subway in Allston and rode the train all the way downtown to Park Street, then up the stairs of the train station, across three large city blocks, and then down the basement stairs into the little fire control room. Then I would sit all night long and log into BBSs using that one active phone jack I had found on the wall. I didn't dare make any long-distance calls; I was sure that someone would notice this one phone line suddenly racking up big phone bills, so I only called the local systems. Boston wasn't Lewiston-Auburn, so there were more than a few BBSs within the local calling area.

FINDING THE LØPHT

One of the first things I would do when calling a new BBS was to check out their list of other BBSs and scan it for boards I hadn't called yet, especially local boards. This is how I stumbled across the underground systems, or the elite boards in the Boston area. I started with completely legit and above-ground boards like the Boston Computer Society (BCS) BBS and from there branched out to boards with names like Buckman's Tavern, Mud Hut, and Myron's Manor. Looking for Macintosh bulletin boards, I quickly found Sinbad's Galleon, a two-line Mac BBS specializing in pirated high-end graphics and animation software like Photoshop, Pro Tools, Maya, Aldus 3D, and other premium packages that would normally cost several thousand dollars per copy. Not that I would have had any idea how to use them or that my Mac SE was fast enough to even run them, but Sinbad's had very active message bases about all things Macintosh.

The Works was the preeminent underground board in Boston, but despite that, it was relatively easy to find. It ran a customized version of Waffle BBS software, customized so much that I barely recognized the interface. It had special custom commands like "fnord" (I don't remember what it did) that weren't listed anywhere. You had to find them on your own. The Works was a unique environment; I felt connected to the message bases and by extension the people that wrote the messages. I became intimately familiar with individual writing styles and looked forward to when certain people would post. Even though I had never met them, I began to feel connected to people with names like "The Death Vegetable," "Bubble Sorter," "White Knight," "GarbageHeap," "Tweety Fish," and other nonsensical handles. I spent months reading every single message on The Works, not wanting to miss out on anything. It took so long because The Works, like most other BBSs, had a daily time limit so that one person wouldn't keep the phone line busy and other people would be allowed to call in. So I would read through as much as I could with each call, absorbing as much information as possible. Much of it was inane banter, simple chat, and, of course, flame wars, but tucked in between were small flakes—and sometimes huge nuggets—of information gold. Maybe a default password to some rare computer system, a useful command for some other system, an explanation about how certain telephone switches operated, or the simple breakdown of how internal computer communications worked. I found it all immensely fascinating and didn't want to miss any of it. I didn't want to jump in at the end of a conversation and start talking about things that had already been discussed or that everyone else already knew. The ebb and flow of the messages, the long-forgotten flame wars, the nuggets of information here or there really made it feel like home to me, and by the time I got through all the messages and started posting my own, I felt like I had known everyone else on the board my entire life.

One of the unique things about The Works is that it had a UUCP (Unix-to-Unix Copy Protocol) gateway, which was basically a connection to the internet. This was my first exposure to the Internet in a format that I could consume. I had Internet access at Boston University but didn't really know about or understand it. It wasn't talked about in class, and I didn't know anyone at the time who could explain it to me. I didn't even discover Usenet, a worldwide distributed messaging system, until the last few weeks I was at school. It was like drinking from a fire hose. When I left BU, I lost all access I had to the Internet. So having this UUCP gateway, this extra connection to the Internet just a phone call away via The Works, was a big deal.

A UUCP gateway to the Internet was nothing like Internet access today. First, it was still all text-based, and there was no web or graphical interface. About the only thing you could do through the UUCP gateway was send email, but back then you could do a lot with email. For instance, you could send a command via email to an FTP (File Transfer Protocol) server and receive files from other computers on the Internet via email, all through The Works email system.

From The Works and Sinbad's Galleon, I eventually found my way to more elite and deeper underground boards. Boards like Calvary, Black Crawling Systems and ATDT East. Many of these underground boards were run by folks who would later be pivotal in the creation of the L0pht. L0pht cofounder Golgo13 ran the Calvary BBS and

L0pht cofounder Brian Oblivion ran the Black Crawling Systems BBS. Magic Man and Omega ran a board called ATDT East and later handed over SYSOP duties to Count Zero, also a L0pht founder.

I get asked about how I chose the handle Space Rogue a lot. I wish the story was a little more exciting. Shortly after I left Boston University and was working as a rent-a-cop at the Lafayette Place Mall, a new BBS I called for the first time (I think it was simply called "M") requested users to create a unique username, something totally new, that had not been used on any other system. The goal was to foster open communication without the baggage an existing identity would bring with it. I thought anonymity was an intriguing idea—no one would know who anyone else was. Elite or lamer, old timer or newbie, it wouldn't matter; everyone on this new BBS would start out at the same level. I thought really hard about a new handle.

Your handle became your identity. It was the only unique item you took with you online. Your handle was linked to your reputation, your hacking capabilities, and your previous exploits. It was essentially a full resume summed up in one word or phrase.

BBSs were all text at the time—no graphics, icons, or avatars to go along with your posts and musings. The only thing that set your messages apart from everyone else's was your username. Your status was based on what you wrote, and it was all attached to your handle. Many early systems could only accommodate eight-character usernames, often not enough for a full first or last name, so people started to get creative, and handles became the norm.

I wanted something cool for this new BBS. When the only thing separating your electronic bytes from someone else's bytes was your name or handle, that moniker takes on a greater significance. I started looking around my bedroom for inspiration, and I hit upon the book I was reading. *Cyberpunk: Outlaws and Hackers on the Computer Frontier*[6] by Katie Hafner and John Markoff. The book was over the top, full of exaggeration and inaccuracies, but still enthralling. While I didn't know it at the time, the book had a significant influence on me.

I began free associating with the title, especially the cyber part. Even at that point I knew using any handle with the word "cyber" in it would not be a wise choice (In these early days of the Internet, "cyber" was considered an almost dirty word.) But "cyber" lead me to "cyberspace," so I started working with "space" instead and somehow hit on "Space Rogue." I spent maybe all of ten minutes coming up with it. There was a new BBS that I wanted to get into; I didn't have time to stand around trying to pick the perfect handle. I just need something new that was good enough for right now. I thought it would be a throwaway, one-time use; I would use it on this board and that would be it. I had no idea that "Space Rogue" would stick so well that I would still be using it nearly thirty years later.

It wasn't until a year or two later when I was pawing through a discount software bin at some corner computer store when I came across the video game *Space Rogue*, which had been released by Origin Systems in 1989. I remember standing there dumbstruck in the middle of the store, staring at the box with the words "Space Rogue" in huge letters across the top and some goofy looking guy with a helmet, leather jacket, and scarf of all things. Why would you

SPACE ROGUE

need a scarf in space? It was a very newbie mistake to pick a handle from popular culture—anything from a popular movie or TV show was generally considered lame. An obscure reference to some minor unknown cyberpunk novel was the height of eliteness, but a name from a video game? That just screamed "noob."

By that point, it was already too late. Sure, I could have changed my handle then, or even now for that matter. Some people change their handle all the time, but constantly changing handles make it hard to keep track of who people are. I had worked hard to get Space Rogue into some sort of elite status, and I wasn't about to throw it away and start over just because I found a game with the same name. Besides, the game was already several years old; I had never heard of it before, and most other people around at the time probably hadn't heard of it either. I figured the game would disappear into obscurity, but my handle hopefully wouldn't.

Of course, a decade later, Steam happened. Steam is an online video game digital distribution platform which has resurrected many old video games and made them available for play online. So now you can connect to Steam and play *Space Rogue* as it was on an Apple II or Commodore 64. Instead of fading into obscurity, the game had a minor resurgence in popularity in the late 2000s. Now I constantly get the question, "Space Rogue? Is that from the game?" Um, no, no it's not.

The Works was an online collective gathering place, the central point of community for all the hackers in the 617-area code. In 1991 or

'92, the board started having what they called "Works Gatherings," which sounds like exactly like what it was. People would physically gather to meet each other and talk face to face. I had never met anyone that I knew online before, so there was definitely a bit of nervousness the first time I ventured out to the landmark Au Bon Pain café in Harvard Square. I would saunter up to the counter and order my large iced Americano and then find a spot to hang around outside near the cement chess tables where Harvard students would try to win against old men. When the weather was bad, we would gather in the far corner of the pizza restaurant on the second floor of The Garage, a mall built out of an old parking garage, until the owner realized we were just taking up space and not actually buying anything. He kicked us out.

Despite meeting in person, most people still used their online identities and handles. So Count Zero simply became Zero in person, or Kingpin would get shortened to KP. Although most people already knew each other online, there was still a small level of mistrust between individuals within the group. Sharing a real name with someone was considered a high form of trust (This may be related to an early cyberpunk novella by Vernor Vinge, *True Names*[7].) Thirty years later, I still keep in touch with some of these people and yet still do not know their real name, just their handle.

These occasional Works gatherings eventually morphed into "2600 Meetings" and occurred regularly on the first Friday of the month. *2600* is a print magazine that covers hacker topics and is named after the long-distance telephone signaling frequency of 2600 hertz. The magazine has endorsed hacker meetups in large cities around the world for decades. As the Boston 2600 meeting grew larger, sometimes as many as forty people showed up. After the Harvard Square pizza joint kicked us out, we ended up moving to the food court at the Prudential Center. It was a good mix of people, from preppy to grunge, from high school students to people in their late twenties, but most of the group was male. There were a few women who would attend regularly, but they were vastly outnumbered. We would hang out on the patio in the summer and in the corner of the food court away from everyone else during the winter. The Boston 2600 meetings still happen on the first Friday of the month. Last I checked, 2600 meetings were back in Harvard Square at The Garage (now in the new food court instead of the pizza place).

My security job at the Lafayette Place Mall ended when the mall finally closed. The recession of the 1990s had taken its toll, and a large poorly designed mall stuck between two neighborhoods with high crime rates was a quick casualty. The security company kept me on, though, and sent me to work at Lotus Development Corporation, one of the first large software companies across the river in Cambridge. They had hundreds of employees and occupied space in at least six different buildings. Lotus was also seeing the effects of the recession and had just started outsourcing its physical security force. This allowed me to casually tell people I worked *at* Lotus; I just didn't mention that I worked as a security guard for a different company.

My job was to sit at the front desk of one of the many Lotus buildings and check ID badges of employees entering, as well as check the paperwork of employees leaving and wanting to take computers home with them. Laptops were pretty much unheard of, being too large and underpowered for any practical use. Instead, Lotus had standardized a brick-shaped PC that could easily be connected to a keyboard and monitor for its employees to take home. These weighed eight to ten pounds and required the security guard—me—to verify the serial number and the paperwork authorization from their manager before the employee walked out with it.

I could verify the employee information from one of the two terminals at each guard station. One was a PC running Windows 3.1 and Lotus Notes 3.0, and the other was a dumb terminal, usually a Wyse WY-60 connected to the company's VAX mainframes in another building. This setup allowed me to look up employees by name, see the corresponding office and phone numbers, and view a list of what equipment the employee was authorized to remove from the building.

Just like at the mall, I worked as many shifts as I could get, often pulling doubles or even triples, especially on weekends and holidays when the pay was better. One reason I would volunteer for so many shifts, especially at some less busy buildings, was because I had found access to the Lotus modem pool via its mainframe VAX system.

Two of my fellow employees, a man and a woman who were obviously dating, would only work the night shift and only in the Lotus Development Building (LDB). The LDB building was across the street from Lotus's main Rogers Building and was next to the Charles River, bordering Edwin Land Blvd. They never volunteered for any other shift and for some reason always resisted working at any other building. One day, I relieved them at the end of their shift at LDB, and I noticed the terminal screen still displaying some unusual information I hadn't seen before. It wasn't the normal employee roster; I didn't recognize it and had no idea what it was.

I pointed to the screen and asked, "Hey, what's that?"

"Just our homework," one of them replied.

"Homework?"

"Yeah, MIT? Just our homework for our Computer Science class."

I was a little surprised. "Oh, you can connect to MIT from here?" I asked, assuming it was some sort of network connectivity thing as a special arrangement between Lotus and MIT, which was literally a few blocks away.

"Yeah, just enter 'CONNECT 9600,' and it drops you to the modem pool, and you can dial out," he said as he logged out of MIT, disconnected, grabbed his bag, and then left with his girlfriend.

9600 baud was the top speed of high-speed modems of the day.

I stood there stunned, trying to comprehend what he had told me. Did he say "modem pool?" No way, I thought. I slowly sat down at the terminal as they walked away, trying to remember what he'd said. I was thinking there is no way this will work.

I looked at the terminal command prompt and typed:

CONNECT 9600

and hit return.

The screen went blank.

Nothing.

I pressed return a few times, and the cursor moved down the screen but still no response.

I knew it couldn't be that easy... and yet, somehow, they were connected to MIT. And he'd told to me enter "CONNECT 9600." It had to work. I tried entering a basic Hayes AT command. The Hayes command set is the near-universal set of commands that control all modems and having spent so much time with my modem at home, I knew large portions of the Hayes modem protocols. I entered

AT

and hit the return key. The system immediately spit back

OK

I almost fell out of my chair. It worked, unbelievable! I tried dialing one of the local boards whose number I knew by heart.

ATDT 4923208

No response.

ATDT 6174923208

No response.

ATDT 16174923208

Still no response. Hmm, I was definitely connected to a modem but couldn't figure out why it wouldn't dial the number. Not being able to hear the annoying modem sounds or see the blinking lights wasn't helping, and in fact, the silence gave me a rather uneasy feeling. Oh, wait, let me try...

ATDT 9,16174923208

Success! It connected; the BBS welcome screen scrolled down the terminal. The modem needed the "nine" first because the modem was connected to the internal office telephone system. The "nine" told the system to connect to an outside line before dialing the rest of the numbers. I looked up to see if anyone was watching, but it was the first thing in the morning, and I was the only one there. I logged into the BBS and read some messages in the neon-green-on-black color of the Wyse terminal.

My work life immediately changed. From then on, I would purposely try to get shifts at some of the buildings with fewer employees like One Canal Park or the Lotus Manufacturing Building a few blocks away. Overnight shifts were the best. Usually, the only actual job requirements were to answer the telephone and make a walk around the building once every hour. I would just sit there calling BBS systems in between building patrols for eight hours. At some point I took a risk and called long distance. I found boards that required voice verification and sysops who thought it very odd that I could speak on the phone while I was connected to their BBS.

"You have two phone lines?"

"Ah, yup."

"What do you do for work that you can afford two phone lines?"

"Ahhh, I work at Lotus."

"Oh."

Long distance from the modem pool was a bit scary. I didn't have any codez (a string of numbers used to bill long-distance calls) or tricks to get free long-distance calls like so-called l33t hackers. So, I made a couple of long-distance calls and then waited. Wondering what would happen when the phone bills came in and they tried to figure out who was dialing out of the modem bank at three a.m. for an hour-long call to Boise, Idaho. But nothing happened. I assume the bills came in and they got paid and no one ever audited who made what calls. I suspect my few phone calls barely made a difference in the overall phone bill, at least not enough for anyone to notice.

The downside to this arrangement was that I had no way to download and save files, let alone upload. And even if I could have saved the files locally, I had no way to get them off the Lotus VAX system, so I again concentrated on the message bases and mined for those small flakes of useful and interesting information. I would scroll through messages for hours on end, most of it inane banter, but occasionally a message or even an entire thread would fill my screen with nearly magical nuggets of information.

Since I had no way to save files, I would often just let random text files scroll down the screen, attempting to read them as fast as the modem could deliver them. There were files detailing the inner workings of the telephone system, various computer systems, how to pick locks, lyrics to popular songs, arcade game cheat codes, lists of custom AT commands for various modems, bomb recipes, lists of credit card numbers, lists of common passwords and the systems they worked on, guides on how to bypass software copy protection, guides on how to get onto the Internet and what to do when you get there, fan fiction, humor, erotica, lots of UFO-related stuff, files on how to write computer viruses, and even the viruses themselves. There, in a few paragraphs scrolling by in a monochrome glow were the secrets to the universe. If I could only read them all, then I would have all the knowledge—everything would be known.

Most of this information could have been found in a well-equipped library if you looked hard enough. The difference was that someone had rewritten and typed in all this information. It was all text. Photos or graphics on the computer were too large for the systems of the day; they would have taken hours to transmit at modem speeds, not to mention that most home computers didn't have color monitors (let alone the ability to display photos on the screen). Text was king, but someone had to type it in. Scanning and OCR (optical character recognition) weren't available to the average BBS user and were not very robust technologies yet. During the process of information transcription, the data changed. While the source may have been a college textbook or a dry, dusty volume from the library, seldom were the words copied exactly; instead they were often paraphrased and reworded, making the information more digestible than the original academic format it may have been in, and also prone to errors.

BBS text files also had this aura, a mystique, of forbidden knowledge. It didn't matter if it was about a telephone switching system or humorous fan fiction. They often conformed to the community's anti-establishment, anti-government leanings. This mentality arose after numerous run-ins with law enforcement, such as the 1990 Secret-Service-led Operation Sundevil,[8] or the passage of numerous vague laws such as the Computer Fraud and Abuse Act (CFAA),[9] the Electronic Communications Privacy Act[10] and the Stored Communications Act,[11] all of which made some part of exploring the Internet illegal.

There was also the prosecution of Knight Lightning, the editor of the underground electronic magazine (e-zine) *Phrack*, for publishing a document about the Enhanced-911 system.[12] A document that was later found to be publicly available for thirteen dollars. Then there was the raid on the game publishing company Steve Jackson Games[13] on the suspicion of facilitating online crime—in other words, the Secret Service rousting a bunch of teenagers for simply hanging out in a mall food court.[14] This persecution of hackers helped to perpetuate the use of pseudonyms or handles in an attempt obscure identity. What hackers saw as an overreach and overreaction by authority generated a culture of secrecy in the online world and began a long distrust of government rule.

One unexpected advantage to working really late shifts at nearly abandoned office buildings was the trash. The building at One Canal Park was getting cleaned out as the lease was up, and Lotus had already moved most of the employees elsewhere. The clean-out process took months, and there was a construction dumpster parked in the loading dock area of the building. I checked it nightly as part of my patrol rounds in between using the modem pool to call out to BBSs. Usually it was nothing more than the paper contents of people's desks, but occasionally I would find printed manuals or even old hardware. I would rescue all of this from the landfill, carry it back on the subway to my apartment in Allston, and add it to my growing pile of cast-off computers, manuals, cables, parts, and pieces.

Eventually I felt it was time to leave the security company and therefore Lotus. I ended up at another security company doing residential security of apartment buildings, most of which were residential buildings in economically depressed areas around Boston. One of the job requirements was that I drive from one location to the other in the company car. The car was white with the name of

41

the company emblazoned on the side in big gold letters. The only problem was that when I accepted the position, I didn't have a driver's license. I never really needed one up until then. I wasn't aware during the interview that the job would require you to drive, so when they asked me if I had a clean driving record, I figured it was just part of the background check. I truthfully answered yes. Technically, since I didn't have a license, my driving record was not only clean, but it was also spotless. I had my learner's permit for some time at that point, so I quickly scheduled and took the driving test. Thankfully, I passed on the first try.

This job is where I ran into my first evil boss: alcoholic and verbally abusive. He would drunkenly call me late at night while I was driving around checking on the security guards at various sites. He would just yell at me over the phone for half an hour, sometimes about the game he was watching on TV, or how I wasn't doing my job well enough, or whatever he happened to want to yell about that evening. It was soul crushing. Needless to say, I didn't stay with that job very long. After six months, I was ready to just quit with no other prospects, no longer caring about how such a short employment time looked on my resume, or even how I would cover my rent.

Out of the blue, I got a call back from an application I had sent months earlier to CompUSA, a national computer reseller, which I had completely forgotten about.

Receiving that call was surprising. At that point I had no professional computer experience at all and had mostly only ever used Macintosh. IBM-based PCs and their IRQs, memory limitations, and various ports and bus types were alien to me. I applied because I had met several people at one of The Works gatherings that were employed at CompUSA, and I really wanted to get away from that abusive boss.

CompUSA was the primary computer store in Boston. It was a national chain based out of Texas that went public in 1991 and expanded rapidly across the country. They sold hardware, software, and accessories, and were one of the few places to buy a Macintosh outside of an independent, authorized Apple reseller.

Eventually, several hackers from the Boston underground computer scene wound up working at the CompUSA in Brighton, just outside of the Boston city limits. L0pht cofounders Brian Oblivion and Golgo13 worked there. Stefan, a L0pht member who joined later, as well as Tweety Fish and several other local hackers also worked at that CompUSA. I imagine it was probably much the same across the county. I mean, where else was a retail store going to get people willing to work for slightly above minimum wage who knew enough about these newfangled home computers to work in their stores? The employees were going to be people who already used home computers, people who called BBSs—often hackers.

I started in sales and stayed on the Mac side of the sales floor. Within a few months, I had risen to the top of the sales charts, both for number of sales and average amount of each sale. My numbers were so good not because of any special sales prowess on my part but because most of the other salespeople at CompUSA only knew the PC and the Macs scared them. So the Mac salespeople stayed on our side and the PC salespeople stayed on their side. Since I was working as many hours as I could, when anyone came in looking to buy a Mac, I was often the only person there with enough knowledge to sell one.

CompUSA was a dream job for me when I started. I got to hang out with other cool computer-minded people all day, many of whom at that point I considered good friends. I also got to use equipment and software I could never have afforded on my own: high-end Macs with big monitors and color printers, CD-ROM drives, and all the software. Of course, the big downside was having to deal with the public, which is a negative with all retail jobs, I think.

One brush with fame I had there was with Alan Dershowitz. I'd had no idea that he was a high-powered Harvard lawyer who represented OJ Simpson. All I knew was that his family came in with him to buy a computer for their vacation home in Martha's Vineyard, so they wanted something small. They were initially interested in the Macintosh Classic II, which was old and underpowered even then. I was able to talk them into the Color Classic but could not get him to spring for the more expensive HP DeskWriter 500 over the Apple StyleWriter II. After I rang them up and sent them on their way, all my coworkers were like, "Dude, that was Alan Dershowitz!" And I was like, "Who?" I had no idea.

Eventually I tired of sales, finding it boring and not very mentally challenging. I started feeling like getting people to spend more money wasn't doing them a favor; instead it felt a little slimy. I've been suspicious of all salespeople ever since, whether business or retail. Some of my friends had already left CompUSA for other jobs, so it quickly turned into a grind. When the person responsible for handling Macintosh repairs decided to leave, the company naturally looked to me as the senior Mac salesperson to fill the job. Since sales at CompUSA were not commissioned based, I'd still be making the same hourly wage but would not have to deal with the public as much. This was appealing.

The problem was, I really didn't know the first thing about repairing Macs. So I winged it. I found it really wasn't that hard. Most of the problems were straightforward: a bad floppy drive or power supply. Simply swap them out for new parts. Then of course there were basic memory and modem installs. For machines like the Centris 610 or the LC III, this simply meant popping the top off the case and inserting a couple of SIMM cards. It would take longer to get the machine onto the bench than to get the cover off and install the memory. Then there were machines like the PowerBook 520 and 540 that required an almost complete disassembly of the laptop to install the modem. Apple standards established an hour per install of a PowerBook 520 modem; I had it down to about twenty minutes and would sometimes do nothing but laptop modem installs all day long.

On the other side of the spectrum, I would occasionally get machines with serious problems that were hard or nearly impossible to fix. One such problem machine was a Quadra 610 that would not format 800K floppy disks. The machine could read them just fine but would fail to format. Newer 1.4 MB disks worked fine, just not the older 800K. I swapped out the floppy drive, the cable, and the motherboard, which really should have fixed it but it didn't. I eventually convinced Apple to give the customer a brand-new machine, which Apple seemed to do rather easily, I thought. Apple never replaced entire machines. Years later, I ran across an Apple tech note describing a weird bug when formatting 800K floppies having to do with the power supply of all things.

The failure to properly troubleshoot and repair a machine like that was rare, but those failures really shook me. Another time I was working on a Color StyleWriter Pro with one of my favorite tools, which had a big magnet on the end. This magnet made it easy to grab screws you dropped into the bowels of a system. However, unbeknownst to me, it also made it really easy to wipe out the magnetic tracking that the Color StyleWriter Pro used to determine its print head location. The few times I encountered something that I couldn't fix, I took it personally. I had to remind myself that I had no training and was just winging it. Today, people in the information security industry call it "imposter syndrome," and this was really my first taste of it.

I first met Count Zero and just about everyone else online via a BBS. I probably met him for the first time in person at one of The Works gatherings in Harvard Square. Zero had a certain aura around him, not so much a cult of personality but a coolness factor that I found both magnetic and intimidating. He and Brian Oblivion were probably the two people at The Works Gatherings who I most looked up to as the experienced hackers. I also considered Golgo13, Magic Man, and a few others as elite, but Zero and Oblivion were whom I gravitated to the most.

In the real world, Count Zero worked at Mass General Hospital (MGH) Neurosciences Department on the research campus in the Charlestown Navy Yard, just down the street from where Old Ironsides, the USS Constitution, was berthed. Zero had set up the department's first web server and did tech support for the department's users. I assumed he did other medical-type stuff as well, but he only ever told me about his tech work. He had a tightly cropped beard and longish hair and would often wear skinny, futuristic-looking sunglasses, like his namesake from the book by the same name.[15] Count Zero often looked like he could have stepped off the page of a William Gibson novel.

Zero recommended me for a position at MGH in the OCD (obsessive-compulsive disorder) clinic under Dr. Michael A. Jenike. The OCD clinic had a handful of doctors who all used Macs, and they had one pizza-box-style Sun Solaris machine that they used to run statistical analysis on. This machine wasn't a PC that ran DOS and Windows, or a Mac, but a high-powered workstation from Sun Microsystems that ran Sun's version of unix called Solaris. The job was part-time and was supposed to be only ten hours a week, mostly helping the doctors troubleshoot their Eudora email programs on Mac SEs and making sure the department's small AppleTalk network could communicate with the larger hospital network. The job also came with root access to that Sun Solaris box.

I had little unix experience at that point, just the small bit I had picked up during my short stint at Boston University, which really didn't amount to much more than navigation commands such as `ls` and `cd`. But here I was, the systems administrator of my very own unix machine with a handful of users.

I picked up a book on unix administration and started reading. I more than once got stuck inside of `vi`, a powerful and supposedly simple text editor with no way out. The first time, I rebooted the machine and then sat there for fifteen minutes waiting for the entire system to come back online. Another time I had to kill the process after using ps -aux to figure out which process it was. Eventually, slowly, I found my way around and learned how to create users, change passwords, move files, and run programs.

I spent a lot of time in the little office closet at MGH that housed that Sun workstation; more than the ten hours a week, I was paid to be there. I would finish my shift at CompUSA in Brighton, grab some takeout Chinese from the restaurant across the street, and then drive my white, stick-shift, four-door, rusting ten-year-old Ford Escort (which I had bought for $700) down Memorial Drive to Charlestown. I stayed in that little office until it got late enough to be a little creepy being in a large, mostly empty office building.

On the way home, I usually made a short detour to the artist loft space I and some other hackers had begun simply calling "the loft." Of course, we later stylized that name into leetspeak, an online slang way of replacing vowels with numbers, and it became "the L0pht." It was in an old south-Boston factory building. I would spend a few more hours of hacking time there before either crashing on the couch or, more likely, driving all the way back to my Newton apartment in the wee hours of the morning. Then I'd do it all again the next day. But I'm getting ahead of myself; I haven't even mentioned how I got involved with the hackers at the L0pht yet.

###

The online world of the late eighties and early nineties was one of exploration and learning. But it was also one of not damaging things, of following the outdoor explorer mantra of "leave no trace." The norm was that if you gained access to the system, it was okay to look around, to explore, but it was not okay to cause damage or even a disruption in service. You were there to learn. Inadvertently causing a system to crash or reboot was mildly okay if you took steps to minimize that possibility. It was not okay to delete files, change information, lock out accounts, or in any way prevent the legitimate users of the system from using their system.

None of these norms were written down anywhere. There wasn't some guide with a list of dos and don'ts for new people to follow. There was no handbook of what was acceptable and what was taboo. It was just community knowledge and culture passed from one to another. You were exploring and learning, and that was it. Anything malicious was definitely verboten.

In his book *Hackers: Heroes of the Computer Revolution* Steven Levy called this need to explore and learn a "hands-on-imperative,"[16] an unrelenting curiosity, a drive, a compunction, a need to push the boundaries and discover new things or acquire new knowledge. To learn by doing, by typing and entering commands. An imperative that compelled you, required you, to seek out computer access to fulfill this hunger. Any barrier—physical, legal, or electronic—became an annoyance, a challenge to bypass. The motivation at the time was seldom profit, or power, or to further your career, or even anything to do with security; that all came later. The motivation then was mostly intellectual curiosity and the ability to participate within the community.

Sharing was considered an important part of that community, also known as "the scene" as well, but the sharing only went so far. Often sharing meant that a resource would get overused and eventually lost as the owner realized his or her resource was being abused and locked everyone out. While sharing might have been seen as a way to help someone it was often done as a way to prove "eliteness" to others within the social group—sort of as an electronic "look what I can do" exclamation, like a toddler seeking attention. In many cases this information exchange went beyond simple sharing and advanced into trading and bartering: a long-distance code in exchange for a special dial-up number or a password to a certain system in exchange for yet another email system exploit.

Sharing, helping, or teaching, was a double-edged sword. On the one side you wanted others to know what you had discovered, what knowledge you had gained, just how "leet" you had become. To be considered elite, or leet, or l33t, or 31337 was considered the highest honor. On the other hand, if you shared too much, you might enable someone else to become more elite than yourself. It was always a game of one-upmanship, of constantly trying to find that next bit of knowledge, the next system no one else has gotten into. The next thing you could wave in the air and say "look what I can do."

One thing about the BBS and early Internet scene in the '80s and '90s that many people like to wax poetic about today was the so-called meritocracy that governed the hierarchy of people within that social group. The more tech you knew, the higher in the hierarchy you would get, and the more elite you would become. It kind of felt that way. The hackers at the head of our social structures seemed like smart people, and I at least assumed that the reason they got there and became leet was because they knew a lot.

Another aspect about hacker culture that people like to reminisce about today was the inclusivity of the social order. And in some ways, it was. Mostly we were all social outcasts, kids who had been picked on in high school and somehow found refuge in technology and online conversations that separated the individual from the face-to-face reality of interpersonal relationships. Something in those shared experiences drew us together and kept us there.

At the same time, the culture was extremely exclusionary. For the most part, we were all upper-middle-class, white males. There was little tolerance for newbs or noobs or newbies who hadn't achieved the same level of knowledge of those who were leet. Asking a simple question would often result in a brash reply of RTFM, or "read the fucking manual" if the question wasn't outright ignored. While we were all outsiders, so to speak, if you were *too* far outside, you weren't welcome. People would get ignored, or worse, harassed, both online and in person. Some would give up and find some other social group to be a part of.

This exclusionary aspect of the culture has been hard to change. Even now, some of the old guard thinks things were just fine the way they were. They still believe that things should be run by a strict meritocracy without mentioning which merits should be considered important. This mold has been difficult to change. Although things are getting better, we still have a long way to go.

I took part in this culture then and make no excuses for it. It was wrong then, and it is wrong now. I did my best to learn things on my own and attempt to become leet. I like to think I also did my best to help new people, but chances are, I was just as big of an asshole as everyone else. If you were one of the people I was an asshole toward, I apologize. Today I make a conscious effort not to do that and try to help where I can.

EARLY LØPHT

At one of those early 2600 meetings during one of the warm months in 1991, Brian Oblivion was sitting next to me wearing his standard brimless hat over shoulder-length balding hair, his black bike messenger bag draped over the back of his chair. He leaned in close and whispered, "Hey, you wanna go to the loft after?"

We were sitting outside in Harvard Square in front of the Au Bon Pain café at the monthly 2600 meeting. I was nursing my large iced Mocha Americano and listening to the surrounding conversations and watching the old men play chess.

I said sure, trying to sound nonchalant and cool like it was no big deal, but getting an invitation to the artists-workshop-turned-hackerspace in South Boston was a major deal, at least for me. I had been there a few times before, but each time was unique.

A hackerspace was a physical location where hackers could work on projects in a communal setting. Today, many hackerspaces are setup as nonprofit organizations with official memberships, elected boards, and other structure. The L0pht predated most of these spaces and was formed from a group of like-minded people who originally just needed a place to store equipment.

At this point the loft had not yet become the "L0pht," the famous (some would say infamous) hackerspace it would soon become. Of course, this was in the early nineties, long before anyone knew what a hackerspace was. I knew it as a cool place where the elite hackers of the 617 area code could hang out. There was a ton of old computer equipment there, mostly in boxes, but some of it was up and running. The place had a certain vibe, a secrecy about it that made you feel in awe. I considered an invite to hang out there a pretty high honor.

As I mentioned earlier, Brian ran one of the elite bulletin board systems in the 617 area code called Black Crawling Systems. It was your basic hack/phreak/anarchy/virus or h/p/a/v system with heavy influence on radio and earlier wireless communications. He only gave access out to people he had met in person or otherwise trusted. I had met him at a few Works gatherings and 2600 meetings before and had been lucky enough to get an invite to his board six months or so earlier.

Brian Oblivion and Count Zero lived on the same block in South Boston. Their wives, Mary and Alicia, started a business together decorating and selling women's hats. They rented a loft in an old factory building that had been converted into artists' spaces. It was just around the corner from their apartments, and it quickly became a dumping ground for all the random computer equipment

Brian and Zero had been storing in their apartments. But even with all that equipment, there was still a lot of space, so Golgo13 and White Knight, two other local Boston hackers, also stored their old computer equipment here.

Mary and Alicia's hat business didn't last long. Within a few months, they could no longer afford their share of the rent from the small amount of income generated by hat sales. Unbeknownst to me at the time, this was why I had been asked to the loft that evening.

I had been at the L0pht a few times before to hang out. Count Zero had moved his BBS out of his apartment and into the space. That BBS was called ATDT East and was one of the most elite underground BBSs on the East Coast. It was cool to monitor the computer screen and watch people as they logged into the system and poked around. There was a lot of interesting equipment in the place, equipment I didn't get a chance to see anywhere else. Golgo13 had his original Apple Lisa, and Brian had soldering irons and other fun gadgets. There was even a huge VAX computer, which took up about four or five half-height filing-cabinet-sized metal boxes. It ran in a row just inside the main entrance, creating a short hallway. Not to mention the detritus of who-knows-how-many trashing runs around Boston, old PC parts, manuals, boxes of software, and cables of unknown purpose that littered the floor or were piled haphazardly wherever there was space.

That particular evening, I was there with Kingpin and Weld Pond—two other people I had known of from BBSs, Works Gatherings, and 2600 meetings. Count Zero told us that the hat business was failing, and that Mary and Alicia were moving their stuff out. That's when he asked Kingpin, Weld, and me a question that would change our lives forever. Would we be interested in renting space with them there at the loft?

The offer surprised me immensely. I had no idea that it was coming. Obviously the four of them—Brian Oblivion, Count Zero, White Knight and Golgo13—had all discussed this plan prior to inviting me over that evening. The four of them were pretty much "it" for the Boston 617 hacking scene, and for them ask me to join them was amazing. I was told that my share of the rent would be something like $120 a month, way more than I could afford on my barely-above-minimum-wage security guard salary, but I didn't care. I hadn't collected very much computer equipment yet, but I didn't care about that either. A big part of why I didn't have stuff was because I didn't have anywhere to put it and renting space at the loft would solve that problem.

I think what attracted me to joining a bunch of people I barely knew and sharing a working space was a sense of belonging and camaraderie. After being discharged from the Army, moving to Boston, and having to leave school, I was feeling isolated. Yes, I had coworkers and even a girlfriend I had met at school, but I'll be honest, I didn't have much in the way of friends. Francyne, my girlfriend, had gone on to graduate school and wasn't around much. Eventually my relationship with Francyne grew very strained, and we just grew apart. This situation left me with little else other than the routine of going to work so that I could make money to sleep and eat. So when Brian presented me with that offer, I considered it a pretty big deal, even if I didn't consciously realize all the reasons why.

The rules were laid out during the meeting. Everyone would share in the rent, which came with electricity and heat included. That was pretty much it for initial rules other than respecting each other's stuff and the space. My share of the rent would get me an eight-foot square space. Kingpin, still in high school and living with his parents at the time couldn't even afford that much and so ended splitting a space with Weld.

###

Like goldfish that grow to the size of their bowl, hardware at the L0pht accumulated items to fill every corner and horizontal surface. If someone was throwing out some old computer equipment in the trash, we would stop, pick it up, and drop it off at the L0pht. If our day jobs were in the middle of an upgrade cycle and needed to purge out a few dozen old dot matrix printers, we would volunteer to take them off our boss's hands, and they would end up at the L0pht. If we heard one of the many tech startups in the area had flamed out and was going under, we would make a trashing run to their dumpster at night and look for whatever they were throwing out. We knew where all the "good" dumpsters were in town, and on warm summer nights, we would drive around Boston, climb into dumpsters, and pull-out equipment we could later sell at the MIT flea market.

Some of this hardware would get repurposed and put to good use. I built my first PC from parts that had been thrown out at CompUSA. When BBN, a high-tech defense contractor where Mudge, Weld Pond, and Brian Oblivion worked, disposed of one of their multi-processor parallel processing machines, it never made it to the landfill. When another one of my employers decided it was finally time to ditch all their old Mac Pluses that had been sitting in a closet for a few years,

I volunteered to take care of all of them so they wouldn't have to pay a hazardous waste disposal fee. I would load them up in my trusty old Ford Focus (and after it died, my less trusty Ford Tempo) at night and drop them off at the L0pht.

If we did not find some way to purge ourselves of this cast-off detritus of the computer world, it would eventually overwhelm us and drown us out. Most months we would load up as much as we could and head to the MIT Ham Radio and Computer Flea Market, or more colloquially, the "MIT Flea" or just "The Flea." Currently the official name is the MIT Swapfest.[17]

The MIT Radio Society has run The Flea since the mid-eighties. It usually holds it in an empty parking lot or parking garage in and around Vassar Street, just off Massachusetts Avenue in Cambridge. It is every third Sunday from April through October, rain or shine. We used to say if it runs on electricity, you can find it at the MIT Flea. This isn't a normal bric-a-brac flea market; the organizers stringently police what gets sold, and if you try to bring in your large collection of costume jewelry or old pottery, you will be politely asked to leave, or at least asked not to return the following month. However, if you are looking for a capacitor the size of your fist, an old oscilloscope, ham radios, antennas or parts to make one, microwave equipment, a five-and-quarter full-height 5 MB ISA hard drive, cartridges for old gaming systems, an HDI-30 to DB-25 SCSI disk cable or any of thousands of other obscure and outdated tech items, chances are you can find it at the MIT Flea.

The market's proximity to MIT and its students with no money, engineers from the local tech startups, and, of course, hackers, means the variety of stuff you can find and sell at the MIT Flea can surprise you every month. One purchase I still remember was a dual 20 MB SCSI Bernoulli drive that actually worked. That's the thing about The Flea, it's really hard to tell standing in the middle of a parking lot if something works or not. It always seemed like you were playing the lottery. Dare I risk ten dollars on this item that probably won't work, or should I try to haggle down to five dollars on a maybe? In the time before eBay and easy online sales, it was hard to compare prices on old equipment; you had to gage whether the price you could haggle down to was worth it and whether it was worth the risk of the item not working. If whatever you bought "popped smoke" when you got it back home and plugged it in, there was a very small chance you would be able to return it for a refund.

So as the L0pht filled with random bits of cast-off technology, we would truck items over to Cambridge and wait in line to get a space, which was limited. Well, at least the good spaces were limited. The gates didn't open until seven a.m., and all the good spaces got taken very quickly. We would try to arrive at five a.m. or even earlier to get in line; we were never first in line as some people arrived the night before. What do you do at five a.m. in the middle of MIT on a Sunday with two hours to kill? First you head over to the MIT Student Union a few blocks away and get some bad coffee, as it's the only place open. Then on your way back you poke around in some dumpsters and get some more hardware that you could sell a few hours later at the flea market.

We didn't go to The Flea every month, but some months we had so much stuff that we would rent a U-Haul. Once I went to pick up a U-Haul the night before The Flea, and all they had left was a twenty-year-old, large box truck with a four-speed manual transmission. The truck was so big it wouldn't fit in the garage at the flea market, and we were stuck out in the parking lot in the rain. But that month we made more money (about $700) than any other month, enough to cover most of the rent and utilities. Another time I drove my Ford Escort packed full of junk to The Flea and was pulled over by the Massachusetts State Police for speeding, right in front of the State Police barracks. It was five a.m. on Easter Sunday. I remember the trooper looked at the contents of my car with utter disgust and then said, "Slow down, I'm going to give you a warning today but only because it's Easter and shit." Yes, The Flea still happens on Easter Sunday, and I think that trooper was a little upset that he had to work on a holiday.

For me The Flea was both good and bad. It was a shared task that we all took part in, so it helped cement the camaraderie among the group. It also reminded me heavily of going to the farmer's market with my father when I was younger. Those were also very early on Sunday mornings, and we sold things out of our car to random people in a parking lot. Unfortunately, it didn't always feel like the work preparing for and selling stuff at The Flea was split evenly, especially the waking up at four thirty a.m. part or the loading up of the truck part. But The Flea was more than just a way to make some money, it was also a social event. Not only would we go together as the L0pht, occasionally even hanging up an enormous handmade banner with our name and logo, but also a lot of other Boston hackers would show up. Sometimes this was the same group from 2600 meetings, and sometimes there were people we would only see at The Flea. Some we knew would not arrive before ten a.m. and then complain about how they missed all the good deals. And then after The Flea, there was often food and video games in a basement pizza joint just outside of Harvard Square or a trip back to the L0pht to play with whatever new equipment we had bought.

There were some people who I was certain made their entire income selling things at the MIT Flea Market. As far as I could tell, it was their only job. Or at least I didn't see how they made any other income other than selling stuff at not only the MIT Flea Market but other ham fests and flea markets up and down the East Coast. We would see them every month, always selling the same old things, and it was obvious they lived in their cars. We nervously half joked that The Flea was the prototype of society "after the fall" when the cyberpunk dystopia foretold by Brunner, Dick, Sterling, Gibson, and Stephenson would become reality. I, at least, would also wonder how long I would go to The Flea, and if I would end up as one of these old-timers living in a van packed full of ancient electronics trying to make gas money at flea markets.

L0pht was not the only physical hacker space in Boston. Other places like Messiah Village, Hell House, Sin House, and New Hack City were actual houses with four to eight hackers living in each one. No one lived at the L0pht, and we actively discouraged people from sleeping there. In fact, the L0pht space in South Boston, located in an artist loft building, didn't even have its own bathroom. It had a shared bathroom space down the hall. The lease specifically mentioned that the space wasn't to be used as a living space. Occasionally crashing on the couch because we were working late on a project was one thing, but it wasn't common. The fact that no one lived at the L0pht made it different from the other hacker houses around town.

###

One of the first motivations for us at the L0pht to network our machines together, and for me to build myself a PC from spare parts instead of using a Mac, was to play the video game *Doom*. *Doom* was released in 1993 and helped define the first-person shooter genre. *Doom* is one of the most popular video games of all time and has had a major influence on many technology lovers then and now. People still try to port *Doom* onto various pieces of computer hardware, such as a refrigerator or a bank ATM, just to see if they can.

Doom was also one of the first video games that could support multiplayer network play, and this was one of the incentives for us to network the L0pht. 10BASE-T networking, which used cables like telephone cables but larger, was around then, but it was expensive and too new for us to find discarded networking cards and cables in the trash. So we used what we could find: coax 10BASE2 (aka Thinnet or thin coax) cabling to connect our computers together. This coax cable was very similar to the cable most people still use today to connect their cable TV set-top box or cable modem to the cable network.

We quickly ran into problems. We could get it to work, but once in a while things would die for no apparent reason; connections were lost, and the game would just end. The problem would only occasionally manifest itself, and we lived with it for weeks with no solution. My PC, being rather slow and built out of pieces from the trash, was constantly blamed for causing the network failures. But one night we finally grew frustrated enough to do something about it and started swapping out the network cables themselves. One cable we ripped out had the brand name Cheapernet written on it; its removal made the network stable. We held the Cheapernet cable up in triumph, knowing this piece was the culprit. After we replaced that cable and game play continued without interruption, we cut the cable up into tiny pieces to ensure that not only would we never use that cable again, but also so that no one would mistakenly pick it out of our trash to use on their network. It also helped to work out some aggression and frustration on a piece of bad network cable.

I saved a piece of that cable, and I still have it tucked away in a drawer as a reminder to always check the things you least suspect and that anything, even a lowly unsuspecting cable, can be the source of your problems.

When the L0pht moved from South Boston to Watertown, we got rid of all our old 10BASE2 networking gear, including the coax cables. By this point, 3Com 3C509 Ethernet cards were readily available in the trash and elsewhere, so when we moved, we upgraded our entire infrastructure to 10BASE-T, or what is more commonly referred to as Ethernet. It used cables that looked like telephone cords, just bigger.

###

We purchased two USRobotics 56K modems with our MIT Flea Market earnings. Based on the date that we registered our domain name, L0pht. com, this purchase probably occurred at the MIT Flea in April of 1994. The USRobotics Sportster modem was not the slightly faster flagship

Courier modem with HST, which all good software pirates used, but the less expensive consumer model. I drove one of these modems up to Billerica about twenty minutes North of Boston and dropped it off at a small new company known as TIAC, or The Internet Access Company. It was one of the first companies in the Boston area that would allow you to connect to the Internet for a monthly fee. One service they offered was a dedicated line; this was a phone number that only your account could call and connect to. No busy signals, no waiting for a line to become available, and best of all, no time limits forcing you to hang up.

Once we had a modem up in Billerica and another one at the L0pht, we were set. We were online 24-7. Well, as long as we could keep the machines up and running. Granted, it was only at 56k, which is extremely slow by today's standards, but moderately fast for the time. A standard two-hour movie that would only take a few minutes to download via broadband today would literally take days to download over a 56k modem, not that full movies were even available online back then. These circumstances made most people very frugal with their file sizes. Things like JavaScript, advertising, and auto-streaming videos that you find on today's web pages did not exist. In some ways the web of the mid-nineties was even faster than today. Web designers took great pains to make sure their web pages were small and svelte; the rule-of-thumb was that a page should download within seven seconds at 56k. Today, even with super-fast broadband, we have some web pages that don't download in twice that time because they have been stuffed full of tracking cookies and ads, and are now a "multimedia experience."

Once we had the modem and an always-on connection, it wasn't long before someone decided to set up a web page. I think it was Weld

Pond who somehow secured a Sun SPARC station motherboard. We made the motherboard fit inside an old stereo case with a front glass panel and then downloaded Slackware, an early version of the Linux operating system. Count Zero downloaded it floppy disk by floppy disk on his machine on one side of the L0pht. As soon as the system finished writing to the floppy disk and was ejected, I would run it over to the other side of the L0pht where Weld and Brian were doing the install. This procedure happened over and over for dozens of floppies' worth of data until we finally got it up and running.

Soon after we switched L0pht from Slackware to OpenBSD, a security-oriented BSD Unix distribution like Linux, and moved from Intel x86 to a DEC Alpha architecture, which again, we had rescued out of the trash. Naturally.

When the Internet got popular in the mid-nineties, people stopped dialing into regular BBSs and opted instead to call into an ISP (internet service provider). Within a few short years, the thriving communities of tens of thousands of BBSs across the world screamed out in pain, and most were silenced. Some of those communities found new life on the Internet, but most faded away and died. Those communities were missed but only briefly, as they were quickly replaced by new communities often centered around various web forums.

Count Zero had moved ATDT East, the bulletin board that he now lead, from his apartment into the L0pht. With the rise of the Internet, telephone calls into this system quickly dropped off. After we had the L0pht.com computer system and website up and running, we quickly installed a BBS package. You couldn't dial into this BBS, but you could access it using the telnet protocol over the Internet. It was no longer limited by telephone exchanges. If you didn't live in the Boston area, you didn't need to make a long-distance phone call; if you had Internet access, you could use telnet to connect to bbs. L0pht. com. The BBS didn't have any files, but it did have a few message bases.

A small community grew up around this BBS, as people would connect to it from around the world. Unfortunately the user base never became what it had been as a dial-up BBS. The BBS was never super busy, but it was a connection for us to our recent past when we would all call local bulletin boards and talk to people we would never meet. Despite the low number of users, I still run into people today who tell me they used to visit the L0pht BBS.

Besides the website and BBS, all the L0pht members had a directory on the L0pht.com system where we could store files and make them available to the Internet. I ended up using some of my storage space on L0pht.com to create the Whacked Mac Archives. I had been collecting what could be best described as an underground Mac software for years: software that wasn't readily available on most Mac BBSs. With the demise of those BBSs, underground software was becoming even more difficult to find—software such as war dialers that would dial phone numbers in sequential order with your modem looking for other modems, or software for bypassing the passwords on FileMaker Pro databases, or lists of serial numbers for software packages, or utilities for cracking unix password files and the dictionaries to go with them, or utilities to decode credit card numbers to determine the issuing bank. None of these files were explicitly illegal (not that any software was illegal then), and most had very legitimate uses. While the software itself wasn't illegal, some things the software accomplished might have been depending on who used it and how.

I quickly taught myself HTML,[17] the language of web pages, and coded up a few dozen pages listing the pieces of software I had downloaded over the past few years from calling BBSs. The software that I had collected had only been traded on underground systems, and most of it hadn't made its way into the larger software repositories on the Internet. Back then many universities had large collections of what was called "shareware." Shareware was free to try and share and if you liked it. If you wanted to keep using it, you were supposed to pay the developer a small amount of money. Archives like the Info-Mac Archive at Stanford, the U-M Archive at the University of Michigan, or any of the dozens of smaller archives that were usually run by universities held thousands and thousands of small shareware titles. Those repositories usually wouldn't host anything at all related to "hacking."

The Whacked Mac Archive's small collection of programs, maybe a couple hundred titles, became very popular very quickly. I hosted the files themselves on an old Mac IIci, the motherboard of which I had rescued from the trash and then somehow squeezed into an even older Leading Edge XT case that had been painted a deep blue.

I had to limit the FTP[19] server to a maximum of three concurrent connections at a time; otherwise it would lock up and become nonresponsive. But even three users at a time were enough to saturate our tiny 56K modem line—so much so that it became difficult for anyone else to use the Internet connection. Unbeknownst to me, Weld had created a script that could run from the L0pht.com box called UpWhacked and DownWhacked. When run, it would do just what it said: either take the Whacked Mac Archives offline or put them back online. I would check on my FTP server and notice that sometimes people were connected and sometimes they weren't, but it never occurred to me that people weren't connected because their traffic wasn't allowed through. I just assumed that the site wasn't being used right then. I didn't learn about the UpWhacked/DownWhacked scripts until years later.

Before I found the elite BBSs of the 617 area code, they were already holding physical get-togethers like Works Gatherings. Another gathering came to be known as Grill-A-Thon or simply Grillathon (GAT). It was an open invitation potluck barbecue for the Boston area's elite hackers. The first Grillathon was on the roof of Count Zero's apartment building, and it soon became an annual event. Later additions were held in the Arnold Arboretum and at the Beaver Brook Reservation, a park in Belmont just outside of Boston. The Grillathon's limitation was always that the location had to be accessible by local public transportation and allow outdoor grilling. Both requirements were extremely difficult to fill, and I'm not sure we did any actual barbecuing at the Arboretum.

Grillathon's Four and Five were held at my apartment in Newton; I think this was in 1995 and '96. My apartment had the added benefit of also having a pool. I'm not sure what drove me to host a bunch of drunken hackers at my apartment—twice—but I think it was partly so that Grillathon wouldn't die. I was worried that if I didn't host it, no one else would, and a budding tradition would cease to be. So I picked up the mantle for two years and opened my home to anyone who wanted to show up. The next year I was living in a tiny little attic apartment in Waltham with no pool, so I passed the mantle of Grillathon on to one of the hacker houses in town. FreqOut and Silicosis, two local hackers, lived at a shared house called New Hack City. They hosted Grillathon Six in Ringer Park, Alston. The moniker of "park" is little bit of a misnomer; while it is technically a city park, it is more like a garbage-strewn series of small hills and dirty sandlot playgrounds frequented by drug users and alcoholics who used it mostly as a toilet. In later years Grillathon eventually found its way to Golgo13's backyard, where it has stayed every year for close to two decades.

The original official invite for Grillathon that was posted online on local bulletin boards and through direct email specifically said that everyone was invited. This wasn't just a party for elite hackers but anyone who wanted to show up.

```
* * * * * * * * * * * * * * * * * * * * * * * * * * * * * * * * * * * * * * * * * * * * * * *

              L0phT Heavy Industries

                   Grillathon

* * * * * * * * * * * * * * * * * * * * * * * * * * * * * * * * * * * * * * * * * * * * * * *

Yes folks, it is that time of year again. Time
for Roof Throwing, Island Hopping, Pool Ball,
Flaming Chili, Jack the Crack Fiend, watching
```

them copulate in the woods, and who knows what else. Are you ready for the mayhem? the carnage? the free for all? Are you ready for Grillathon 5.0?

I am ready, I think I want it, but what is it?

ATDT and ATDT East may be dead but Grillathon lives on as a tribute to those that have gone before. A yearly gathering of the characters that make up our world. A gathering to meet face-to-face those you may have only known through the transferring of electrons across great distances. A time to interact via analog methods over some potato salad, a burger and a dip in the pool. You have heard of Summercon, Defcon, HoHocon, Pumpcon, and all the rest, but this is not a con, it's a Thon. There will be no guest speakers, no scheduled demonstrations, no hotel rooms to trash, no fee to pay at the door, just a day of merriment and laughter.

Well, gee can I come?

Yes, Virginia, you can. Everyone is invited as always. Basically if you can read this you're invited. However, this being a worldwide accessible page, let me point out that Grillath0n has traditionally been a local event. Local pretty much to the 617/508

AC. You are still welcome to show if you like, but if you spend all your hard-earned cash on plane fare and then have nowhere to stay, or someone throws you in the pool, or if you're shunned into a corner and no one speaks to you, don't come crying to me.

Alright! Now I know what it is, but when is it?

Saturday, August 12th is the magic day. If for some reason you can't make it, let me know and I will reschedule the whole thing. Wait a minute, what do you mean you can't make it? This is Grillathon! It comes but once a year! How are you gonna tell Dem0nSeed you can't make it? I could see telling Santa Claus you that you couldn't make Christmas, but Santa Claus is a big fat red guy, what the hell is he gonna do? Dem0nSeed, however, is a two-ton flaming orange Monster Truck who would crush your skull without a moment's hesitation. Face it, you will be there. Besides, how could you live with yourself if you missed something legendary like the Flaming Chili Incident, or if you missed those heartfelt moments with Jack the Crack Fiend. Face it, you will be there.

OK, OK, I 'll be there. What do I need to bring?

Yourself, a bathing suit (or go au naturel if you like), and a towel. Maybe a small pool toy; my pool will be available again this year, so bring a towel. Someone might want to bring a basketball. I need someone to mix the tunes. Your own booze. Most importantly you must bring food. Grillathon has traditionally been potluck, and it will continue to be, so everyone should bring one item that can be shared by all. We almost always have enough ketchup but never enough hamburgers, so screw the condiments and think BIG. Think pounds of hamburger, gallons of potato salad, watermelons, etc.... (Note: Last year I had four bags of hotdogs left in my freezer when it was all over, so we won't need any hotdogs this year.)

Got my towel and some food, I'm ready to go. Wait a minute, where the hell am I going!?!

To Grillath0n you fool! Oh, you mean the location. Well for those that were there last year, it will be in the same place. So you can ask one of them or you can send me mail at spacerog@tiac.net, and I will mail you directions.(NOTE: Any inquiries made to spacerog@L0pht.com will be IGNORED! I get way too much mail there already.) This being a worldwide accessible forum, I'm not inclined to post directions to my house here,

even if I will only be living there for a few
more weeks.

Ahhh, I just woke up. What was this page all
about?

Grillath0n 5.0, Saturday, August 12th around
1 p.m. or so, bring a towel and some food,
email me at spacerog@tiac.net for directions.

* *

This was long before Facebook existed, so I was pretty certain that only people we knew would be there. Still, there was one guy... he claimed to be from Florida (no one knew who he was) who showed up anyway. We all thought it rather odd that he would come all that way just to attend a barbecue where he didn't know anyone. Everyone was friendly towards him, and he was an outgoing, polite person, but we all whispered behind his back "who is that guy?" in a quasi-paranoid sort of way, wondering if he was from some sort of three-letter agency sent to investigate us.

One year the inhabitants of Messiah Village, another local hacker house, made some "magic" chili to bring to Grillathon. The "magic" evidently came from a Habanero pepper that gave it a little kick. I was busy running around doing party host things such as throwing away empty beer bottles and telling people not to jump off the roof of the garage into the pool. I noticed Lemon, one of the younger women who called the local BBSs, running around the house screaming, stopping every so often to bend down and pick up dirt and shove it into her mouth. I came outside to find out what was going on. Someone told me that on a dare, Lemon had taken a huge bite out of the Habanero from the chili pot. I just sighed and went back inside to finish cleaning. Lemon was maybe twelve or fourteen years old. She was a hacker who had been hanging out at 2600 meetings at the Prudential Center and somehow got her parents' permission to hang out at some stranger's house for a barbecue. Lemon eventually changed her handle to Lady Ada, graduated from MIT, and founded the maker startup company AdaFruit. I will always remember her running laps around my house, trying to do anything to get the fire out of her mouth.

After Grillathon was over I did what anyone who had just held a hacker party at their house would. I cleaned the place up, put the beer bottles in the trash, and put the trash out on the curb.

At the next 2600 meeting Deth Vegetable asked me, "Hey, do you still have that pot we brought the chili in?"

"You mean the burnt, dented, beat-up, aluminum pot you probably got at Goodwill for two bucks?"

"Yeah, that one, the magic chili pot."

"Umm, no. You didn't take it with you, so I assumed it was trash, and I threw it away."

To this day I am known as the guy who threw away the Messiah Village magic chili pot.

Grillathon is still a yearly event that happens in the Boston area. Most recently it has been held in the backyard of Golgo13's house in Cambridgeport. A lot of old-school hackers show up, and some new people too. People still bring their own food, Golgo13 often makes his special ribs, and there are usually a couple of watermelons. Since a lot of us have our own kids now, there is one watermelon for the little kids and one Vodkamelon for the older "kids."

At various points the L0pht had at least three different DEC VAXs (or is the plural "Vaxen"?), a type of mainframe, or "big iron" computer system from the late seventies. We had a VAX 11/780, an 11/730 and a MicroVAX II. I'm not sure where the 11/780 came from, but it never worked. It was a huge multi-filing cabinet-sized machine. We ended up dissembling it and using its metal carcass as a wardrobe of sorts. We would often use it to store old monitors and dot matrix printers before we carted them off to The Flea. The numerous large, nearly square circuits boards with their dozens of ram chips that made up the system's insides became a hanging wall at the L0pht's Watertown location. We tied them together with small bits of wire scavenged from old telephone cables. The wall created a great backdrop for many photo shoots and outstanding eye candy for video photographers.

The VAX 11/730 was physically shorter than the 11/780 but comprised many more cabinets; I think we had five cabinets n all. It had been rescued from destruction from some place in Virginia. A few months before I was asked to join the L0pht, Count Zero, Brian Oblivion, White Knight, and possibly others drove a U-Haul to Virginia or New Jersey to bring it back. They carried it up the flight of metal stairs and into the L0pht in South Boston and attempted to get it to work. The artist's loft space we had rented came with free electricity, mostly because the landlord was too cheap to break out the spaces with different electric meters. Our lease specifically prohibited air conditioners but said nothing about mainframe computers. The 11/730 did work, briefly, and then we realized just how loud the thing was, how much heat it generated, and that we didn't really have any use for it. When the L0pht moved from South Boston to Watertown, the 11/730 did not move with us.

The MicroVAX II had only a brief stay at the L0pht. It was not an enormous machine compared to its older siblings, the 11/780 and the 11/730. I don't remember its original origin; we probably rescued it from a fate worse than death as we did most of the hardware we had. It was a little larger than your standard PC at the time, and it stood vertically (an unusual orientation for most systems of that size) with a large pedestal on the base.

The MicroVAX II was first introduced by the Digital Equipment Corporation (DEC) in the middle of 1985, so by the mid-nineties it had little usefulness left. The one we had still worked, but compared to the other VAXen we had around MicroVAX was woefully underpowered. Since we really had no use for it, off to the flea market it went. One Sunday morning it moved from the hardware pile into my car, and we set it on the pavement of a parking lot in the middle of the MIT campus for the MIT Ham Radio and Computer Flea Market. This is when we met RosieRiv, or Rosie the Riveter, or Window Snyder, for the first time.

Occasionally I would post what we thought we might take to the MIT Flea Market on the L0pht BBS. The L0pht BBS never really saw much activity, and I think it was only active for a year and a half, but when I remembered I would post a notice for people to come down to the MIT Flea and list some of larger items we thought we might take with us for sale. One month in the spring, that included the MicroVAX II.

It was a standard flea for MIT, and the weather was nice. We were outside in the parking lot up against the fence next to the train tracks, our preferred location, much better than being in the garage. We had our usual selection of one-dollar "guaranteed dead" hard drives (if you got them working, you could return them for a refund), a pile of miscellaneous cables, a few monochrome monitors, maybe a printer or two, a box of random PC expansion cards, the MicroVAX II, probably one or two things even we couldn't identify, and enough other random stuff to fill whatever vehicles we had drove there with that month. We hovered around our tables, taking turns between trying to sell stuff and walking around looking at other people's junk and trying to haggle them down in price. Every once in a while, we would hurry back to our table to tell everyone else about some unusual piece of equipment or amazing deal we saw on the other side of the parking lot.

In the morning, a young woman walked up and asked, "Are you the guys with the VAX?"

I would learn later that this was RosieRiv, Window Snyder. She would go on to hold high-ranking security positions at Microsoft, Mozilla, Apple, Fastly, Intel, and others. She literally wrote a book[20] on threat modeling. She had read my post on the L0pht BBS detailing what we were bringing to The Flea that month and specifically came looking for the VAX.

She had on a pink T-shirt with blue jean cutoffs and black heels. She had brown curly hair pulled back into a bun on the back of her head. I was a little stunned at first, not understanding what it was she was asking for; I'd heard VAX and was thinking about one of the huge ones still back at the L0pht, and she didn't quite match the ripped jeans, dirty T-shirt, and black-leather-jacket cyberpunk aesthetic of most of the other people at The Flea.

Brian responded right away. "Yeah, it's right over here." He pointed her to the side of the table where we had displayed the MicroVAX II.

I recovered quickly and started right in on my normal sales pitch, which was usually just talking bullshit about whatever it was we were trying to sell. I think we offered to throw in a terminal, and the deal was about done when she asked, "Do you deliver?"

Until that point, we had never delivered anything to anyone. Everything was sold cash and carry. We might hold something for you until the end of day so you didn't have to lug it around, but we didn't deliver. At least not until that day.

"Sure, I can deliver it to you," I heard myself say and could almost feel the quizzical gazes of the other L0pht members. "If you don't mind waiting until after The Flea. Umm, where do you live?"

I didn't think anything of offering to deliver it, or at least I told myself I wasn't thinking anything of it, that it was just another part of the sale. And no one else said anything either, although I am sure everyone noticed such an out-of-character offer.

After we sold everything we thought was going to sell that day and we packed up what was left, I made a stop at a local MIT dumpster to deposit whatever would never sell. I then drove over to Chestnut Hill near Boston College with a MicroVAX II and a Wyse terminal in my trunk. I rang the doorbell and unloaded my trunk when she opened the door. "Would you mind carrying it upstairs?" she asked.

"Umm, sure," I again heard myself say. The MicroVAX II weighed at least forty pounds, probably closer to fifty. It was an old turn-of-the-century apartment building with steep narrow winding staircases. I lugged it up without pulling a muscle or falling backwards down the stairs, and I set it down on the floor in her room.

"Let me plug it in and make sure it works," she said.

We plugged in the power cables and hooked up the terminal and just started geeking out. She was way more familiar with VMS, the operating system the VAX used, than I was. The whole thing was pretty alien to me. We got the system to boot up, and then of course we had to figure out how to login, and after a little while she had figured that out to. During all this we talked about different things, well, as best as we could. What was she studying in school? Where did I work? Where did she grow up? Why where you at the flea market? What was this loft thing? Come to find out she had already been doing sysadmin work on VMS for a while, hence her interest in owning her own VAX. I was still self-conscious talking to women at that point in my life, so it was good that there was an unfamiliar computer there that I could focus on during the lulls in the conversation. Typing on the keyboard helped hide the nervous shaking in my fingers, I hope.

There was an attraction building between us, or at least there was definitely an attraction building in one direction, anyway. I found out she was nineteen years old, nine years younger than me, which seemed like a rather large age gap. Although I didn't think about that part right then.

After a few hours I figured it was time I should go home. I was still conflicted over my growing attraction toward her, the difference in our ages, and my own nervousness. As I took one step outside of her door, I decided. I took the other step and turned around to give her a goodbye kiss, but the door was already closed. The opportunity was lost. I convinced myself that it was just as well. Nine years is not a small age difference, especially when one of us was nineteen.

Over the next few weeks, we would occasionally chat on the L0pht BBS. I invited her over to the L0pht to hang out a few times, and we even ended up going to a party at Messiah Village. We hung out at my apartment a few times, geeking out over something or other and eating black olive and mushroom pizza. Nothing ever progressed beyond the friend stage, though. The attraction, at least for me, didn't fade. The age difference still gnawed at me, until finally I decided I needed to do something about the situation. That year I was going to host Grillathon at my apartment, and I was certain I was going to do or say something.

I was renting a first-floor apartment in a house with a couple of other guys in the Nonantum area of Newton. The big draw was the pool behind the house. There was no yard to speak of, and after we crammed in about forty-some-odd hackers, there was hardly room for the grill. I was busy running around mostly picking up empty beer bottles so that the place wouldn't get too messy. I tried to keep the volume down on the music so that the neighbors wouldn't get too upset and tried to avoid the pool area lest I get thrown in, which in the days before cell phones was always a possibility.

That year was definitely one of the better Grillathons. This was the year that Deth Veggie made the famous Messiah Village chili in the supposedly magic chili pot, and the year that Lemon bit the habanero and did laps around my house screaming. Eventually the party wound down in the late afternoon, and those that were still full of energy moved the party over to Messiah Village. I was trying to work up the courage to say something to Window, but I didn't. I told myself when I finished cleaning, I would say something, but of course you're never done cleaning and soon she had left. After everyone had gone, I decided staying home would not accomplish anything; I was still determined to say something. I got in my car and headed downtown.

The route from my house in Newton to Mission Hill took me down Beacon Street, right past the CompUSA (which is now a CVS, I think) and across Market Street. As I passed through the intersection, blinking blue lights appeared in my rearview mirror. Money for me at that point in my life was tight; I was constantly making choices of which bills to pay and which ones could wait another month. Well, that month I had chosen not to pay my car insurance bill. As a result, one broken brake light resulted in a fee to the towing company, a storage fee for the car, the fine for the brake light, another fee for driving without insurance, a few taxi rides, a day off from work to go to court to get everything sorted out, and a trip to the tow yard to pick up my car. Obviously, it would have been much cheaper to just pay the insurance bill. As a result, I did not make it to the Messiah Village after-party and ended up never saying anything to Window.

After that I would see her occasionally at the flea market or when I visited one of the hacker houses around town. At the end of the summer, she told me she was thinking of moving into New Hack

City, the hacker house in Allston composed of many of the same people who had lived in Messiah Village. I didn't think that was the right choice for her and told her so, but she didn't take my advice. A few months later she told me she and another hacker in the house were now seeing each other, and that was the end of that. She ended up working at @stake, a company later formed by L0pht members during the early days, but eventually moved to the West Coast.

Twenty-five years later it is easy to look back and imagine what the course of history might have been if... But I have no regrets. I was a shy, nervous, inexperienced, geeky, almost-thirty-something kid. It was what it was, and I am happy where I am now.

Not everything with the L0pht was roses and honey. As you can imagine, with any group of late-teen to early-thirties guys, there is likely to be some friction within the group. And with people that have spent large amounts of time online instead of interacting face-to-face with other humans, that social friction likely wouldn't be handled as smoothly as it could have been.

We were nearing the end of our five-year lease on the South Boston space, and we decided that we needed a new space instead of renewing the lease on the current one. As I remember it, the evening we discussed the next step, everyone was there except Count Zero. Which was odd, because he literally lived just around the corner from the L0pht space in South Boston.

There were a lot of reasons to move The L0pht. We wanted more actual physical space, we had crackheads on our doorstep getting high (South Boston back then wasn't as pretty as it is now), and we wanted to get outside of downtown so that random people wouldn't stop by and end up sleeping on our couch.

At the time Count Zero wasn't being a team player. He would come by and use his equipment, but he wasn't engaging with the rest of us. He seemed disconnected from the group for several months, possibly because of his recent divorce from his wife, Alicia; we weren't sure. He was keeping to himself and not following any of the unwritten communal house rules. His desk area had become a mess with stale pizza and cigarette butts strewn all over. We didn't see any sign of things changing anytime soon. So we made the hard decision not to bring him with us when we moved.

We debated about who would tell him. Eventually we came up with the totally awful idea of sending him an email. This is, of course, what young socially maladjusted computer geeks do when they can't handle the social responsibility of a friendship.

The wording of the email and the actual sending of it was agonizing. It was a group effort, and it took us several hours to compose, but eventually Brian Oblivion pressed the send button around one or two in the morning.

Count Zero and I both worked in the same building at Mass General Hospital; in fact, he had recommended me for my job there. I ran into him in the elevator the next day after the email had been sent on the way up to my office. It was quite awkward. I just stood there in the elevator and stared at the floor, the elevator buttons, or my feet. I didn't say anything. Eventually he asked me what was wrong. I asked him if he had read his L0pht email, and he said no.

I told him he should go read his L0pht email and then the elevator doors opened, and I walked out quickly.

Eventually there was an in-person meeting at Pizzeria Uno. Unfortunately I missed the meeting because I had to work, so I'm not sure who was there or what exactly was said, but I am sure it wasn't pleasant. The actual meeting part did not last long; evidently Count Zero stormed out before they even placed an order.

Things would get mostly patched up years later. Count Zero and Weld Pond even shared space with a few other folks in another hacker space in the Boston area in the late 2000s.

In the spring of 1996, those of us at the L0pht decided that we really wanted to make the L0pht pay for itself. We were already pretty good at generating revenue simply by selling old equipment at the MIT Flea Market. The lease on the space at 46 Waltham Street in South Boston was just about up. The space was not in the best part of town; we often had to walk past public drug use and urine puddles on the way to the front door.

This was about the time that we brought both Mudge and Tan into the L0pht. Despite being members, neither of them ever had any desk space at the original South Boston L0pht. We brought in Tan specifically because he worked in finance; I believe it was Morgan Stanley, and we assumed he knew how to do money stuff. At first Tan set us up as an S-Corp in Delaware under the name of LHI Technologies, which was an abbreviation of L0pht Heavy Industries. Then Massachusetts passed a new law that allowed for the creation of LLCs or Limited Liability Corporations. An LLC had much easier paperwork and tax filing requirements so LHI Technologies became one of the first LLCs ever incorporated in Massachusetts.

Despite Tan being the money guy, I was somehow elected to handle the bank accounts and cash. I remember protesting this decision, but my protests fell on deaf ears. They placated me by suggesting that the responsibility would rotate each month, and I grudgingly accepted knowing that there was no way paying the bills would ever change out of my hands. Rotating the responsibility of that task was impractical, so for all intents and purposes, I became the CFO/COO of the L0pht, not only making sure that the rent got paid each month but also handling our mail orders of CDs and other items, and eventually accounts receivable and payroll.

Besides the drug users at the front door, the South Boston location of the L0pht had another problem: random people stopping by all the time. This was a problem because often people would show up expecting they could crash there, or just wouldn't leave when we wanted to go home. It was interrupting work on our projects, and we didn't feel comfortable leaving some of them alone in the L0pht with all our equipment. So we looked for a different space, something that wasn't as centrally located and maybe a little more upscale.

There was no Craigslist back then, and we knew we couldn't afford a real estate agent, so Brian Oblivion and I would spend Saturdays driving around various Boston warehouse districts in my twelve-year-old Ford Tempo and write down phone numbers off the sides of buildings with "Space Available" signs. Most of these spaces ended up being way too expensive. We almost pulled the trigger on two different spaces in Cambridge, but both had major issues that turned us off.

Eventually we found a place at 294 Pleasant Street in Watertown. It was about half a mile from the nearest bus stop, more than far enough to prevent the casual interloper from dropping by but close enough to not be too burdensome. The space was an old warehouse that the owner had divided up into various offices. Downstairs was a woodworking company that made furniture. Across the hall from our space was a publishing company for a Russian Language newspaper (which, now that I think about it, wasn't suspicious at all!) and a few other companies. The space we ended up renting was a five-room chemist's office. It had its own bathroom, an emergency chemical shower, and an access hatch to the roof. It was probably twice the size of the original L0pht space in South Boston. We got a slight discount on the space accepting it "as is," meaning that the landlord did not have to replace the threadbare rug, and we promised to replace the broken and missing linoleum tiles and paint the walls before we moved in.

Moving day itself was quite the experience. We rented a large fifteen-foot U-Haul truck and started carting stuff down the stairs of the old L0pht. I don't think any of us realized just how much stuff we had accumulated. It was the standard hazy, hot, and humid Boston summer evening. We started loading the truck around four or five p.m. when we got off from work, and when it was finally loaded, we drove to Watertown and started carrying everything upstairs and into the space. I think we had to make two trips and finished completely exhausted sometime around eight a.m. the next day. I felt bad for Tan, as he had only known us for a short time, but he hung in there all night long helping us lug stuff down the stairs and then back up again. He was probably asking himself what exactly he had gotten himself into.

MEDIA ATTENTION

T he first bit of media that the L0pht got was in a 1994 independent documentary called *Unauthorized Access* by Annaliza Savage.[20] This was the first time any of us had really been in front of the camera. She had made contact through Count Zero and was probably referred to us by Emmanuel Goldstein from *2600* magazine.

The segment on the L0pht had appearances by quite a few people who weren't actually in the L0pht, such as Rogue Agent, Death Vegetable, and Tweety Fish. They just happened to be hanging out there when she was filming. The slightly longer than two-minute segment took her the better part of two days to film. We had to turn on the main lights for the space so the camera could film, which was unusual because we usually only used the glow of the various CRTs to find our way around.

Shortly after participating in Annaliza's documentary, the L0pht appeared on a TBS show called *CyberMania '94*,[22] which was just as bad as it sounds. It was a cheesy video game awards show hosted by Leslie Nielsen and child actor Jonathan Taylor Thomas. It was so cheesy that the winners of the awards' names weren't in sealed envelopes but displayed on a soon-to-fail handheld device called the Apple Newton. For some reason, in the middle of the awards show, they did a news magazine piece on hackers. There were clips from Emmanuel Goldstein, Count Zero, Death Vegetable, and some background footage filmed in the L0pht. There was a really, really bad shot of me grabbing a Mac SE from a dumpster and running away with a gleeful look on my face. And, of course, they used a random shot of Count Zero eating a slice of pizza while wearing an old Nintendo Power Glove. In fact, the show was so bad that twenty years later, *College Humor* would do a riff show called *Bleep Bloop: Cybermania '94*[23] in which they used a few seconds of the L0pht footage and a spoof on Count Zero eating the pizza with the Nintendo Power Glove.

I think the *Cybermania* piece and an equally terrible episode of a show called *Net Café*,[24] which had a very short segment from Mudge, and some awful segments from other folks we knew, were a wakeup call for us. Up until that point, I think we were just excited that someone with a big camera wanted to pay attention to us. The novelty wore off quickly. We realized that the media could easily use bits and pieces of what we said to fit their own narrative, which usually wasn't the narrative we were trying to tell. Most media pieces at the time that dealt with hackers often focused on hair color and how many Mountain Dew cans were on your desk. We came to realize that until then, we didn't have a specific narrative at all. We were just a bunch of people with a clubhouse and a lot of computers, which made it very easy to be manipulated by the media. This was not a cognitive realization at the time; we didn't sit around and debate our mission statement, but those early media pieces got us thinking and realizing just how powerful the media could be.

By the time we did a segment for New England Cable News in 1997,[24] not only had we formed the beginnings of a message about the fragility of the internet but we had also learned to control the content. We didn't control it by scripting it or doing the editing or anything; instead we educated the reporters both before and during filming (or writing) so that when they sliced their story together, we knew it would come out close to what we were trying to say as opposed to the idea the reporter may have had.

We could have easily turned down all the press requests, but we also knew that the press was a valuable tool. Sure, we could have just published our findings on our own website and maybe to a couple of security-minded mailing lists, but we recognized that the problem of security on the Internet was much bigger than that. We realized that the only way to affect any sort of meaningful change, or as Mudge put it, to "Make A Dent in The Universe,"[26] was through broad dissemination of our discoveries on the problems with software and hardware. To do that, we needed the press.

Eventually I came up with a protocol of sorts for dealing with press requests. First, we would look for prior material the reporter or journalist (yes, there is a difference) had published on hackers or just technology. If every story the writer published had a negative slant, or we thought there was no way we could bring them around to our way of thinking, we would politely decline. In fact, I even kept a list of reporters who had done terrible technology stories to make sure that if we ever dealt with them, we were extra careful with what we said or didn't say, if we said anything at all. If we decided that their past performance was acceptable, we would agree to a dinner meeting first, no cameras and everything off the record. (And yes, we realized even then that there is no such thing as "off the record.") We would usually hold these dinner meetings at a restaurant called John Harvard's in Harvard Square. It was a good excuse for a decent beer and a free meal, as they would always pick up the tab. (I would recommend the chicken pot pie, but unfortunately, that location of John Harvard's closed in 2019.)

This first meeting over beers and food was the perfect opportunity for us to question the reporter, determine their motives, and find out what sort of story they wanted to do. This meeting is also where we would suggest alternative viewpoints and different angles to the proposed story. In the end, of course, the reporter always made the final decision on what sort of story they were going to produce, but I think we were able to influence more than one reporter to change their story from the "evil hacker" story they had originally planned to one that painted hackers in a better light.

Press stories seemed to snowball one after the other. The Internet was new and shiny and exciting, and yet most people knew almost nothing about it. The media tried to fill the demand, but there just weren't very many stories about the Internet that weren't flat out boring or way too technical for the general population. Hacking and hackers, however, was one of those angles that had a mystique about it; throw in a Robin Hood and a David-versus-Goliath angle, and the press couldn't get enough. We just happened to be in the right place at the right time.

We got a half-page spread in *Wired*[27] magazine, including a picture, in August of '96. We got a nice extended segment on New England Cable News[28] at the beginning of 1997, followed by BBC, CBC, and PBS segments. One of first important print pieces was a series of articles that ran in the *EE Times* in March and April of 1997. The articles covered our recently released L0phtCrack tool (see Chapter 5), the vulnerabilities that lead to its development, and Microsoft's response. While a few articles in a technical magazine may not seem like a tipping point, I think those articles did more to establish L0pht as hacking experts than the half page in the vastly more popular *Wired* magazine.

During the summer of 1999, Emmanuel Goldstein told us he had been dealing with a producer from MTV who seemed really cool and wanted to know if we would be interested in speaking with them. We told him sure, as we would always at least talk to media to see what they wanted, and well, this was MTV. Weld took the lead in dealing with the producer while we went through our normal vetting process. Evidently the guy had some decent credentials. He graduated from the Columbia School of Journalism and had won a few journalism awards. We did not do our normal pre-dinner meetup prior to agreeing to film with him—the guy already had some decent credentials, we figured Emmanuel had already checked the guy out, and it was MTV.

By this point being on TV was no big deal for us; as a group we had been on CNN, *MacNeil Lehrer NewsHour*,[29] and *New England Cable News*.[30] I had done several individual shots for CNN, *ABC News* with Sam Donaldson, not to mention the dozens of print interviews. Usually the media centered around L0phtCrack or hacking in general. We figured we had this dealing-with-the-media thing down pat. If we could master CNN, we could master MTV. We had all grown up watching Kurt Loder, Tabitha Soren, and Daisy Fuentes, and it was going to be damn cool to be on the same network.

I remember feeling a little cautious about the whole thing, especially since we had not done our normal pre-filming dinner, but I glossed over the uneasy feeling in my mind and reminded myself this was MTV. Besides, Weld told us we would meet with the producer and find out what he was all about on the day of the shoot. I remember during the weekly meeting before MTV's visit that we all coordinated our wardrobe so that we wouldn't all be wearing the same L0pht T-shirt on camera.

On the day of the shoot, they were late. Very late, like over an hour. We knew this was going to take all day, so it wasn't that big of a deal, just annoying. When the producer finally knocks on the door, he was ready to shoot right away. He was in a big hurry to get the "in the door" shot, or the shot of Serena Altschul as we open the door and meet her for the first time. We tried to tell him we really don't do things that way and that we would like to meet Serena and the rest of the crew first and discuss what it is they want to shoot before we get into it. The producer, Anthony, was in such a big hurry, so we just say okay and let Serena in for the "in the door" shot (which the show never even used).

We spent the entire day filming, showing them everything in the L0pht, going over a lot of the cool projects we were working on, discussing our philosophy on finding software flaws, describing what L0phtCrack was all about and how we were the good guys. They probably got at least six hours of footage while they were there.

Of course, having an attractive and famous woman in the L0pht was a little intimidating. There was more than one stutter and a few trips over equipment, but I don't think we made too big of fools of ourselves.

Then we waited. We knew post-production of a piece like this would take some time. It wasn't due to air until the fall anyway. In the meantime, we started hearing rumors floating around that the show was going to suck, that they had totally morphed everything that we had been trying to educate them, and by proxy, the public on. By the time the air date came around, we were more than a little nervous knowing that they had over six hours of footage to cut up and remix in any order they wanted. We tried to remember if anyone had said or did anything that could make us look really bad.

When the show finally did air, we were relieved that they only used about fifty seconds of L0pht footage, and most of that was of Weld using his laptop to pull down Aircraft Communications Addressing and Reporting System (ACAR)[31] data and watch planes in real time. Nothing too bad. The rest of the show, however, was complete and utter crap. Some of the other people interviewed for the show didn't seem to take it as seriously as we did and decided to troll the producers with some cloak and dagger stuff about government agents and international secrets or something... Even after watching the show a few times, I'm still not sure what they were trying to do. Of course, the producers ate it up, didn't verify anything, and ran it as truth.

A few months after the piece aired, Weld sat on a panel at the HOPE 2000 hacker conference in New York City and talked about how terrible the show was and how the producers had completely warped the message we had been trying to tell them. Some of the better quotes by Weld from that panel…[32]

"We were pretty duped about what the whole thing was going to be about. We were pretty experienced with sussing out reporters before. We didn't want to be involved with a show about criminal behavior. We want people to understand the message of what hacking is all about of questioning technology and exploring."

"MTV chose to completely ignore reality and called it a documentary."

"They were very, very clueless, completely clueless; sometimes no matter how much education you try to do, if the people are dumb, it just doesn't matter. Some people just don't get it."

"We find this all the time with the media, a lot of time they just can't understand."

"I think there are things we can do, 'cause a lot of the reason at the L0pht we want to do these things besides the fun and glory of being on MTV is because we actually think we are going to actually educate young and impressionable people about reality as opposed to yet another story about someone's idea of hackers."

"People in the hacker community need to go outside of the media in a lot of ways... One of the reasons we started HNN, the Hacker News Network, is to have an alternative voice."

"I don't know what we were thinking being involved with MTV. That won't happen again."

And it didn't.

One of the other hackers profiled on the show, Shamrock, was also host of his own online hack/phreak TV show called *ParseTV* that was part of the online TV network Pseudo. He was part of the... I'm not even sure what to call it—*hoax* seems too strong of a word—prank maybe? Shamrock was replaced on the *ParseTV* show immediately after the MTV piece aired, and the show was abruptly canceled a few weeks later. He ended up sending us a long diatribe, which we later published on our own news website, "The Hacker News Network," that at first apologized for his involvement in the piece and then blamed MTV for being gullible enough to air it.

But the MTV piece was a reminder of why we were always so careful with the press. It was a double-edged sword. The press is an invaluable tool for reaching a mass audience with a positive message and at the same time can turn and cut you to shreds without a moment's hesitation or second thought.

###

The Works gatherings eventually morphed into the slightly more formalized 2600 meetings promoted by the magazine of the same name. *2600* magazine was named after the radio frequency used to seize control of a class-4 telephone switch.[33] This frequency was immortalized in a free plastic whistle found in the bottom of Captain Crunch cereal boxes in the 1960s. When blown, the whistle would emit a tone of 2600 Hz and allow someone to seize control of the tandem telephone switch to make free phone calls.

After 2600 meetings got kicked out of the pizza place in The Garage in Harvard Square, they moved to the food court at the Prudential mall. One, because there were pay phones nearby, so you could theoretically call another meeting, and two, it was warm. Outdoor meetings in Harvard Square are nice in the summer, not so much in the winter.

When 2600 meetings were over for the evening, those of us who were over twenty-one would often head to a nearby bar. There was a rundown, seedy Chinese restaurant, across the street from the Prudential mall, which I think was known as Peking Tom's, where we would often end up. We would try to use this meetup to weed out some of the younger crowd of 2600 meetings. But a few of them realized that the Boston Blue Laws would allow underaged people into an establishment before 8:00 p.m. without checking IDs. They still weren't supposed to drink, but if they left 2600 a little early, they could get inside and then try to hangout until the rest of us showed up hoping the staff wouldn't kick them out before then.

Eventually these post 2600 meeting gatherings became known as 2621, signifying the legal drinking age. That name may have originated in other cities, or it may have started in Boston, but soon many cities started referring to get-togethers in bars after the 2600 meeting as 2621.

As far as I know, Boston was unique in at least one way: we would buy beers for people who brought exploits, or computers flaws that allowed unintended access. People would write up the description of an exploit, print out a few copies, and bring it to 2621 for a free beer. This is how the L0pht's infamous Filter Fresh Exploit[34] was first released, which basically allowed you get a cup of coffee for twenty-five cents instead of thirty-five by manipulating a Filter Fresh coffee vending machine. This is also where Hobbit released his first version of Netcat,[35] a still popular port-scanning tool for unix systems.

NEW LØPHT

We divided up the large primary office of the new L0pht into two smaller rooms using some bookshelves and a hanging wall made from old VAX circuit boards that we tied together. One side of that wall became our chill-out area with a couch, several VCRs, a stereo system rescued from the trash, a small refrigerator, an old payphone we converted to work without coins, and an original standup arcade cabinet that played *Battlezone.* We would sometimes trick visitors into depositing coins into the payphone, even though it was on a standard phone line and didn't need coins to make a call. The other side of the wall became our library and conference room. It was our library because all the manuals we had rescued from various dumpsters were lined up on bookshelves and our conference room because we had made a large table out of a smooth door laid across two old minicomputers.

We knew right away that the two smaller rooms would become our workspaces. In one room would be hardware and in the other software. Even that early on we understood the marriage of software and hardware—you could manipulate hardware to cause issues in software and vice versa. Many vendors have taken twenty years to reach that conclusion, some still haven't figured it out. Microsoft only recently merged its hardware and software teams.[36] So Brian Oblivion, Kingpin, and I each set up desks and built a couple of long work benches in the area that became known as the hardware room. Weld, Tan, Stefan and Mudge set up desks in the slightly smaller software Room.

The small room to the left immediately off the main entrance became our network operations center (NOC). This is where we stored not only the L0pht.com system but also the parallel processing machine we had rescued from the defense contractor BBN. The last small room near the entrance, which we had at one point fantasized becoming a receptionist's space, became a storage area for the junk we would sell at the next MIT Flea Market. This was fine in the summer when we would clean it out every month, but in the winter months, this space would fill up and stay filled up until we could empty it at the first flea in April.

The rest of the space became a semi-organized dumping ground for old equipment. We had the shell of a VAX 11/780 in one corner of our conference room, which was the size of a large wardrobe. I remember one time it was filled with various dot matrix printers from some company that wanted to throw them away. Another time we filled it with old CGA monitors. Everything was eventually carted off to the flea market to make money to pay the rent and make room for the next pile of equipment. It was amazing that we never had to go looking for stuff; we just stumbled across it, and eventually people knew if they had old equipment to get rid of to let us know, and we would come take it off their hands. So much old computer equipment flowed through the L0pht, working or not. Some of it we fixed, some of it we hacked on, and almost all of it ended up at the flea market.

Most of us used large old metal desks—usually cast offs from Harvard, MIT, or Boston University—with big rolling cushioned metal chairs in various states of disrepair. I had a folding banquet table that I had purchased from the office supply store Staples and an old wooden desk that had originally been in a Harvard dorm room. I still have both pieces of furniture in my home office and work on them every day.

We kept the large overhead fluorescent lights off, preferring to work in the dim glow of CRT monitors and an occasional indirect lamp here and there. We had a few strings of Christmas lights, both colored and plain white, but we usually reserved those for parties. Occasionally we would need to turn on the big overhead lights when digging through a box of hardware looking for one specific part or trying to find a SCSI cable in a box of parallel printer cables; or when you needed a 5 V, 1.2 amp brick power supply with a certain power plug on the end. It was considered rude to just flip the lights on and blind everyone, and if you did you would suffer the wrath of insults from all corners. Instead, etiquette demanded that someone would yell "LIGHTS!" before switching on the large overheads, and while this action may still result in some groans and insults lobbed your way, it was preferable to the quantity of such outbursts if you failed to announce the warning beforehand.

Despite the constant moving in and out of old computer equipment, I kept the place somewhat clean and mostly organized as best I could in the evenings and weekends when I wasn't working at the real job. The Hardware Room had one huge metal cabinet with boxes inside for different cables. The Software Room had an old metal filing cabinet; I used one drawer of the filing cabinet to store the L0pht's bills and other paperwork. We used the rest of the drawers for printed-out manuals and other paper. We had a small refrigerator for cold drinks next to the *Battlezone* arcade game in the Chill-Out room. Later, when we had some actual paying clients and people were in the L0pht every day, we added snacks, mostly ramen, Cup-A-Soup, pretzel rods, and Cheez-Its.

Getting network access at the new L0pht was a challenge. Even getting a phone line installed so we could use our old dial-up was an issue. The local phone company NYNEX wanted us to get an expensive business line, since we had a business address. I was able to use a little social engineering (the art of convincing someone to do something they probably shouldn't) and convince them to install a less expensive service, telling them that while it was a business address, the phone would not get used much. We also knew that our little 56K modem dial-up would not cut it any longer. We needed more bandwidth. Traffic to the L0pht.com domain, even without people downloading files from the Whacked Mac Archives, had clogged our pipe to the extent that there was nothing left for us to use. The latest and greatest of high-speed bandwidth at the time was a 128K ISDN line. It was twice the speed of 56k dial-up but a still just a trickle of bandwidth compared to today's broadband. This system took us forever to get installed. It seemed we were constantly fighting with NYNEX, or later Bell Atlantic. Techs would come out, try to get things set up, and one thing or another would prevent them from completing the job. They would leave us with our old pokey dial-up. It got so bad that during our weekly meetings, we joked about a "Plan B" and even a "Plan C" if that didn't work. Both Plan B and C involved various quasilegal and straight-out illegal actions to either get our ISDN line connected or extract our revenge on NYNEX or both. Neither plan B nor C was ever enacted to my knowledge.

During these early days at the new L0pht, I was pretty much there every day. Others would show up for our weekly meetings or on the weekends, but I was usually around. I lived less than a quarter mile away across the river in Newton. Instead of going home after work, I would go to the L0pht and hang out by myself, work on the Whacked Mac Archives, pay some L0pht bills, watch a little *Babylon 5*, maybe solder together a few POCSAG decoders, or have an impromptu dance break by myself with the music turned up wicked loud to the musical stylings of Utah Saints, The Chemical Brothers, Covenant, The Prodigy, Fatboy Slim, or The Crystal Method. If I needed to do some heavy Internetting and didn't want to fight the mass of users attempting to hit our website, I could log in to the L0pht box and turn the web server off for a little while. Occasionally there would be an email to our internal mailing list, Resident@L0pht.com, mentioning that the web server was down and whoever was over there next if they could look into it. I had the L0pht to myself in those days. Everyone would show up for our weekly meetings and occasionally someone would stop by on the weekends, but mostly I was there alone. If I wasn't working or at my apartment sleeping, I was at the L0pht.

In at least one way, it was good that I was there almost daily. The L0pht.com box wasn't the most stable. We ran the OpenBSD operating system on top of a DEC Alpha, which are both respectable systems, but then we also had Mudge. Mudge customized multiple subsystems. He stripped much of the kernel and user space functionality, had telnet run on port 25 instead of 23, custom tweaked all the shells, and more. Mudge did stuff like that to add a little obscurity to the box and to reduce its overall attack surface. L0pht was a huge target of other hackers. If the L0pht.com domain was compromised, someone could acquire a lot of bragging rights as well as sensitive information, and that made us a little paranoid—enough to make weird minor changes that would alert us to someone trying to break in. An early IDS system, if you will. Anything to raise the bar a little, make the attacker expend a bit more effort and lower their chance of success.

Often I would come into the L0pht only to find that the box had crashed with some cryptic message about needing to reboot and run fdisk, a utility to repair the file system. The crash may have been due to someone poking at it from outside, or more likely, was unstable from all the custom alterations and changes. I was a heavy Mac user at the time, and anything outside of the basic text editor Nano, or Pine for email on the command line, was pretty alien to me—not to mention that this was L0pht.com, an important machine. Throw in all the tiny little tweaks that Mudge had made, and the system was a little twitchy to say the least. However, since that box was also running a lot of other critical services, if I didn't do something, the entire L0pht network would be unusable until someone more knowledgeable came in and fixed things. It could be days before anyone else could make it over there. And so I taught myself how to reboot the machine, run fdisk, and make notes of any errors. Between troubleshooting L0pht.com, my experience poking around the Boston University mainframes, and working on the SunOS box in my job at the Mass General Hospital OCD clinic, I became a pretty a decent unix system admin. Not a wiz mind you, but decent.

Tom Icom was an interesting character. It is hard to talk about him without also mentioning his really crooked front teeth. He got them fixed years later, but at the time it was a defining facial characteristic. When I first met him, he lived in Danbury, Connecticut. At Brian Oblivion's request we stopped by his apartment on our drive to a hacker conference, either Pumpcon, at a Best Western in Philadelphia (which is now a Whole Foods), or one of the HOPE conferences in New York City. He was very much into radio communications, hence his handle, Icom, taken from a popular brand of radios. On our way to the con, we passed a large building near the George Washington Bridge that Tom knew to be an office of the State Police. He pulled out his handheld radio, tuned to a frequency he obviously knew by heart, and started burping and yelling "pig" into the radio and then cackling with laughter. That's the kind of guy he was.

Tom was also the editor of *Cybertek* magazine, a short-lived printed and electronic magazine, or zine, with limited circulation that made it to at least sixteen issues. *Wired* magazine described *Cybertek* as a cyberpunk technical journal that published information relating to survival or personal freedom.[37] Tom and *Cybertek* magazine were associated with the International Information Retrieval Guild, or IIRG, a hacking group that Brian Oblivion was also a member of.

At some point Brian convinced Tom to move to Boston, got him a job at BBN, and invited him to become a L0pht member. Tom was only around for about a year, but while he was there, he wanted to publish a L0pht technical journal of sorts. Something we could get corporations to pay huge subscription fees for. At the time I thought the idea was a lot of work, especially with producing content, not to mention meeting hard deadlines. We couldn't attach our name to some self-published hacker zine and try to charge one thousand dollars a year or more for it. But looking back now, I think we could have made a viable product out of it. Three or four good articles a quarter with some slick glossy publishing, it could have been a success. Unfortunately, we soon learned Tom wasn't the most reliable person. He had a hard time fitting in at the L0pht or at BBN, and within a year he had left the L0pht and moved back to Connecticut. Last I heard he had gotten his teeth fixed, got married, and moved to Wyoming.

I'm not sure exactly when the idea hit me, but we were constantly on the lookout for alternative ways to make money. So at one of our weekly meetings, I brought up the idea of selling a CD of the

Whacked Mac Archives. There was some pushback at first because we considered selling something that we had gotten for free partly wrong. I argued that we would still have the FTP site up. If people wanted to wait in line, they could still get all the files for free, but if they wanted things a little faster, they could pay us twenty-five dollars to ship them the CD.

The first problem was that we didn't have enough money to professionally master a CD, but Weld said he knew a guy and could get us a deal. Then we realized we didn't have a CD-ROM drive needed to burn a master required to send out for duplication. So I suggested we could just take pre-orders. We would put the CD up for sale but tell people that it would take six to eight weeks for delivery. It was pretty common for things you ordered via mail order to take between four and six weeks back then. Free overnight or second-day delivery was pretty much nonexistent, so everything went via snail mail and took time. It was basically an early crowdfunding effort way before Kickstarter or crowdfunding were a thing. Within two weeks we had enough money to pay for the CD-ROM drive and the duplication, and within four weeks we had a stack of one thousand CD copies of the Whacked Mac Archives.

Over the next few months, sales remained steady. We had a PO Box at the US Post Office at the Prudential Center, and I would check it now and then. It was surprising how many people sent actual cash through the mail, sometimes wrapped in aluminum foil or five pieces of paper to prevent the mail man from seeing it through the envelope. It was also surprising how many checks bounced. Unfortunately, I didn't have the time or energy to sit around and wait for checks to clear before shipping the CD, so I would ship them and then wait for the checks to clear. A lot of people ended up getting a copy of the CD for free. I would enter the address from the order into a FileMaker Pro database, print out mailing labels, and take a trip down to the post office to mail the CDs out.

After we realized how popular the Whacked Mac Archives CD had become, Brian decided we should also make the files from his bulletin board into a CD, so we also created the Black Crawling Systems Archive CD. Black Crawling Systems was the name of Brian's old BBS. After we put L0pht.com online, he had moved all his old BBS files onto the www.L0pht.com website. By this time there were several other people also selling CDs of their old BBS files, which by now, you could easily find on the Internet if you looked hard enough. CDs such as Knowledge Phreak, Weasel Enterprises and High-tech Hustler were all sold the same way by other people and contained nothing but files that people had been trading for free on BBS systems. The CDs made it easy for people to get a ton of files all at once and not have to wait for them to download over slow and often expensive modem links.

We had an order page up on the website, but I also placed ads for the CD in the back of *2600* magazine.[38] It became so popular that a music and culture magazine in Italy called *Brain* published a review of the CD in October 1996.

In 1994 *2600 Magazine* held a conference in New York City to mark the magazine's tenth year in publication. They called it the Hackers

110

on Planet Earth Conference, or HOPE. Brian Oblivion went and volunteered to run the registration table. He took an old Mac II that had a video capture card from the L0pht and used it to create photo badges for the attendees. I heard later that the setup did not work very well and caused some rather long lines at the registration table.

Six years later *2600 Magazine* did it again, only this time they called the Conference Beyond HOPE, and they didn't bother trying to do photo ID cards. They did attempt to have a live two-way video link to some place in Europe, probably Germany. It was grainy and spent a lot of time buffering, but it mostly worked, at least from what I saw on the New York end; I have no idea what the quality was in Europe. Video conferencing was innovative technology at the time, especially going halfway around the world, and to have anything resembling that tech actually work at a hacker conference was pretty amazing.

This is where I first spoke with Captain Crunch. He was an older, white-haired, bearded, heavyset guy. I had seen him years earlier at my very first hacker con, HoHoCon, at a Motel 8 in Texas in December 1992. At HoHoCon he was constantly yelling at people to stop smoking and complaining that the conference room was full of smoke. I thought he was some cranky old dude and wished he would just shut up so I could focus on the presentations on Van Eck phreaking and hacking .gov systems for information about aliens. By Beyond HOPE in 1997, I understood that he was the person who had taken credit for discovering the whistle in the Captain Crunch cereal that would blow a 2600 Hz tone that was useful for taking over telephone switches and making free long-distance calls. For a long time his choice of handle, "Captain Crunch," led people to believe that he had discovered the whistle; today it's pretty clear he did not, but he didn't try to correct the record. Regardless, the community considered him OG, part of the Old Guard in hacker circles.

At HOPE he came right up and started talking to me; he knew who I was and asked for my autograph. The people I was with quickly tried to get me to move into a different room and not talk to Captain Crunch. I didn't understand what they were doing. Here was a pretty famous hacker asking me, Space Rogue, for my autograph. I was extremely flattered and wanted to stay there and talk with him. Someone took a picture of me and Crunch while I was signing something for him. Whoever was with me pulled me away and into another room. And only then was I warned,

"Crunch is bad news. Stay away from him."

"What, why?"

"Just stay away from him."

I didn't learn until years later that evidently Captain Crunch liked to enjoy questionable activities with younger men or even boys that involved piggyback rides and back massages.[39] Obviously the flattery and autograph request was a part of his craft to ingratiate himself with his victims. It is a shame that we sometimes hold people up as revered figures and that once they reach that status almost nothing can touch them. Even now when Captain Crunch's and other's characters are well-known, people still try to defend their actions as being misinterpreted, misunderstood, or somehow defensible when in fact they are immoral, unethical, and possibly criminal.

###

The entire L0pht was at Beyond HOPE in August of 1997, which at the time included Mudge, Brian Oblivion, Kingpin, Stefan, Weld Pond, John Tan, and me. The conference gave us a speaking slot, and we conducted a panel on stage.[40] We each discussed some of our recent projects. Brian mentioned a potential universal wireless decoder that he wanted to build with Kingpin that would handle not only POCSAG but also FLEX, ReFLEX, Mobitex (protocols used by cellular pagers), and even the MDT protocols used in police car terminals. Kingpin discussed some of his work on PalmPilots and plans for various hacks on that platform. I discussed Macintosh stuff, specifically the Whacked Mac Archive CD. Stefan talked about how power companies could become major ISPs by transmitting data over electric lines, which would make them a big hacking target in the future. He also encouraged people to look at the AppleShare IP protocol since there weren't many people looking at it yet and there were probably some big, easily discovered holes. Weld told people if anyone wanted to publish stuff on the L0pht's advisories page that we would be more than willing to do so and that it would be an excellent way to share information among the community. Tan briefly mentioned his work on Netware. Mudge then gave a really abbreviated and rushed talk on the failings of Windows NT LAN Manager passwords, scrunching a forty-five-minute talk about how our new software tool L0phtCrack worked into about twenty minutes.

This was my first time on any sort of stage and talking in front of a large group of people. It helped tremendously that I wasn't alone and was on stage with six friends, but it was still extremely nerve-wracking. I think my speaking time totaled a whopping two and a half minutes.

Beyond HOPE was also important because I think it was then that I realized how popular L0pht had become. We were more than just some people playing around in our spare time, or a popular website. L0pht was something bigger than that. I don't think I understood exactly what, and maybe I still don't, but Beyond HOPE was where I realized that L0pht was more than just the sum of its parts. Many people already knew of us, and when people we knew introduced us to others, it was always with, "He's a part of L0pht," to which there was always a reaction of recognition. So while people may not have known us as Kingpin or Tan or Space Rogue, they did know the L0pht name. That feeling of strangers recognizing me at Beyond HOPE was alien to me then but would become extremely familiar as time went on.

One year it worked out that Mudge and I were both looking for a place to live at the same time. I think I suggested the idea that we should get an apartment together and not worry about finding new roommates. So we ended up renting a two bedroom apartment on the top floor of a triple decker next to a gas station on Trapelo Road in Belmont, just on the other side of Watertown, less than two miles or a ten-minute drive from the L0pht.

It was a large apartment for a two bedroom with a conjoined living room and dining room. Mudge took one half of the large room and I took the other, and we set up our computers on desks. When we weren't at the L0pht or working, we would sit there back-to-back hacking away. At one point Weld stayed with us for a few weeks, sleeping on the floor in the middle of the living/dining room. It was a great setup. At the end of the lease, we both moved to separate places. Mudge rented another apartment with his then-girlfriend, I think, and I moved into a house in Acton with my then-girlfriend, Lori.

In July 1997, L0pht somehow got involved with a company known as Cambridge Technology Partners. CTP was a software consulting company that eventually got bought out by Novell and later Atos. They had IPO'd in 1991 and hit peak revenue in 1999 at $628 million. They were going strong in 1997 and looking to expand their consulting business.

The L0pht and CTP relationship was rather touchy-feely at first, as neither side really knew what to think of the other. We were a bunch of T-shirt-and-ripped-jeans hacker types, and CTP was a more of a polo-and-khakis yuppy type. Since both sides seemed interested in the other but neither one knew what to expect, we proposed a simple penetration test of CTP's systems. This would allow us to see how CTP worked and allow CTP to see exactly what we could do.

And so we executed a master agreement with terms and conditions and a statement of work, all professional like a real company. The process was that LHI Technologies, the business name that we incorporated L0pht under, would perform a black-box external penetration test over a few weeks. We would then provide CTP with a written deliverable detailing our findings and any obvious recommendations, and an in-person briefing covering our activities after it was all over.

One stipulation in the agreement was that we had to get liability insurance. I thought this was going to be a major issue, but I went down to the insurance agent who handled the renter's insurance for my apartment, and he had a quote for me that afternoon. It was somewhere near one hundred dollars for something like a million dollars' worth of liability insurance. I'm sure if we ever had to file a claim against it, getting a payout would have been a challenging exercise. But I had the insurance certificate I needed to show CTP that yes, we had liability insurance.

We finally got the paperwork ironed out by the beginning of August, and we divvied up the work. Mudge, Weld, and Tan would hit the network from the outside. I had already been doing open-source intelligence gathering for weeks in anticipation. (Of course, back then we didn't call it open-source intelligence, we didn't even call it Googling, since Google didn't exist yet.) Brian and I would do a trashing run outside one of their offices in Newton, a suburb of Boston, and Kingpin would explore their telephone system.

The trashing run was boring; the dumpster was on the other side of the parking lot from the space they rented out of a multi-tenant building. I basically drove up in broad daylight, opened the hatchback of my ten-year-old Ford Tempo, threw a couple bags of trash in the back, and drove away. I got lucky, as two of the bags came from the CTP offices. One bag contained what looked like the full contents of someone's desk, like it had just been cleaned out and dumped in the trash. There was more than enough information to build a complete profile on this employee. He had been fighting a traffic ticket for driving in the breakdown lane of Route 128 South just before the Route 9 exit. His argument was that his then-pregnant wife was experiencing abdominal pain, and he was trying to get her to the hospital. He didn't mention why he didn't just stop and call an ambulance. I don't know if he beat the ticket or not, but there was more than enough information in that one trash bag for some threat actor to completely compromise that employee.

Mudge and Weld went after the web server first. There was a popular bug at the time known as the PHF vulnerability, which was in a CGI-bin file that came preinstalled with the Apache web server. This PHF file was vulnerable to a simple command injection attack, which normally should not have been that big a deal. However, Mudge and Weld quickly found that the http.conf file on this web server had the wrong permissions set and by using the PHF command injection vulnerability, they could force the web server to run as the root user on the system's next reboot. The problem was that the web server had been running for over three months straight without being rebooted, and there was no way to tell when the admin would decide to reboot the system next. Without the machine rebooting, there was no way to get the web server to run as root, which made this attack ineffective for one's needs.

Mudge and Weld moved on to different attack surfaces of the network and quickly found other ways of getting in. But as luck would have it (luck being a very relative term here), a few days later there were a series of sewer explosions in Kendall Square[41] in Cambridge just a few blocks from the CTP offices. One person died and four people were injured in the terrible accident. The electric company responsible shut off power to a large section of Cambridge for over five hours while they made repairs. After hearing the news, the next day Weld checked the remote machine and, sure enough, the power outage was long enough to drain any UPS batteries the web server had been using, and the server had rebooted. Apache was now running as root, which allowed us to use the command injection vulnerability in the PHF file to access any file on the system.

Between the vulnerability on the Apache web server and other issues elsewhere on the network, Mudge and Weld had access to everything the company owned. Everything from payroll to staffing, forecasting, monthly reports, pricing and costing models, Oracle databases, network diagrams, corporate credit cards, network routers, etc. Everything was just laid wide open, one big flat network.

Kingpin also struck gold in compromising the telephone network. He had gained access to every employee's voice mailbox—including the employees we had been speaking with about setting up the penetration test and an acquisition they were working on. He only needed to make a recording of one voicemail to show that we did indeed have access. To minimize privacy concerns, we figured we should grab one voicemail from one of the people we had been dealing with at CTP instead of just some random employee. Somehow we got lucky and grabbed the one voicemail message in which they discussed the L0pht.

This is a transcript of the voicemail intercepted by Kingpin during his test of the CTP voicemail system.

> Received, Five forty-nine PM, Thursday, August 14th, three minutes, to listen press 0
>
> Got your messages but its late in the day so instead of beeping you I'll just leave this message. With regards to the guys at LHI, ummm, heheheh, that is a bit frustrating

that they keep bringing up the million-dollar thing and have this one-thirty number in their heads. Here's where I am and maybe this will get us there as a group. Ummm, What I have in mind is to give them a base of, umm, let's start with a base of eighty, and a bonus of twenty, umm, and so that's going to be set on performance metrics, the bonus will be, that are outlined in the business plan, if they hit that, that gets them then to the number of one hundred, which I think to begin was their magical number, umm, now of course, that's thirty grand short of what they're putting out there as one thirty so ah, we could do that through options, ah what I'm thinking of is if we give them three thousand options across the board, which is a bit rich, but at the same time I think we're thinking initially we would have to do that regardless. If you go with that, if you do three thousand I'm thinking if we're at thirty-five right now in terms of a stock price in four years' time, let's say the stock is seventy, which I think is extraordinary conservative umm, but nevertheless if the stock is at seventy within a four-year timeframe umm that means that the overall valuation of those three thousand shares would be a hundred-and-five thousand dollars, so ah, if you divide that by four then that gives you twenty-six thousand

dollars per year, which is the valuation
of the stock, so you add the twenty-six to
the hundred and then you come out with one
hundred and twenty-six umm, and where I would
be willing to move with that, maybe we should
go in with that as a going-in position, ah we
could maybe move to eighty-five as a base,
that would get them to a hundred and five,
and then of course you throw in the twenty-
six, that gets them to one-thirty-one, which
is what they are asking for, and again I
think that is very conservative because I
think the stock will perform much better than
that. Umm, yeah one thing I would have to do
is walk these guys through the logic because
I don't think they really understand what
stock options are all about. Umm, but I think
this would be a very fair offer, and would
probably get us there and also keep us in
line from a ah, a uh, pretty much in line at
least, from a salary perspective. Still not
real comfortable in shelling out that kind
of money for Brian and Joe, but if that's
how the package comes together, then that's
how it comes together. So ah, anyhow, that's
where I am with that, why don't we chat about
it tomorrow. I'm going to be in the Cambridge
office from probably 7:30 till 10, then I
have to meet with Jim at 10 and after that I'm
going be at Travis Street in the NorthEast

```
review with Bill and Diane. Umm, for the rest
of the day. So ah, let's try to hook up one
way or another, talk to you later, thanks.
```

We realized from this voicemail that they didn't get it. They didn't understand the value that L0pht brought to the table. They didn't understand our vision of software and hardware working together or of fixing problems to protect users. Brian and Kingpin didn't like this voicemail one bit. Despite this message, we realized early in the test that we would not be a good fit with CTP. However, even knowing that a L0pht and CTP marriage would never happen, we continued with our contractual obligations. We wrote up our deliverable and prepared a final presentation.

Before we realized that this was not a match made in heaven, we were still working on the penetration test and negotiating how CTP and L0pht might eventually work together. It was a heady time, for me at least. I was thinking this might be it, my ticket out of dead-end tech support jobs. I screamed along loudly in my car whenever the ska-punk song by Reel Big Fish "Sell Out" came around on the radio.

> So I signed on to the record company
> They say they're gonna give me lots of money
> If I play what they want you to hear
> They tell me it's cool, and I sure believe it
>
> Sell out, with me oh yea
> Sell out with me tonight
> The record company's gonna give me lots of money
> And everything's gonna be all right

Before we presented our final deliverable, our negotiations with CTP progressed far enough that CTP prepared written offers of employment for each of us. The offer amounted to $90K salary, 22 percent yearly bonus based on corporate profit, and 3000 stock options. This was a very attractive offer, especially for 1997. It was three times what I was currently making and a good bump up for others in the L0pht as well. Despite having no interest in accepting the offer, Kingpin used his letter to get a raise at the company he was working for. Despite the offer letters, there was no job guarantee, no mention of what would happen to the L0pht name, the group, or anything. I often wondered what would have happened if one or two of us had accepted that offer.

Mudge went to CTP with our report in hand and gave the presentation on our findings. He tells an amazing version of this story—how their mouths were agape the entire time, and how when he got to the point about the voicemails and what we must have heard, their mouths just about hit the floor.

After Mudge basically pointed out how CTP had their pants down around their ankles security wise, we responded to the job offers. We knew things were over at that point, so we asked for some big stuff that wasn't completely outrageous but that they would be very unlikely to accept. Basic things like a job guarantee, that L0pht would stay together for a certain amount of time, and a mobile hacking unit with a list of equipment that made the panel van in the movie *Sneakers* look like a Hot Wheels car. It was all legit needed equipment for a fully kitted-out SigInt (Signals Intelligence) vehicle but with a boosted price tag. We figured if on the off chance they accepted our counteroffer, then it would be worth it to get to use so many toys. Needless to say, they didn't respond.

Mudge had left a backdoor open in the CTP network, a way to get back into the system in case they had discovered our primary access during the test, or it otherwise became disabled. The plan was that after we finished the test that we would remove the backdoor. However, the relationship after our last presentation to the board of directors was such that there was no way we could go back and ask for access to remove the backdoor. We had listed the backdoor in our report and mentioned it in the presentation, so they knew about it and could have removed it any time. We no longer had an active contract, so we could not legally go into their network to remove it. Now and then it would call out to us electronically over the Internet and let us know it was still there and active. It kept trying to connect back to us for years.

One of my coworkers at CompUSA was Stefan. Stefan later followed Brian when he moved over to working at University Computers, and then I followed Stefan. Brian eventually invited Stefan to join the L0pht while we were still at the old South Boston location. Stefan was a Mac guy like me, but he also knew a lot about high-voltage power connections. Like the kind needed to get old VAXen or large parallel processing machines up and running.

Stefan was around a bit, as much as anyone else, and he had a decent collection of machines he stored at the L0pht, but I don't remember any of the projects he worked on. He was a good guy, and everyone got along with him. He was very helpful in hooking up the power for the larger machines, but I never really knew what it was he was hacking on.

There was a point, though, after our first buy-out offer from Cambridge Technology Partners and after our Congressional testimony but before we started talking with @stake, where we decided Stefan wasn't contributing to where the rest of us wanted to go. At least this time when we had to say goodbye to one of our members and good friends, we didn't do it over email as we had with Count Zero. We told Stefan in person during one of our weekly meetings. It was still super awkward, uncomfortable, painful, and probably not handled as well as it should have been. We tried to explain our case and tell him it wasn't personal, but I am sure he took it pretty hard. When six of your good friends basically all break up with you, it cannot be a good feeling.

Camneerg is "green mac" spelled backwards. It is what I named a weird Frankenstein machine I created out of a Mac Plus and a Pac Bell Data terminal. The Mac Plus originally came with a nine-inch black-and-white screen, and I swapped out the screen with the green and black one from the Pac Bell terminal. The screens were the same size, so that part was easy. I had to mess with the wiring a bit to get it to work. Looking back I'm not sure how I didn't either shock myself with the high voltage inside the tube or blow myself up. But somehow I got it to work.

Well, I mostly got it to work. Everything on the screen was backward. On the one hand, I thought this outcome was wicked cool, and I had no desire to mess around with the wires again for fear of a high voltage shock or worse. So it stayed backward and green. During a late night online chat session via IRC (Internet Relay Chat), when I was describing my franken creation, Lady Ada, the same person who ran around my house at Grillathon after taking a bite of a Habanero, gave it the name Camneerg, or "green mac" spelled backwards. The name seemed appropriate, so it stuck.

About a year later, I painted the machine black and augmented it even further. I worked up the nerve to mess with the internal video cabling again and added a cable that routed outside the case and enabled me to hook up an old monitor with an orange-and-black screen to it. I then installed a web server on it. So I ended up with a black-painted Mac Plus with a green-and-black internal screen that displayed everything backward and an external orange-and-black screen that ran as a web server. Because, why not?

Marcus Ranum, who many credit to inventing the network firewall[42] while he worked at Digital Equipment Corporation, was running a company called Network Flight Recorder (NFR) early in 1998. Marcus, of course, never gave himself that credit, saying that many others had come before him, but in his own words, it was the first firewall to have "a part number and a manual and a corporation behind it." While Marcus's firewall may not have been the first, Network Flight Recorder was a product ahead of its time. NFR was not a firewall; it was designed as an evidence collection audit tool and to help determine what had happened on a network, mostly after some sort of incident like a breach or other intrusion. By 1999, Marcus discovered that network forensics and analysis wasn't really a hot seller yet. A general-purpose network analyzer, data monitor, and recorder just weren't sexy enough to grab many dollars in the marketplace, regardless of how good a product they made. At the time the new shiny, blinky light solution was IDS, or intrusion detection systems. The market's shortsighted thinking probably being that if you can prevent the intrusion, then you don't need forensics.

And so, like any good CEO, Marcus pivoted his product ever so slightly to take advantage of the current market until the market would, hopefully, catch up with his product.[43] However, as an intrusion detection system, NFR was severely lacking, as it had no signatures. In the 1990s most defensive security tools, including firewalls, anti-virus, and IDSs, were signature-based. You needed a small snippet of code, or a signature, that was present in an attack. You then compared this signature with the data analyses from network traffic. When the system saw a match in a signature and some network traffic, it would trigger an alert. The difficulty came in developing a signature for a specific attack that would not also trigger an alert on legitimate traffic. When Marcus added IDS capabilities into NFR to take advantage of the current market, he only had a few rather basic signatures.

As Mudge, Brian, and Weld worked at the defense contractor Bolt Beranek and Newman (BBN), they got early access to NFR and easily recognized the product's power and adaptability. Mudge; Weld; and another BBN employee, Silicosis, wrote some early signatures for Marcus to include with the product. Marcus was so impressed he asked them to write more signatures. They could not do that work through their current employer, a defense contractor, so it was arranged to pass the work off to the L0pht instead. To help facilitate that work, Silicosis left[44] a comfy government contractor job with full benefits and a nice office to work in a dingy wooden mouse-infested warehouse that was literally down by the river. In addition to Silicosis, we hired Dildog to assist with the module/signature writing. (Years later Dildog claimed he turned down an interview with Google before they launched because he thought search engines were boring.[45]) Silicosis and Dildog became the L0pht's first two paid employees, and NFR became our first major contract.

The agreement was officially announced with a press release in March of 1999[46] that quoted Marcus as saying, "L0pht has an amazing depth of information about system vulnerabilities and are the ideal source for cutting edge intrusion detection signatures." Our work with NFR went a long way in establishing our credibility and legitimacy as trusted experts with both the hacker community and the business world.

We continued to push out dozens of signatures for NFR over the next several months. Silicosis took it a step further, pushing Mudge who pushed Marcus that NFR shouldn't rely on simple signatures alone but should also add protocol monitoring that would look for attacks. Protocol monitoring gave NFR an advantage over other IDSs. When new attacks were discovered, other products had to wait for a signature to get written and then installed, whereas many of those attacks were already covered by the modules Silicosis had written and deployed.

Eventually Marcus sold off NFR to Check Point,[47] another firewall company. At the time much of the code the L0pht had wrote and pushed to NFR remained in the product; in fact, I wouldn't be surprised if some of that code wasn't still shipping in other products today.

By late summer of 1999, L0pht was earning enough money from NFR, HNN, L0phtCrack sales, T-shirts, CDs, and other disparate sources that we had four or five of us drawing at least part-time salaries. Some months were touchy; if someone was a week late in paying us, we wouldn't have made payroll. Some months I had to delay in paying the electric bill so that everyone could get paid, but somehow we never missed payroll, which is more than I can say for some startups I worked with later in my career.

Despite the number of advisories we published on some of the largest companies in the word and the numerous threats from various software vendors, the L0pht only had a few minor legal issues. We were tight-lipped about our real-world identities. We were very careful not to link our online handles to our actual names to help prevent a lawsuit from happening. However, when we incorporated as the first LLC (Limited Liability Corporation) in Massachusetts, we obviously had to use our real names. The corporate name wasn't L0pht; we used LHI Technologies. LHI obviously stood for L0pht Heavy Industries. We had a separate domain and website at Lhi.com, but the link between LHI and L0pht was transparent for even early search engines such as Alta Vista. Despite the link, no one had ever made the connection between the two until we got served with a lawsuit.

That is, Brian Oblivion got served with a loud knock on his door at five a.m. from the local sheriff's deputy. The lawsuit wasn't from

Microsoft or Novell or any other large company we had shamed by publishing their dirty laundry but by someone we had never heard of known as the "Supreme Law Firm." It sounded like a joke, but it wasn't.

The Supreme Law Firm[48] is still around, with a website that hasn't much changed since the mid-nineties. The website has a bunch of information related to things like the IRS and various court cases. Some of those files had found their way onto Brian Oblivion's Black Crawling Systems BBS years before, and from there onto L0pht.com when Brian moved his old BBS file archives online.

The lawsuit was a complaint about copyright infringement, about how we had published copyrighted materials from the Supreme Law Firm's BBS. When you get woken up at five a.m. and served with a lawsuit by a sheriff's deputy, it can rattle you. It wasn't just Brian; we were all a little scared. So we called the only lawyer we knew, a distant relative of Kingpin's—an Uncle or cousin—who was a real estate lawyer or something equally innocuous. We told him, "Just make this go away." And so he did. By the time he called us back a few days later, we had time to calm down and think about our options. The lawyer told us we could settle by just removing the files from the website. But by now we didn't want to. It pissed us off that this guy would try to sue us over a couple of text files that had been floating around on BBSs and various other websites for years. But in the end, we caved. We didn't have money to pay for a protracted lawsuit and a lawyer who could actually handle the case. Since Supreme Law Firm had an actual lawyer, his costs would be minimal, so not really a fair fight. Brian took down the files. The lawsuit went away, and it left us with a bitter taste in our mouths.

Another time, I received a random email from some group claiming to be the greatest Macintosh hacking website in the world. Here they meant hacking as in coding and routinely holding some sort of hackathon for coding challenges every year. Their complaint was that the Whacked Mac Archives were infringing upon their Great Mac Hacking website moniker. I checked out their website and guessed that they didn't have any money either, so I put on my best legalese writing hat and responded to their email saying that I could find no record of their copyright claim with the US Copyright office, which at that point had just begun putting searchable stuff online. I said that the likelihood of confusion between their greatest Mac hacking site and the Whacked Mac Archives was slim to none. I emailed it off and never heard from them again.

Besides Brian Oblivion's BBS archives of the Black Crawling Systems, the L0pht website also hosted several other archives, including text files from the Cult of the Dead Cow, the Information Retrieval Guild, and Dr. Who's Radio Phone Archive. This last archive contained a ton of information on various cellular telephones. By the 1990s computer hackers had realized what the phone phreakers had known for years: that cell phones where really computers, and even better, they were just endpoints of a much larger network. Like anything else, cell phones could be hacked and information about how to hack them was included in Dr. Who's Radio Phone Archive. And before you ask, yes, this is the same Dr. Who from the (in)famous hacker group Legion of Doom.

In May of 1997, Custom Computer Services, Inc. (CCS) filed a lawsuit against LHI Technologies in the Eastern District of

Wisconsin. The complaint specifically mentioned software piracy or a violation of US Copyright Act 17 U.S.C. § 101. They claimed L0pht was distributing copyrighted DDI software via our website. DDI, or digital data interpreter, analyzes digital data used to control cellular telephones.

According to the legal complaint, CCS had notified someone, presumably Dr. Who, via email the previous June about the infringing software. Of course, receiving legal complaints via email in 1997 usually resulted in a quick chuckle followed by a prompt hitting of the delete key. Dr. Who obviously never informed us of these complaints, so the legal filings came as a complete surprise to us. Unlike Supreme Law Firm, a law firm with five people in its name represented Custom Computer Services. A name you couldn't help but take seriously, as it provided the correct amount of fear. I mean, there was no way we could afford a lawyer to fight this, let alone travel to Wisconsin to fight it even if we wanted to. But this was a legitimate complaint, despite how we may have felt about the copyright law itself or how it specifically applied to software, or strings of ones and zeros. CCS was right, and we were wrong according to the law. So to avoid any trouble, we quietly asked Dr. Who to remove the software, which he did reluctantly, and we quickly settled with CCS.

The Radio Phone archive also had some trouble with Motorola, not with the company's software but with use of the company's logo. This time Dr. Who didn't ignore the initial email and handled the issue on his own. At first he tried to just turn the Motorola logo upside down and call it a derivative work, but they didn't fall for that. Then he tried replacing it with an upside-down Williams Pinball logo, which looked eerily similar to the Motorola logo, but again, Motorola demanded that all logos be removed. In the end, they were.

One thing L0pht did really well was throw a party. If you can imagine the best cyberpunk scene out of any Brunner, Gibson, or Stephenson novel, you have a pretty good idea of what the L0pht looked like. Monitors stacked on top of monitors, each displaying different images or scrolling text; strings of Christmas tree lights, both white and colored hanging on the walls; a hanging wall of circuit boards from a VAX computer; and everywhere you looked, power-on LEDs from some piece of equipment. Mannequins decorated with ribbon cable sashes, and computer chips stuck at random places into their soft torsos. Even a keyboard from an old point-of-sale terminal rested on top of the toilet water tank in the bathroom. Like a nightclub the lights were low, and the music was loud a techno, goth, and industrial remix of Brian Oblivion's own collection of vinyl. When the DJ was taking a break, Mudge would play live progressive rock in the software room to the accompaniment of a homebrew laser light show from Hobbit.

We had a holiday party every year in the middle of January, and somehow it often ended up on the coldest day of the year. That was always fun for people trying to get a cab home at two a.m. from the outskirts of Watertown.

We invited everyone we knew, not just the local hackers in Boston. Anyone we had met online or elsewhere and that we had an email address for received an invitation. Many people would take a flight to Boston just for the L0pht party.

One year I was near the front entrance to the space, probably organizing some trash bags full of beer cans and other detritus from the party, when I looked up and saw a police officer standing in the doorway. It was late at night in a run-down industrial area of town, and they probably heard the thump-thump music and saw the lights flashing through the window outside. I stood up and stood in the doorway directly in front of the officer and assumed the parade rest position with my hands behind my back, blocking his path.

"Can I help you, officer?"

"What's going on here?" he asked as he attempted to peer over my shoulder into the darkened room.

Someone else must have noticed him standing there because the music and the commotion behind me got a little quieter right then.

"Just having our office holiday party," I said calmly.

"Is anyone underage in there?" he asked

"I don't think so, but I didn't really check IDs."

He took a step toward me expecting I would step out of the way and let him enter, but I just stood my ground. It was the same tactic old drill sergeants would use to get you to break formation. Invade your personal space and see if you step away. I didn't.

He stepped back, turned to his partner, and shrugged. His partner looked at me and said, "Have a nice day," and then they both turned and walked down the stairs.

While we knew everyone at our parties, we didn't trust them enough to be at the L0pht without one of us present, just like you probably wouldn't trust party guests alone in your home, so we would usually shut things down at three or five in the morning.

One time Mudge had a few folks over to the l0pht for a wine tasting party of some sort. Since I wasn't into wine, I didn't hang around. I went in the next day to find the place a complete mess with half-empty wine bottles nestled in between computer monitors and trash everywhere. So I cleaned up, took out the trash, and then started hacking on something as one does at the L0pht. Later in the afternoon, or maybe the next day, Mudge comes in and says, "Hey, where are all the wine bottles?" The wine tasting was of rather rare wine, so rare that even the bottles were valuable, some of them being over a hundred years old, apparently. He jokingly gave me shit about throwing away those bottles for years afterwards.

Besides our yearly huge invite-everyone-we-know party, we also had quieter, smaller parties for just us and a few close friends. New Year's Eve was one of those traditions where a few of us and some friends would gather and see in the new year. I would also spend the Fourth of July at the L0pht, usually by myself. I'm not sure anyone else knew it, but you could see about four different towns' fireworks from the roof of the building.

One thing I liked to do at the L0pht was to resurrect old hard drives. especially old Mac SCSI hard drives. At the time 20, 40, and 80 MB hard drives were abundant when people were upgrading to 120 and 250 MB drives. We would rescue them from trashcans at our day jobs, or pull them out of hardware we found lying around, or people would just give us boxes of them.

I had an old Mac SE setup on a L0pht workbench that I had dedicated specifically to testing hard drives. Sometimes, I had to remove the circuit board from one drive and replace it with another board from the same make and model of drive. Most of the time, though, it was just a matter of executing a low-level format that would force the drive to map out bad sectors, and boom, the drive was usable again. Really dead drives were dead drives and were pretty much useless. You could only take so many of them apart and remove the magnetic parts because eventually your refrigerator is covered in old hard drive magnets. Instead of throwing the really dead drives away, we sold them at The Flea. We became well known for selling "guaranteed dead" hard drives for one or two dollars each.

Occasionally someone would stop by our table and tell us, "Hey, you know that dead drive you sold me last month? I got it working again."

"Do you want your money back? We guaranteed it dead," I would reply.

No one ever returned a drive.

Sometimes low-level formatting a drive didn't work because the driver or the software on the drive used to control it would get in the way, usually because it was corrupted and would prevent the format. Forcibly replacing the software driver, which you could do by using different software, was a solution that often worked. I had an entire collection of Mac formatting utilities with names like Anubis, 1st Aid HFS, VCP Formatter, Symantec Utilities, SCSI Director Pro, Silverlining, FWB, and a few others. If one didn't work, I would try another.

FWB specifically also had the option of applying a password to your drive. This would prevent a disk from mounting and being available to the system unless you knew the password. Somehow I realized that even if a password was set, you could just forcibly replace the FWB driver without destroying the data on the drive, bypassing the password and still getting access to the data.

This information became my first official L0pht advisory. We posted it to our website and to the BugTraq mailing list[49] as we did with most of our advisories. I also sent a few copies to the major Mac news websites like MacInTouch and others. I was pretty proud of it.

Post Office Code Standardization Advisory Group (POCSAG) is a wireless protocol used to transmit asynchronous data to pagers. Pagers were very popular before cell phones achieved wide adoption, and pagers stayed popular for quite some time. Wireless coverage for cell phones wasn't all that great in the early days, and pagers worked on a lower frequency that had wider coverage. The earliest pagers didn't receive data and would only beep or vibrate to alert the wearer to find a telephone to call in to check messages. Later pagers had small screens, usually used for someone to enter a phone number for the person receiving the page to call back. The display on most pagers could fit about ten characters, and people got very creative on how to use those characters. It was always numbers, no letters, because you could only enter numbers from a telephone touch pad. It wasn't long before people developed their own codes to enter instead of a phone number. Something like 99-911 might mean "call home it's an emergency." Eventually more complex codes arose, like 143 would mean "I love you," or 411 would mean "where are you." Even more complex codes like 170 90-02, which might mean "I'm not coming home, Mike."

By the early 1990s, multiline pagers or alphanumeric pagers were common. These usually had about three lines of twenty characters each where someone could write a message. You could either call an operator and have them type in your message for you or use some sort of online pager gateway. Some large companies had their own gateways to send messages, and by the mid-nineties, most pager companies had both dial-up and Internet gateways where you could send someone a message via a pager from your own computer. Sort of like one-way texting, you would send your message out but seldom had any way to know if the receiver got it or for them to respond unless they found a phone and called you.

There are several paging protocols in use today, but by and far the most common in the mid-nineties was POCSAG. It had no encryption or any obfuscation at all but broadcast in the clear over the air for anyone to receive.

Kingpin had a keen interest in wireless data transmissions. As part of his research, he stumbled across POCSAG and discovered how easy it was to intercept and decipher the messages people were sending to pagers. Eventually this action became one of our products, the POCSAG Decoder Kit. The kit allowed off-the-air decoding of pager and Mobitex data traffic. It could decode both numeric and alphanumeric messages, and an optional hex dump of raw POCSAG codewords. The kit included a one-inch-by-one-inch printed circuit board and the various resistors and capacitors needed, and it fit inside a DB25 connector hood. We powered it from a PC-compatible serial port and required input from the speaker or the discriminator output from a radio scanner.

We sold these decoders in both kit and assembled form, and they became very popular. The circuit for the decoder was well known, and the specifications were readily available, but no one had thought to condense it down into a one-by-one circuit board that fit inside a DB25 hood. The kits were easy to prepare, just put all the pieces into a little baggy and drop it into the mail. Assembled ones were a little more work intensive. This is where I cut my teeth on soldering. Using an old Weller soldering iron I had bought at The Flea for twenty dollars, I would spend hours sitting at our work bench soldering these kits together. Despite its small size and limited components, each decoder had over thirty-five solder joints. I specifically remember spending entire Saturdays doing nothing but sitting at the workbench of the L0pht soldering POCSAG decoder kits together.

In one of our media shoots, New England Cable News recorded the reporter receiving a page on his alpha numeric pager and then the same page showing up on one of our monitors as we captured it over the air with our POCSAG decoder. I always thought that shot was kind of neat.

LØPHTCRACK

In late August 1996, Microsoft released Windows NT 4.0, a computer operating system designed for use on servers in large corporations, as opposed to Windows 95, which had been released the year before and was designed for personal home and office computers. Windows NT 4.0 had a slew of security improvements over prior versions, including the use of protected memory and a hardware abstraction layer that allowed software to run with various different pieces of hardware. Accompanied by a strong marketing campaign touting its server capabilities, it made many inroads into corporate IT departments. This brash newcomer to the network operation center rubbed many unix systems administrators (sysadmins) the wrong way. They didn't like this introduction of a "consumer" OS without a real command line interface into their unix playground. Why would anyone use a GUI (graphical user interface) when a command line would do?

However, the biggest complaint was how Microsoft positioned the new OS as secure enough to use on servers in large corporations. Most sysadmins took this marketing copy with a grain of salt, knowing full well that while NT 4.0 was more secure than previous versions of Windows. It was nowhere near as tight as a well-maintained and fully patched unix system. In addition, NT broke a lot of things that worked on UNIX networks, making sysadmins do much more work and therefore not winning many friends.

One of the many security features that Windows NT lacked that UNIX systems administrators relied on was a way to audit their users' passwords to ensure that they complied with internal password complexity policies. Things such as number of characters, upper and lower case, numbers, punctuation, etc., things sysadmins take for granted today. Windows NT sysadmins had no way to audit passwords for these controls. Microsoft considered the inability of a sysadmin to see the password a security feature, while UNIX admins, understandably, did not agree.

Windows NT stored passwords in its registry, a database that stores configuration information for Windows and some applications. These passwords were scrambled before they were stored by using a one-way hash function. Every time you would enter your password, the system would run what you entered through the hash function and then compare the result with what was stored in the database. If the two matched it would grant you access; if they didn't, then access was denied. You could not figure out the password from the hash, as the function only worked in one direction. What you could do was hash every possible password until you got a match. The thought was that such an endeavor would take a considerable amount of time. As a result, many people, the engineers at Microsoft included, thought that hashing alone was sufficient. However, it was not; the solution to the hashing problem was to add salt, or random bits, to the password to prevent any attempt at comparing hashes to determine the original password.

Microsoft was pushing for its proposed Common Internet File System (CIFS) that was included in Windows to become a standard in late 1996. This drove Hobbit, a unix sysadmin, to try to get the unix protocol SMB to work with the Microsoft protocol CIFS so that both systems could talk to each other and share files across platforms. The result of this effort was a paper Hobbit published in January 1997 entitled *CIFS: Common Insecurities Fail Scrutiny*[50] which detailed numerous weaknesses in the CIFS protocol.

On March 22, 1997, Jeremy Alison, who was working for Cygnus software, released a program called PWDump, which dumped the hashed[51] (but unsalted[52]) password database of a Windows NT machine from the NT registry into a valid smbpasswd format file.[53] The SMB protocol required passwords to authorize users access to files. The PWDump tool had two uses: it helped systems administrators to migrate users to unix systems from Windows NT, and it helped to keep password databases in sync between Windows NT machines and their unix/Samba servers. These tasks were critical if a network was to allow unix systems to share files with Windows NT systems. A side product of these uses was that it also revealed the hashed versions of passwords of Windows NT users. Of course, the tool required the user to have administrative access to the Windows NT server already to dump the password database. As a result, Microsoft downplayed the severity of the security risk since the passwords were hashed and, in their mind, the only people who could derive any benefit from seeing Windows NT user passwords already had legitimate access to the system.[54]

This excuse is the same one Microsoft would use years later when presented with the vulnerability that would become known as Mimikatz.[55] Microsoft didn't think storing encrypted passwords and the encryption key in memory was a security issue. They figured the only people who could access both would already have legitimate access to that machine. Mimikatz proved otherwise. Mimikatz, in conjunction with a few other vulnerabilities, resulted in an attack allegedly launched by Russia, known as NotPetya,[56] which caused hundreds of millions in damages worldwide.

Just five days later on March 27, 1997,[57] Jonathan Wilkins of Secure Networks Inc. released NTCrack, which took the hashed (but not salted) output of PWDump, the valid smbpasswd format file, and attempted to crack the password, similar to the way a unix administrator would run the utility Crack over their own password files. Windows NT actually stored two different hashes of a user's password, one for the older LANMAN protocol and one for the newer NTLM protocol. NTCrack could only extract the LANMAN version of the password which would allow network but not console logins to Windows NT systems. Someone else wrote and released a dictionary attack module as an add-on to NTCrack, further increasing the effectiveness of the tool in revealing user account passwords.

After various security experts enhanced its release, PWDump made it even easier to access, acquire, decrypt, and view user passwords, all in plain text. On April 1, of all days, Microsoft posted a response to the rising popularity of PWDump and other Windows NT security tools claiming that the issues were not security flaws in Windows NT and encouraging users to protect administrator accounts from unauthorized access.[58]

All this activity following the release of PWDump really set the nascent security community a buzz. Weld and Mudge had been working on their own version of NTCrack and were slightly dismayed that someone else had released a cracking tool first. Finally, On April 11, 1997, just a few weeks after the release of PWDump and NTCrack (a mere ten days after the Microsoft notice), a post to the BugTraq mailing list announced the availability of both a command line and a graphical user interface (GUI) version of L0phtCrack.[59] L0phtCrack had the ability to crack not only the LANMAN hash, like NTCrack before it, but also the NTLM hash which would allow console login access. This was not the first Windows NT Password cracker; NTCrack and others had come before it, but it was one of the first, if not the first, to offer a GUI interface with point-and-click functionality and offer to crack both the LANMAN and NTLM hashes.

The whole point of L0phtCrack at the time was to just add to the growing chorus trying to point out the insecurities of Windows networking. Microsoft was still attempting to downplay the issues and claim that cracking Windows NT passwords was theoretical or would take thousands and thousands of years. The more voices added to the growing chorus would make it more difficult for Microsoft to ignore the problem. L0phtCrack quickly gained the attention of a wider audience beyond just systems administrators, the press, and Microsoft.

Microsoft was still insisting that as long as users kept tight control over administrative accounts and paid attention to other security issues, cracking encrypted passwords on any NT network was still inherently difficult.[60] In some press reports Microsoft claimed they weren't familiar enough with L0phtCrack to comment despite the fact that L0pht had reached out to Microsoft several days prior to L0phtCracks release, and we could see internet addresses from Microsoft.com hitting our web server looking for information and downloading their own copies of L0phtCrack.[61]

L0phtCrack itself had no way of breaking into a WindowsNT machine to recover the password database. Someone would already need admin privileges to access that file either as a legitimate admin or an attacker exploiting a vulnerability. It was well known that WindowsNT had several published holes that would allow an attacker administrator level access, but that was outside of L0phtCrack's functionality at the time. Commercial network tools like NetXray and TCP Watch, as well as free tools such as Gobbler and tcpdump, were readily available to "sniff," or intercept, login attempts and administrators' passwords off the local network. There was also at least one method of obtaining passwords using an ActiveX control with what we now call a watering hole attack, which relied on an administrator visiting a malicious web page that contained a hostile ActiveX control. That was the thing about most WindowsNT admins that differed from most UNIX admins. Windows admins used their main administrative account to surf the web, read email, and more, leaving them more vulnerable to this sort of attack. Unix admins generally made it more difficult to use the administrator or root account for everyday activity and usually knew not to do that.

L0phtCrack worked on both the LANMAN and NTLM hashed passwords present within Windows NT and would use a brute force method, basically trying all combinations of letters and numbers until it got a match. It could do this for passwords of up to fourteen characters. Technically, Windows NT allowed up to 128-character passwords, but someone at Microsoft decided to limit the login dialog box to just fourteen characters. To make it even worse, the dirty little secret of Windows NT LANMAN passwords was that long passwords were truncated to a measly fourteen bytes and then split in half. If the password was less than fourteen bytes long, the system would pad it with null characters. This system meant that Windows NT passwords were easy to crack regardless of how strong you thought your password was. And it was fast! On a Pentium Pro 200 MHz machine, L0phtCrack could crack forty thousand NT domain passwords in about forty hours.[62]

Microsoft tried to respond to L0phtCrack and the other cracking tools by issuing Service Pack 3 (SP3) for Windows NT systems in May of 1997 which attempted to simply obfuscate the part of Windows NT where the passwords were stored. This was easy to bypass and so L0phtCrack and other tools kept on working. Microsoft's challenge was maintaining backward compatibility with the older LANMAN protocol. This insistence on keeping a link to the past meant that L0phtCrack would keep on working for years to come. In fact a variety of LANMAN remained in versions of Windows for the next decade until Windows Vista shipped in early 2007.

Shortly after the Black Hat Briefings, a large computer security conference held in Las Vegas during the summer of 1997, Microsoft invited Mudge along with Hobbit and Yobie Benjamin to a dinner[63] to discuss their security concerns with Windows NT. Hobbit of course had written his CIFS insecurity paper earlier that year[64] and had just given a talk at the Black Hat conference on the security weaknesses of NT's implementation of CIFS, and Yobie had been a loud voice criticizing the overall security of NT for some time. Paul Leach, Microsoft's director of NT architecture, acted as the dinner's host, and he along with Karan Khanna and few other senior Microsoft managers sat down to discuss the situation.

The gist of the conversation that Mudge told the rest of us afterward was that Microsoft offered to give L0pht early access to Windows NT source code as long as we promised to send any bugs we found to them first. Of course, all of this would have to happen under an NDA. What Microsoft didn't realize is that we already had access to the Windows source code, both legally and otherwise. At the time universities, government contractors, and lots of other people had legitimate access to the source, which made legal access easy and illegal access even easier. Attempting to entice us with an offer of source code access was a pretty weak attempt to tie us up with an NDA. The offer totally missed the point that most of the problems with Windows NT that had been made public up until that point had been found without source code access at all. There were so many problems with NT that access to the source code wasn't necessary.

Despite the face-to-face meeting, it was unclear whether Microsoft really "got it" or not. Mudge suspected they did not. In fact, it would be another five years before Bill Gates would write the now famous Microsoft security memo[65] that created the Trustworthy Computing initiative, which aimed to put customer security at the forefront of all Microsoft products.

We gave version 1.0 of L0phtCrack away freely, mostly as a simple proof of concept, as a way to prove that Windows NT password weakness was not simply theoretical. Soon we started hearing that several large accounting firms, security companies, and even governments were using L0phtCrack in their assessments to determine password strengths and then charging their clients large sums of money for running a free tool. We figured if they are going to get rich off our tool, we should at least get a minor cut. We decided that the command-line version would remain free for anyone to use, but the graphical version would cost you fifty dollars. In July of 1997 we released version 1.5 which not only included a bunch of bug fixes but built-in hash dumping and other features. The US Government Accounting Office was one of the first customers of the new shareware version.[66]

By version 2.0 we had added a built-in sniffer to grab the hashes directly off the network, the ability to grab passwords from the Windows Security Account Manager or SAM file, and had moved from a shareware license to a full commercial release. We also raised the price to one hundred dollars for a single user license, eight hundred dollars for a ten-pack license, or ten thousand dollars for a site license. We sold a few hundred single user licenses and one or two ten packs but unfortunately no site licenses. Since we knew companies didn't want to send credit cards or even checks to a PO box run by a bunch of hackers, we contacted a popular shareware registration service to handle all the money stuff for us. They of course took a sizable cut of the profits. Needless to say, we didn't get rich selling L0phtCrack, but it did help to pay the rent.

In January of 1999 we had recruited a few new members to the L0pht including Dildog, who became the primary developer for L0phtCrack. He pretty much completely rewrote L0phtCrack from the ground up and created a hybrid dictionary/brute force attack which made decrypting passwords even faster.

When L0pht was sold to the Internet consultancy @stake (covered in Chapter 10) they were not really interested in L0phtCrack at all. Despite version 3.0 ready to go with a slew of new features @stake was a little scared of the 'hacker' tool. They wanted nothing to do with the 'hacker' label so they agreed to let Weld and Dildog release L0phtCrack 3.0 as LC3 under a new company called Security Software Technologies in the spring of 2001. But sales were pretty good and so by May of 2001 @stake had repurchased what was now LC3 and poured a ton of resources into it coming out with three different versions and even offering technical support. Within a year @stake had added Rob Cheyne to the L0phtCrack team and released LC4. But by this point L0phtCrack, or LC, was no longer on the cutting edge and other password auditing tools were faster and had more and better features. The final version produced by @stake, under Ian Melvin, LC5 was released in September of 2004, finally adding rainbow table support, audit scheduling and other new features. Shortly after the release of LC5 @stake was bought by Symantec.

Like @stake before it, Symantec didn't really know what to do with L0phtCrack, and eventually just shelved it and declared it end of life. At the very end of 2008 Weld, Dildog, and Mudge convinced Symantec to sell L0phtCrack back to them and after a slew of modernization updates released L0phtCrack 6.0,[67] followed seven years later by L0phtCrack 7.0.[68] In 2020 a company called Terrahash acquired L0phtCrack[69] only for it to be repossessed by Mudge, Weld, and Dildog a little over a year later.[70] Then in October of 2021 L0phtCrack version 7.2.0 was released as open-source, free to the community.[71]

Over the course of some twenty plus years a small little piece of proof of concept code, hurriedly produced within a few weeks, went from an exercise to prove a point, security weaknesses in a major operating system, to shareware, to commercial success, to other companies thinking it was too hot to handle, to being a major tool used by researchers and consultants the world over, to being freely available to everyone. Kind of an amazing journey for something that was once considered theoretical.

Hacker News Network

Besides the web server and other duties, L0pht.com also handled our internal email. We had an internal email list known as resident, or resident@l0pht.com, so we could discuss the regular business of the L0pht, discuss current projects, let others know when one of us would be at the L0pht, and communicate other normal things you use email for. This included sharing links to relevant news stories of the day. Anything from the latest breach report to a new zero-day or patch released by a major software vendor. We all would share whatever we thought the rest of us would want to know about. Of course, being hackers, we had to take this to the next level, or at least I did. It became a game to see who could post a relevant link to our internal email list first. Weld and I quickly became the most prolific posters of worthy links.

I would try to get to my day job, which at the time was in the IT department of Vertex Pharmaceuticals, extra early so I could use their fast network bandwidth to collect and email links. Vertex was an early-stage medium-sized drug discovery startup in Cambridge and was my first taste of a venture capital-funded workplace. They didn't call it AI (artificial intelligence) or ML (machine learning) back then, but Vertex was way ahead of the curve in using such technologies to search for drug targets for certain diseases. As a result, they had a lot of high computing power, which was fun to play with during downtimes. But for my emailed news link competition, they had a super-fast pipe to the Internet. I would arrive an hour or more early every day to search through a dozen or more bookmarked sites for links to stories I thought the others in the L0pht would find interesting and then connect to L0pht.com over SSH and email them out.

By this point we had gone from wanting L0pht to pay for itself to wanting L0pht to pay us. We wanted to be paid to be at the L0pht and basically hack all day long. As our website became more and more popular, it often tempted us to post online advertisements. With the traffic our website was getting and the rates web banner ads were getting, we figured we could easily pay for one person's yearly salary with one banner ad on the top of www.L0pht.com. But we just couldn't bring ourselves to do it. We brought it up more than once during our weekly meetings. Banner ads were making many people a ton of money, but we held out; we were all attracted to the money, but we really felt it would dirty the name, that people might distrust our advisories if they thought advertising influenced our methods. We also feared that we might grow dependent on the money and give advertisers leverage over us to silence our voices. So no advertisements ever graced the pages of L0pht.com

The lure of those web ad dollars was strong. I knew we couldn't put anything on L0pht.com, but I thought, what if we put them somewhere else on a different domain? The question was what do we put on that other domain to generate enough traffic to actually make some money. Then one day when I am writing up an email to resident and copying and pasting links, it just hit me. Instead of writing an email full of links, I should write a web page full of links and I should call it... "hacker news." One thought flowed right after the other. A web page of links to other web pages might not sound like much, but some of the biggest websites of that time were based on that model. Sites like Slashdot.org and Digg.com were two of the biggest websites of the day, and they were really nothing more than link aggregators. Those were the type of sites I envisioned right then that my hacker news idea could become.

That Thursday, at the weekly meeting when most people were watching *Seinfeld* on Must See TV, I presented my idea to the group. I know I was excited about it. I'm not sure anyone else was as excited as I was. I think they were all like, sure, whatever, if you want to waste your time doing that, go for it. So we registered the domain Hackernews.com the following week. It was Weld who added "network" to my "hacker news," and on July 28, 1998 the Hacker News Network, or HNN, was born.

Weld created some really cool circuit board graphics with a red-font logo we used for the basic site design, and I added the back-end HTML. The design of the site was simple; no fancy database, just basic flat HTML, mostly because things like Cascading Style Sheets (CSS) weren't really a thing yet. One of the biggest problems was finding an advertising platform that would allow us to host their ads. There was no DoubleClick or Google AdSense yet. Our very first advertising partner was an affiliate marketing program for Russian wives that we used during the first few weeks of the site. The problem I was having in finding someone willing to display ads on Hackernews.com was the word "hacker." Almost every single platform had a clause in their acceptable use policy that specified no "hacking" websites, and here we were with hacker right in the domain name. Eventually I discovered Burst Media. I'm not sure why Burst Media took us on as a client, but they did, and I was grateful. In the spring of 2000, they even invited me to talk at one of their corporate retreats where they had invited a few other select clients. After my talk, a couple of folks in the back approached me and introduced themselves as the IT Department for Burst Media. They told me they were big fans of the site and checked it every day. That made me smile.

HNN did not take off right away. It took about four months before I started seeing any sort of decent traffic to the site. I would wake up extra early every day, around five a.m. or so, and usually drive straight over to the L0pht, and then I would scour an ever-growing list of news sites to gather my links for the day. I would write a small blurb and an opinion on each one, give it a catchy title, format it all into HTML by hand, and then post it to the site. To post it, I would log in to the server, copy index.html to the previous day's date (like 1998.07.28.html), and then upload a new index.html. It was pretty basic; no funky content management system or anything, just good old-fashioned artisanal hand-crafted organic HTML.

Eventually I gathered a small team to help me edit the site. People like Jericho, Carole Fennely, Cancer Omega, Lyger, and others. We would all hangout in an IRC channel together. After I had finished gathering the news and writing it up, they would help me proofread the copy before I posted it. I made some hilarious typo mistakes sometimes, especially with the names of major cities in Thailand.

HNN took up a lot of my time, roughly twenty hours a week. At the time I was still working a regular forty- to fifty-hour-a-week day job at Vertex Pharmaceuticals' IT department. But I enjoyed the HNN work a lot. I really enjoyed watching something I had created and nurtured grow to become a useful tool to others. The people in the small group that had formed on IRC to help me edit the site every day became lifelong friends. And after a few months, those banner ads started to pay off, and the site made some actual money.

HNN was also starting to produce original reporting as opposed to just copying links from other websites. HNN was the first to report on using PalmPilots as toll fraud devices and the first to report that the FAO Schwarz website was leaking customer information, among other stories. One of HNNs strongest stories came when I denounced a report by the UK newspaper *Sunday Business* that a UK satellite had been hacked and its course altered. Hackers and satellites were an ancient trope, even then. There are a ton of similar stories with very little evidence to support them, and this story was no different. That didn't stop a lot of the mainstream media from picking up the *Sunday Business* report and simply reprinting it, including Reuters, who sent it out on their news wire with no verification or corroboration. HNN also reported on the story, but I didn't just parrot the *Sunday Business* report. I laid out my suspicions in a factual and technical manner, which was supported a few days later by staunch denials from the

British Intelligence Service that none of their satellites had been compromised and a retraction by Reuters. This did not go unnoticed by Brock Meeks, a well-known and respected reporter, who published on the MSNBC website that HNN was the lone voice of reason. That "voice of reason" phrase became a moniker for HNN; I added the quote to the front page of the site as a badge of honor.

It took a while, but HNN found its voice; I focused almost exclusively on breaches, new vulnerabilities, and exploits. We also touched on privacy and new legislation, all with a pinch of sarcastic humor. And ironically enough, I tried to not use the words "hack," "hacker," or "hacking" anywhere on the website. Ironic because it was part of the website's name. I didn't use the word because the debate over the meaning of the word "hacker" was at its peak as to whether a hacker was a good person or a bad person. Was a hacker someone who found new and novel ways of doing things with technology, or was a hacker someone who criminally broke into websites and stole data and information? Since I could not predict what my readers would decide the word meant to them, I decided it was best to remove that ambiguity and just not use the word. There are plenty of other words available with much sharper definitions that didn't introduce confusion.

HNN started to get mentions and links from other major outlets like the *San Francisco Chronicle*, *Wired*, and CNN. Links to HNN started showing up in books and even in FBI promotional videos. In *Solar Sunrise: Dawn of a New Threat*,[72] a VHS cassette produced by the FBI in 1999, you can plainly see computer monitors displaying the Hacker News Network website in the backgrounds of several shots. Years later more than one government acquaintance told me that

HNN was the basis for their daily cyber briefing, as in they basically copied and pasted HNN content into an official briefing document.

In a little over a year, the HNN website was seeing some major traffic. It had become a trusted news source with exclusive content. It was generating revenue from not just web advertising but from T-Shirt sales as well, enough revenue that it was breaking even and some months even turned a bit of profit back to the L0pht.

Late in October of 1998, the Reuters news service profiled a small website at Humanrights-china.org. The five-paragraph article mentioned that an organization known as the Chinese Society for Human Rights was running the site. The group supposedly represented China in expanding its dialog with other countries about human rights. The website contained government-approved documents in Chinese and English from the state-run media covering human rights within the country. The site is still up, and you can visit it today and read about how great China and its people are. When I recently visited the site, there was an article about the many educational achievements China has made over the last seventy years, how China helps fight poverty in the Philippines, and how the Chinese government has made improvements in protecting the environment. The Reuters article about the site's launch in 1998 was a small and almost unnoticed article other than it got republished by Wired.com.[73] It was such a small, unnoticeable article, I didn't even bother to mention it on HNN.

A popular activity among some sectors of the computer underground at the time was to "deface" a website. This action involved gaining access to the web server, usually through some vulnerability or misconfiguration, and then change the content on one or more of the pages. The changed content usually consisted of a graphic or two of whatever crew was responsible and then a list of "greetz," or simple shoutouts to other people. Think of it as technical graffiti—annoying, often ugly, sometimes with a message, but mostly harmless. The cultural significance of these defacements was recognized early on, and copies of these webpages were quickly downloaded and saved in various defacement archives.

Bronc Buster and Zyklon, two members of the hacking group Legion of Underground (LoU), probably noticed the Reuters article covering Humanrights-china.org because their names were both listed on a defacement of the website the day after the article was posted. They had broken into the website, which according to a statement on the defaced page they left behind, took less than two minutes. They changed the website's main page to a page of all black with large white letters. Amid many spelling and grammar mistakes, they made fun of the Chinese government, claimed that the Chinese people had no rights at all, and accused China of censoring, murdering, and torturing its own people. The page criticized the United States and its awarding of most favored trade status to China when the US knew these human rights abuses were taking place. The page provided links to Amnesty International and the Institute for Global Communities, among others. Below that was a cry to let Kevin Mitnick out of jail, that "if they could do it to Kevin, they could do it to anyone." At the bottom of the defaced page was a list of, what at the time was almost obligatory for defaced pages, shoutouts to "everyone in LoU,

#hackphreak, NetJammer, Burrows, Accipter, RLoxley, Optiklenz, Deadguy and Fanggz for getting married!" followed by a graphic logo for Bronc Buster and Zyklon.

News of the defacement made Wired.com the next day and became the top news story for HNN.[74] Random defacements didn't always make the top story for HNN, but Reuters's profile of the site the day before made me think it was worthy enough to be listed at the top of the website. As I was traveling for a few days and unable to update Hackernews.com, the story about the defacement and LoU's involvement stayed at the top of HNN website for several days.

This wasn't the first breach that involved members of Legion of Underground. In July of that year, Optiklenz, Flemming, Tip, and Aphex claimed to have access to a Time Warner control system in the Los Angeles area. Specifically, they said they could move broadcast satellite downlink dishes and send text messages scrolling across home television screens.[75] It was hard to tell if they had the access they claimed, or if it was just bravado, or maybe some combination of the two with a little exaggeration thrown in. Then in the beginning of December, Bronc Buster claimed to have broken into a half dozen firewalls in China. He also claimed to have turned the filtering rules off and committed web defacements in the city of Tianjin.[76] A few days later Zyklon of LoU claimed to have defaced hundreds of different websites all at once.

On December 28, news broke that the Chinese government had sentenced two brothers, accused of online bank robbery, to death. According to the trial in an intermediate court in the eastern city of Yangzhou, the twin brothers had connected a homemade modem to the computer system of the Zhenjiang branch of the Industrial and Commercial Bank of China. They then used a personal computer to dial into the banks' systems and transfer Chinese yuan that equaled about $86,000 US dollars into sixteen different accounts controlled by the brothers.[77] (If someone builds a homemade modem in 1998, you don't sentence them to death. Well, unless you are China, I guess.)

Later that day I received an email inviting me to attend an online chat meeting via IRC of the Legion of Underground. The "meeting" was pretty fluid, with normal IRC chat banter interspersed with server messages such as /kick and /ban, as well as server disconnects or netsplits. People asked who I was and what I was doing in their channel. However, most of the discussion centered on the news of China sentencing two hackers to death and, to a lesser degree, the manufacture of weapons of mass destruction by Iraq. On HNN the next day, I published this excerpt taken from the meeting. Under the headline I added, "War Declared on China and Iraq."

> "The Government controls what goes into our mouths lets not let them do the same with what comes out!" said one LoU member during a press conference held on IRC Monday night.

(The full log from the chat is at the end of the book.)

Since it was the news drought season between Christmas and New Year's, most reporters were on vacation for the holidays. Not much happened. I had posted the news to HNN on December 29, but it was not until January 4 when the *Online Standard*, *National Post*, and *Wired* picked up the story with only the *National Post* giving

HNN credit and labeling it an "online news network." This network amounted to pretty much just me and a webpage I was still pretty stoked about.

The next day on January 5, the hacking group spl0it announced it was going to join LoU in attacking the infrastructure of China and Iraq. A polish hacking group said that they, too, would join the fight. In an email message sent to HNN, f0bic of spl0it said…

```
"It's unjust to put hackers in prison longer
then rapists and thiefs, and now they even
want to execute people for doing this. Justice
has left the world I guess. It's time for
change..Big Time"
```

By January 6, things may have been getting bigger than LoU had originally intended. They released a statement contradicting their earlier IRC meeting—it said they had no destructive intentions and blamed the media for letting things get out of hand. The statement read in part "It seemed like we struck a nerve on the entire internet," which was a mild way of putting it. Despite the lack of mainstream press, the IRC channels and mailing lists where full of talk about what role hackers should play in a nation-state's activities and whether hacking skills should be used in a "war," especially when civilians would be the ones who would be affected by most of the actions.

But LoU's statement was too little, too late. Even before LoU released its statement claiming things had been blown out of proportion behind the scenes, many of the world's premier hacking groups were working on an unprecedented joint statement. The Chaos Computer Club (CCC) in Germany took the initiative, and through IRC and emails, achieved consensus from disparate groups around the world.

From January 4, when the story hit mainstream news, through the next several days, I was working on pure adrenaline; I understand, at least a little, why some journalists love their jobs. There is a buzz, a rush, when dealing with events in real time. Almost the same buzz or rush you get when hacking something. I was staying up all night writing for HNN, checking sources, and conferring with contacts, trying to figure out what was going on and keeping the website updated. I answered media requests of my own and contacted other hacking groups to prepare the joint statement.

Once things were solidified, I emailed the rest of the L0pht members for approval to add the L0pht name to the joint statement. Mudge almost immediately rejected the idea, saying it was better if we didn't get involved. When I read his email in my caffeinated, sleep-deprived, adrenaline-high state, Mudge's response pissed me off. I remember stomping around the L0pht late at night, screaming at the walls. I sent a quick email off to the CCC to ask for a little more time as L0pht debated things internally. They told us we needed to hurry, or they would release the statement without us.

After I calmed down a little, I sat at my keyboard and wrote what was probably the longest run-on sentence of my life. I pointed out how bad it would look if every other major hacking group signed on to this statement and L0pht didn't. I argued about how civilian hackers didn't have any business acting outside the rule of law in the affairs of nations. I mentioned that if LoU's actions remained unchallenged, it would change the hacking landscape as we knew it in one fell swoop.

At the end I closed the email with a line from Geddy Lee of Rush, which I had hoped would be one final push to win Mudge and the rest of the L0pht over: "If you choose not to decide, you still have made a choice."

Whatever I wrote in that email worked, and quickly. Everyone at the L0pht was onboard, and I approved CCC to include the L0pht name alongside 2600, Phrack, cDc, !HISPAHACK, and other hacking groups on the statement and in the press release.

The statement talked about how damaging a country's infrastructure was counter the hacker ethos of free access to information. It said that "we strongly oppose any attempt to use the power of hacking to threaten or destroy the information infrastructure of any country." The statement asked that other hackers and hacking groups lend their support to the document. There was an overwhelming response. The CCC received numerous emails that expressed support for the international coalition of hackers and condemned Legion of Underground's actions. Unlike the original declaration of war that took days to make it to the mainstream press, *Telepolis*, *Wired* and IDG all had stories up about the joint statement that morning.

This media brought condemnation down on the members of Legion of Underground, and some members immediately disavowed their membership. Some stuck around and sent a statement in response to HNN that said that they did "not support the damaging of other nations' computers, networks, or systems in any way" and that they would "not take any actions against the systems, networks, or computers in China or Iraq."

The LoU statement blamed the misunderstandings and apparent contradictions on a few individual members of the group taking actions on their own and not as part of a concerted effort by Legions of Underground. The statement also read that they might "in the future take action against other Chinese systems" but that it would limit those actions to that of pure hacktivism. It read that LoU would not be out to destroy computer systems and the internal information infrastructures of other countries.

On January 11 the original website at humanrights-china.org that started it all was defaced yet again. This time a group called NIS - N3TW0RK 1NTRUS10N SP3C13L1STS took the credit and left GREETS TO : P3EPZ, ADM, PROMISC, PIMP, W00W00, HERT, RSI, EL8, L0PHT, PHRACK, THC, LSD, HFG, SK AND AGAIN TO MY BABY P3EPZ (I LOVE YOU).

Two days later on the 13th of January, the Legion of Underground told *Wired* that the original press conference was a fake and that the people present during the press conference had all been spoofed. Which, if true, seems like a pretty elaborate hoax for no apparent gain other than the "lulz" (laughs). Finally, a week later mainstream media starts to report on the story with articles posted from CNN,[78] MSNBC, Spiegel Online, AP Wire, and Kitetoa in France.

By the beginning of February, the Legions.org website appeared to go legit, with offers of web hosting and security consulting featured on its main page. There were no prices mentioned, but they offered a "lightning fast one-to-three-day external audit." According to the Internet Archive, the website remained mostly active with occasional updates until 2011.

HNN published a statement from Optiklenz at the end of the July that reiterated LoU's claim that because of "some iniquitous media converage" [sic], LoU had been misunderstood. He ranted about the lack of security in many government websites, that script kiddies attacking those sites were only doing it for the press and that people should not archive or call attention to those defacements, as it was only encouraging the attackers.

###

It is interesting to look at this incident through the lens of history nearly twenty-five years later. Back then most governments could barely secure their own websites, let alone attack anyone else's. Today, state-sponsored cyber espionage is the new trend, with governments not only employing their own hacking teams but outsourcing the work to military contractors and quasi-legitimate, shady companies. While the hackers of the world tried to take an unprecedented, principled, and united stand of nonviolence and freedom of and access to information, the governments of the world ignored them and moved in the other direction.

Meanwhile, Stuxnet, the malware designed to disable Iranian nuclear subterfuges, may have been one of the first major state-sponsored hacking activities that became known to the public. Since then, we have seen targeted cyberattacks against corporations like Sony, Saudi Aramco, Colonial Pipeline, wider malware attacks like WannaCry and NotPetya, and numerous ransomware incidents, all with serious state sponsorship overtones. And while no one seems to come right out and point fingers today, it is obvious that the naivete of hackers in the late '90s and early 2000s didn't last long. Hackers no longer explore networks and computer systems from parents' basements (if they ever did); now it is often about purposeful destruction at the bequest of governments.

Government participation or encouragement or even knowledge of activist involvement in cyber operations is no longer necessary. This argument is illustrated in the opening days of the Russia-Ukraine war of 2022 when Ukraine implored the hackers of the world to target Russian infrastructure. Not to be outdone, hackers in China reportedly attacked infrastructure in Russia on their own outside of government oversight. There were even a reported three hundred thousand hackers[79] that came together on their own in a so called "IT Army" to join in the online fighting. While it may be questionable how many of those three hundred thousand were hardened cyber warriors, they were all willing to launch electrons across borders in stark contrast to the stand global hackers took against cyberwar in 1999.

Another way that HNN benefited the L0pht besides the bottom line was that it put us in contact with a lot of journalists. They would start contacting us through the HNN website, which I monitored, for comments on a story. Sometimes it was a story that HNN had covered, but most often it was just another random security story. I got to know some of those reporters pretty well. Some would repeatedly come to me not just for an article quote but to bounce an idea or for background on some other story. I quickly became a trusted source. This was a position I reveled in because I thought it was really doing some good. I felt I could increase the technical awareness of the people who were reporting on these stories and help them get the technical facts straight. It was a good use of my time, and I felt it was important to educate reporters who were covering the hacker and security stories of the day.

Poor reporting has led to many unintended consequences. The much-vilified Computer Fraud and Abuse Act of 1986 was a knee jerk reaction that in my opinion can be directly linked to overhyped and uneducated reporting of online risks. In fact, poor tech journalism has been such a common problem that I gave a talk about media hype and the damage it can cause[80] at a few information security conferences, including the hacker conference HOPE 9 in 2012. I have always felt it was my duty to help educate reporters who didn't quite grasp the online world. Accuracy in reporting is important, even more so today than ever.

I would often commiserate about the poor quality of tech reporting with the small team of folks who were helping me edit HNN via IRC. I floated the idea of holding some sort of conference and inviting a bunch of tech journalists for a day of tech education. I also brought up this idea at one of the L0pht weekly meetings. Everyone at the L0pht agreed that tech journalism was atrocious, but we weren't sure we could get anyone to show up to a conference. This is an idea I have tried to push with several of my more recent employers, but so far, I haven't been able to pull it off.

Eventually Jericho via IRC suggested a mailing list of both hackers and journalists. The journalists would have an easily reachable pool of experts to ask questions of, and we hackers could critique and make suggestions about the tech reporting of the day. Of course we called this list the Voice of Reason after the description applied to HNN by Brock Meeks after the Sunday Business hacker satellite story.

VoR, as we call it, still exists today; it started with maybe a dozen people and has grown to over a hundred journalists and hackers discussing the current state of tech journalism. The list has waxed and waned over the years as mailing lists tend to do. Its non-public status is still maintained, and even mentioning it here in this book may violate the unwritten principles of the mailing list. Still the list has developed some strong friendships and occasionally results in an in-person get together at security conferences now and then.

While I like to think that VoR has made a difference in a lot of the reported tech stories over the years, there are far more people writing news stories about information security now than can fit on any sane mailing list. In addition, the turnover rate of security journalists is huge. The security beat is like the city desk of an old metropolitan newspaper—it's where you send the inexperienced reporters to go report on city council meetings or the police blotter. Pretty soon the reporter has moved on to bigger and better things. The same is true in information security. By the time a reporter has learned the difference between cryptography and cryptocurrency, they move on to report a different subject leaving some other wet-behind-the-ears reporter to fill their shoes and starting the whole cycle over again. Leaving the public to read the stories these inexperienced reporters push out none the wiser and possibly even more ignorant than before.

PHOTO PAGES

Space Rogue's work area at the new Watertown L0pht.

Space Rogue's work area at the old South Boston L0pht.

L0pht taking up two spaces at one of the MIT computer flea markets.

Doc ID: 6791787

NATIONAL CRYPTOLOGIC MUSEUM
REGISTER

DATE	NAME	STATE	COMMENTS
17 MAY 98	JAMES ▮	W▮	
17 May 98	Mark ▮	▮	
17 May 98	Rocky ▮	▮	
18 May 98			
5/18/98	You▮	▮A	
5/18/98	Ted ▮	▮	
5/19/98	John ▮	▮	
5/18/98	▮	▮	
5/18/98	Ming▮	▮	
5-18-98	Rob ▮	▮	
5-18-98	Cmmlin▮	▮	
18 May 98	E▮ Bridge▮	▮	
5/05/98	q. ▮	▮D	
5/18/98	Muriel+Gordon ▮	Mass.	
"	W. ▮	▮D	
5 18 98	Gordon ▮	MA	
5/18/98	Johnson ▮	▮	
6/18/98	Susan + Mathew ▮	MD	
5/18/98	Carl ▮	MA	
5/18/98	The L0pht	MA	World Tour
5/18/98	John ▮	MA	
5/18/98	Tui ▮	MA	
5/15/98	Amy ▮	MD	
5/18/98	Bob ▮	VA	
6/18/98	Bill + Tami ▮	NY	
5/18/98	Frank ▮	MD	
5-18-98	Jim ▮	▮	
5-18-98	Dan ▮	MD	

A copy of the guest book for the National Cryptological Museum of May 18, 1998 signed as "The L0pht." Received from the NSA under a Freedom of Information Act request on October 18, 2022, three years after the original request.

Space Rogue testifying before Congress. Weld Pond to the left
and Stefan to the right. (Still taken from CSPAN video coverage.)

A banner signed by attendees of the L0pht New Year's party in 2000.

Local San Jose, CA TV News interviewing Ted Julian and Mudge
in the @stake booth at the RSA Security Conference in 2000.

From left to right: Dildog, Mudge, Space Rogue, Weld Pond, Silicosis, and Brian Oblivion at Space Rogue's wedding reception in 2014.

Many of the L0pht, @stake, and HNN T-shirts after they were made into a quilt.

CONGRESSIONAL TESTIMONY

At some point Mudge was invited to be on a local panel presentation about the Internet and security. The panel was to be hosted at MIT and include an FBI agent from the Boston Computer Crime Squad. We discussed it during one of our weekly meetings and were a little trepidatious about being in the same room with someone from law enforcement who might actually know what he was talking about. But we decided it was a good thing to make friends on the other side.

The panel was in the evening, so a few of us went: Weld, Tan, Kingpin, myself, and, of course, Mudge. While we were sitting in the audience Tan was like, "I think I know that guy."

"Which guy?"

"The FBI Guy. I think I went to high school with him."

During the panel, Mudge and, as we would later learn, Dan from the FBI both got in a few good-natured jabs at the other, and both promised to work more closely with each other to remove some distrust between hackers and law enforcement. I was surprised at the discourse during the panel and expected things to be a lot more adversarial, but it was a hospitable and friendly atmosphere.

After the panel Tan went up and said hi and discovered that they did in fact attend High School together. Pleasantries where exchanged, a quick trip down memory lane, and then before I knew it, someone had invited Dan the FBI guy over to the L0pht. I figured we were just being friendly with no intention of following through with this invitation, but it was brought up again at our next weekly meeting. The feeling was that we really had nothing to hide and that it would be good to have some friends in high places to vouch for us if anyone got the wrong idea about our activities in the future.

This began an involved relationship. Dan, or Danno, as we came to call him, came over to the L0pht a few times, and he invited us to a shooting range to do some target practice once or twice with some MP5 submachine guns, Remington 870 shotguns, and other firearms. I don't know how he got access to those weapons, or if he had to get special permission for us to fire them or what. But mad minutes with submachine guns are always fun.

I didn't really know Dan, and I kept my distance mostly, but Tan vouched for him. Sure, it was possible that this was all a setup, that Dan was trying to groom us or was maybe conducting some sort of investigation, but I never really got that feeling. My spider sense was never activated, and there was never any sign that anything other than friends hanging out was going on, which I guess if you are great at developing and cultivating sources, is how you would want them to feel.

Looking back years later, it is easy to think that there is no way an FBI agent takes a bunch of unknown civilians out to a shooting range for target practice, with what were probably agency weapons, without some sort of approval process going on. This was quite some time prior to our congressional testimony, but maybe it was part of the vetting process? Who knows? I have often wondered about this myself, even going so far as filing several Freedom of Information Act requests on anything relating to L0pht and the Boston FBI, all of which have come back as "no records found." In my mind this makes things worse and further heightens my paranoia. We knew who Dan was, and he knew who we were. I find it extremely hard to believe that he wrote nothing down officially and filed it away. I mean, that's kind of what the FBI does, and yet all my FOIAs come back as "no records found"? Either the FBI is exceedingly bad at filing and then finding what it filed, or someone is holding something back. Both possibilities are well within the realm of reality.

I kept in touch with Dan for a few years and reached out to him a few times when I ran across bad things happening wherever I was working. The problem with job roles at the FBI and, the same as the problem in journalism, is that the people move around a lot. FBI agents rotate through the computer crime division rather quickly. As soon as they understand that a simple Nmap scan is not really 256 cyberattacks, they move on to organized crime or narcotics or something else and take that insider knowledge with them.

The story of how L0pht met CyberCzar Richard Clarke has been told many times, but I remember it a little differently than the previously published versions of the story. Clarke's official title at the time we first met was National Coordinator for Security, Infrastructure Protection, and Counter-Terrorism under then-president Bill Clinton. The story has been told in books such as Andy Greenberg's *This Machine Kills Secrets*, Fred Kaplan's *Dark Territory*, and Joseph Menn's *Cult of the Dead Cow*. In these books the story says Mudge met Clarke first alone in a bar. Mudge had gotten there early and watched Clarke until he was about ready to leave before introducing himself. Then the rest of us met him later. I don't know if this ever really happened. It sounds all very cloak-and-dagger to me, and Mudge may in fact have had a prior meeting without telling us. I don't know. The first meeting I remember was a group meeting between Clarke and several of us.

I remember the meeting was at John Harvard's, the same restaurant in the basement of a building off Dunster Street in Harvard Square that we would often take press contacts. Usually we would meet press contacts before granting a full interview to sort of feel them out and make sure they saw whatever story they were reporting on from our point of view before we actually did any filming. John Harvard's worked just as well to meet press as it did to meet government officials. They had decent beer and, at the time, a killer chicken pot pie. It wasn't too expensive or too loud, and they had large booths that several of us could fit in.

Clarke was a very amiable and friendly person, and we all hit it off really well. We started talking about government activities in the hacker world, forgetting that a major government representative was sitting right there at the table with us. Clarke, of course, defended his position and the governments. He extolled the virtues of privacy and of defending the constitution. Having been a former government employee, albeit in the military, I recognized some of those old traits. While we were sitting on opposite sides of the table both literally and figuratively, I imagined the table becoming rounder and our positions on different issues being much more closely aligned than I first imagined.

Dinner went exceedingly well, and the conversation didn't stop. We covered a lot of areas on both the hacker and the government side. While slightly unusual but not out of the ordinary, we eventually asked Clarke to come back to the L0pht with us after dinner. After driving to Watertown from Cambridge, we lead Clarke and his assistant up the warehouse stairs to our space. When they walked through the door, you could almost see their jaws drop and their eyes widen. We showed him our parallel-processing supercomputer rescued from the trash pile, our old VAX, piles and piles of equipment, our software and book library, the radio broadcast station, and our video network. We gave him the grand tour. It seemed as though his jaw never returned to its original position.

When it was time to leave, we walked with him back out to his car. We turned to go back inside but noticed that Clarke and his associate were standing next to their car whispering to each other.

Mudge called back to them, "Hey, we opened our kimono and showed you the L0pht. No more secrets. What are you whispering about?"

Clarke started to respond, and we all walked a little closer.

"Well," he replied, "we have always assumed that for a group or organization to develop the capabilities that you just showed us

179

would take the resources only available to a state-sponsored actor. We are going to have to rethink all of our threat models."

On the one hand, we thought this was an amazing compliment. That seven guys in a warehouse with no money and picking stuff out of the trash could rival the best capabilities of an entire nation? That was a heady feeling. On the other hand, the thought that the brightest minds in the US government hadn't thought that what we had been doing for years wasn't even a possibility enough to include in their threat models was sobering.

There have been many stories over the years on how we got invited to testify before the US Congress. Mudge had been doing a lot of work with the US Government at the time doing training classes and lectures for the National Security Agency (NSA) and other agencies. He could also cultivate these contacts through his job at Bolt Beranek & Newman (BBN), a huge government contractor. Mudge now says that it was through these contacts that he met Richard Clarke, who was then the Counter-Terrorism Adviser to President Bill Clinton. Clarke then evidently recommended us to Senator Fred Thompson, who was then the chair of the Senate Government Affairs Committee (which was renamed a few years later to the Senate Committee on Homeland Security & Governmental Affairs). However, I did not learn of this possible chain of events until much later. At the time, I was under the understanding that it all started with an article in the *Improper Bostonian*.

The *Improper Bostonian* was a large-format newsprint biweekly lifestyle magazine that was distributed freely throughout Boston via street side kiosks. By early 1998, the L0pht had already received a lot of mainstream press, including a small spot in *Wired* magazine and a couple of clips on the local New England Cable News; this media was beside trade press in the *EE Times* and online outlets such as CNET and elsewhere.

In March we did an interview with Pamela Ferdinand for an article in the *Improper Bostonian*. It was a multipage article but mostly just covered the human-interest angle of *hackers working right here in Boston!* It was a little sensationalist but also balanced, showing our side about how we were helping make things more secure and not painting the same old trope of "hackers are bad." The article for the *Improper Bostonian* didn't get published until the July 1 issue. They had wanted a group photo for the piece and getting that scheduled with all of us and the photographer was a little challenging. We had been promised a cover shot for the issue, but eventually got bumped off the cover for the Juice Guys of Nantucket Nectars.

While waiting for the *Improper Bostonian* to publish the piece, the journalist rewrote the article and submitted it to the *Washington Post*. They published that version on April 4, 1998. They wisely sent a photographer to us, which was a lot easier to schedule. We were all standing around in a group trying to look all serious, as hackers do. The photographer said something that made us all laugh, he snapped a shot, and of course that's the one picture they decide to use.

My understanding is that someone in Senator Thompson's office saw that article in the *Washington Post* and thought hey, these guys would be perfect to get some press around the reports they were going to push out next month. The reports being *Air Traffic Control: Weak*

Computer Security Practices Jeopardize Flight Safety and *Computer Security: Pervasive Serious Weaknesses Jeopardize State Department Operations.*

Things for us happened quickly. We got the official invitation from Senator Thompson's office on May 5 for the hearing that was to take place on the 19th. That gave us two weeks to decide if we were going to do it or not, figure out how we were going to get there, and buy suits.

The debate on whether to accept the invitation was a lively one. While it wasn't widely remembered, we all knew that Susan Headley (aka Suzy Thunder, a compatriot of famed hacker Kevin Mitnick, and accomplished phone phreak and social engineer on her own) had testified before the US Senate[81] way back in 1983. We also knew that Emmanuel Goldstein, the editor of *2600* magazine, had once testified in front of Senator Ed Markey and the House Subcommittee on Telecommunications and Finance. Goldstein was not treated nicely, essentially being called a criminal, and his magazine, *2600: The Hacker Quarterly,* being labeled a manual for criminals.[82] We were under no guarantees that the same thing wouldn't also happen to us. We knew that once we were in the room, there wasn't much we would be able to do about the response. Unlike our careful dances with the press up until this point, there would be no pre-meeting with the senators at John Harvard's to share a beer and a chicken pot pie and make sure the senators saw our point of view before being put in front of the CSPAN cameras.

As a result, we decided not to announce or publicize our appearance until after it had happened. Our thinking was that on the off chance that things went poorly, we might be able to ignore it and hope no one noticed.

As for transportation, we could have flown but that would present two problems. One, we would have to give up our real names to the airlines. Even in that pre-9/11 era, flying without an ID was difficult, and trying to use a name like Space Rogue to book an airplane ticket would have been problematic. Which probably would have been fine except we were fearful that some enterprising young reporter would dig through public records and be able to match a real name with a handle. We feared this identification would open us up to lawsuits from the companies whose products we were finding vulnerabilities in, or possibly costs us our day jobs if our employers didn't understand the whole "hacking" thing. The second and larger problem was that Mudge had issues with planes. The only way he could fly was if he was heavily medicated. This solution would be fine if we were going to Vegas for a hacker conference, but no one wanted to be in a less-than-optimal state the day after travel because of residual medication, even if it was self-prescribed. So we rented a large van and drove the eight hours from Boston to Washington DC.

Believe it or not, coordination of wardrobes was important for any sort of group outing. We all went to the same conferences, so we all had the same collection of black T-shirts. It would look exceedingly lame if we all showed up to SummerCon wearing T-shirts emblazoned with the Ninja Strike Force logo, for example. When the subject came up during the meeting, I immediately said, "We are wearing suits, this is the United States Senate, we are wearing suits."

That pretty much ended the discussion. At the time we didn't even all own suits, including me. I went straight to the Men's Warehouse the next day and bought a three-hundred-dollar suit I couldn't afford and had to pay extra to get the alterations done in time.

###

We gathered in the L0pht parking lot at about 5:00 a.m. and stood around taking a bunch of what now looks like goofy pictures. Then we loaded up the Dodge 3500 15 passenger van Weld had rented, and headed south. Stefan did most of the driving on the way down, but we quickly found out he was one of the most careful and risk-averse drivers ever. Thankfully the rest of us were busy geeking out in the back of the van to notice. We had set up a bunch of antennas on the roof and did what the military would call signals intelligence, or SIGINT. There wasn't much in the way of Wi-Fi networks in 1998, so we were mostly looking for unusual transmissions and experimenting with what data we could collect. We didn't do any transmitting and definitely no burping on law enforcement frequencies as Tom Icom had on the way to Beyond Hope.

On the way we decided to stop at the NSA's National Cryptological Museum. The museum was much smaller back then, but it was still located right off the highway. So when we saw a sign that said NSA and pointed to a highway exit, we took it. The exit did not take us to a museum and instead took us directly to the parking lot of the main NSA building. We turned the corner on the exit off-ramp, and there right in front of us was the guard shack. Stefan, who was driving, freaked out. "Ah guys, what do I do?"

The guard had just stepped out of the guard shack, and Mudge, who was in the front passenger seat next to Stefan, said, "He has a gun, so go slow and stop next to the shack."

This is when the guard saw a large dark-green van with heavily tinted windows and multiple antennas stuck to its roof coming off the exit at what was probably a faster-than-normal rate of speed. So he did what any highly trained low-ranking guard soldier would do—he saluted. I don't know if he was new to the job, still hungover from the night before, or just didn't care that day, but whatever the reason, he had mistaken our civilian dark-green van with tinted windows and multiple antennas for an official NSA dark-green van with tinted windows and multiple antennas.

As soon as Mudge saw the salute, he immediately sat up straight in the passenger seat, and while he brought up his arm to return the salute, he repeated over and over, "Don't stop. Don't stop. Don't stop." And so Stefan just kept driving, straight into the NSA parking lot.

We were shocked but realized that we had completely blended into our soundings. We were like, oh great, we just broke through the NSA's first line of defense, now let's get the hell out of here before anyone notices. So, we quickly turned around, drove right past the same guard shack when going the other way, and headed to the crypto museum.

Twenty years later the NSA invited me to that same office building, through the company I was working for to give them a security briefing. My coworker and I drove past that same guard shack, only this time they stopped us, and made us show IDs and open the trunk while people carrying submachine guns surrounded us. Much more difficult to blend in there today.

At the time the Cryptography Museum was kind of small and not a lot to look at, but it was still neat; it was the first time I had seen an Enigma machine used during World War II and a Cray supercomputer like the kind seen in the movie *Sneakers*. The Great Seal Bug, also known as "The Thing," really enthralled me. It was a passive bug hidden inside a hand-carved seal of the United States and presented to the US ambassador to the Soviet Union by local schoolchildren in 1945. The ambassador hung it on his office wall where it remained undetected for six years, listening to everything ever said in that office.

###

We arrived at the Phoenix Park Hotel in Downtown DC just a few blocks from the capital and went to check in. Part of the agreement for us to testify was that we would continue to use our handles, so when the concierge asked me for the name on my reservation, I said "Space Rogue." He looked at me strangely and slowly replied, "Do you have any ID?" To which I just kind of said, "Ahhhh…" Thankfully someone else had overheard the conversation, pushed the first clerk out of the way with an "I'll handle this," and a few seconds later I had a key to my room.

Signing in at the hotel wasn't our only problem. Part of the agreement of us testifying was that the government would reimburse us for our travel expenses. They really couldn't write out a check to Space Rogue, so we had to get reimbursed in cash. After our testimony, in the basement of one of the Senate office buildings, they gave us yet another alias to put down in the official bookkeeping register to get our reimbursements. The names we used all had the same first and last initial, like Alan Alda, but each of us had a different initial and each name had something to do with baseball, I think. The clerk behind the counter looked at each name, looked at the amount, counted out the cash, had us sign a receipt, and didn't bat an eye. You could tell he knew something was up, but that he also knew not to ask questions, almost as if he had done this same thing many times before.

After we had checked in to the hotel and got something to eat, we headed over to Senator Thompson's office in the Dirksen Senate Office Building to meet with the staffers to prepare for the testimony the following day. We took a few minutes and sat in the empty hearing room to get a feel for how things would be laid out. This wasn't the first time I had been in a hearing room. In high school I had been lucky enough to get a scholarship for the Close Up program, which takes high school kids around Washington DC to show people how our government is supposed to work. As a result, I sort of knew what to expect in the room, but being there then and looking up at the dais where the senators would sit, the gravity of what we were about to do really hit me. This was going to be a pretty big deal.

Once we had finished prepping for the next day with the staffers, we had dinner and headed back to the hotel. We all gathered into one room and went over our oral statements. We were each going to give a brief introduction, and we practiced reading them aloud in front of each other two or three times.

The next morning we all gathered outside the hotel lobby, dressed in our suits and looking pretty fierce, if I do say so myself. We took some pictures from the sidewalk on the side of the hotel with the capital building in the background.

I don't think I really got nervous until I got to the hearing room, and I noticed that there was already a line outside the door of people waiting to get in. We took our seats in the front row and waited for the hearing to start. Peter G. Neumann was testifying first. I sat in my seat and tried not to fidget as the senators walked in and took their seats behind the dais. I tried to pay attention to Peter Neumann's testimony, but by then the enormity of where we were and what we were about to do was hitting me hard. If I had I been there alone, I'm not sure I would have been able to function, but I wasn't alone. I had six very close friends there with me.

The Senate Committee on Government Affairs, which they later renamed to the Senate Committee on Homeland Security and Governmental Affairs after the 9/11 attacks, was composed of some heavy-hitting senators. The chairperson, Senator Fred Thompson, who everyone knows as the actor who played the District Attorney in the early years of the TV show *Law and Order*; Senator John Glenn, who was the first American to orbit the Earth; Senator Joseph Lieberman from Connecticut; and Senator Susan Collins from Maine were the only four members of the committee, out of fourteen, who appeared that day.

Neumann's testimony was very similar to our own. He pointed out the risks to critical infrastructure and of homogenous environments where everything was running the same software. He worried about the power grids and telecommunications networks and how vulnerable they all were to an electronic attack from a determined foe, and that there really wasn't any security on anything anywhere.

When Neumann finished, we all awkwardly got up and took our seats at the table. The nerves for me at this point were intense. If you watch the CPSAN video of the testimony, you can see I am looking down at my notes for the first half of the hearing, and it isn't until probably thirty minutes in that I'm comfortable enough to raise my head and look at the senators sitting above me.

Chairman Thompson introduced us with our handles, to which Senator Lieberman jokingly replied "I thought *you* were the kingpin, Mr. Chairman" to a few light laughs from the audience.

Senator Thompson continued with, "I hope my grandkids do not ask me who my witnesses were today, and I reply Space Rogue," which got a few more laughs from the audience. I smiled but kept looking down at the table.

We proceeded to each read an opening statement, after which I was feeling a bit relieved, as I knew the hard part was over. All I really had to do from that point on was sit there for the rest of the hour, and I'd be done. I wanted to say at least something during the rest of the hearing, but I knew I wouldn't be required to, and I could just sit there and say nothing.

After the opening statements, Senator Thompson thanked us for being there and then went in for the big sound bite.

"I am informed that you think that within thirty minutes, the seven of you could make the Internet unusable for the entire nation, is that correct?"

Mudge replied, "That is correct. Actually, just one of us with just a few packets." He then talked about some investigation he had been a part of.

Sitting there in the hearing, I didn't really think too much about the statement. I had assumed that Mudge was talking in general terms and not about a specific vulnerability. "Taking down the Internet" was a thought experiment we used to play on BBSs all the time. "Well, if you compromised this one specific router, you could then reach these other routers, and this and that and the other thing, and boom, the Internet would be down." These thought games would always lack specifics and were just an exercise that a lot of hackers would use to illustrate just how fragile everything was and that if just one tiny part breaks, the whole thing comes tumbling down. I did not know, sitting there at that table in front of the Senators, at that specific moment, that Mudge was talking about a specific vulnerability—one he had already disclosed to government agencies. Perhaps he had mentioned it during one of our weekly meetings and I forgot, but there was no prior plan that I was aware of to open the hearing with a dire prediction about taking down the Internet. But this is what the press would latch on to.

About halfway through the hearing, I could calm my nerves enough to answer some questions, enough so that I think I interrupted and cut off Senator Lieberman once without realizing it. But the senators seemed to get it. You could see the beginnings of realization dawn on them. When Senator Glenn started relating his experiences as a pilot to the weaknesses in GPS signals, you could tell he was at least starting to "get it."

When the hearing was over, we adjourned to Senator Thompson's office, where the receptionist told us she had received a call from a newspaper in Maine that wanted to know if there was a Chris Thomas testifying today. The receptionist said she had to say no because she didn't have that name on her list. And then she just kind of glared at us. No one said anything, but everyone just looked at me, and I looked at the floor. My mother, of all people, had blown my hacker cover and doxed me to the US Senate. All the work we did to protect our identities almost ruined by one errant phone call.

Senator Glenn's office was pleasant enough to offer us all autographed photos of himself dressed as either an astronaut or a senator. I chose astronaut and later had the picture framed.

[A transcript of the L0pht's oral testimony before the Senate Committee on Government Affairs can be found in Appendix A.]

I found out during the days after our testimony that when Mudge claimed that a few packets (a small piece of data) could take down the entire Internet, what he was talking about was a specific flaw in the Border Gateway Protocol (BGP). BGP is a core routing protocol that decides how data should travel on the Internet. Basically, BGP helps data on the Internet get from one machine to the next along the most efficient path. Mudge was talking about a cascading flaw that would force a router to stop sending traffic. Before it stopped, it would transmit the key information to the next router in the chain, which would in turn transmit the key packets before it would also stop sending traffic. We estimated it would only take a few minutes to propagate across the entire Internet, locking up all the routers. If you tried to reboot a router to clear its memory, it would immediately receive the key packets from its neighbor routers when they came back online locking up again. The only solution would be to turn all the routers off at once and then turn them back on.

Well before our testimony, Mudge had evidently privately disclosed the problem to the router manufacturers who had already come up with a fix and sent it out to their customers. However, since no one really knew at the time what Mudge had been referring to when he claimed the Internet could be taken down in just a few minutes, we often had people come up to us in the weeks and months after the testimony and ask whether Mudge had been talking about this other specific method that they would then describe to us. Our answer was usually along the line of "No, that is not what we were thinking of; in fact, we hadn't thought about your method at all, but it sounds like that would work too."

The Internet truly was—and still is—held together with bubble gum and bailing twine. BGP specifically is still a problem. While the specific flaw mentioned during our testimony had already been fixed by the vendors before we arrived in Washington DC other flaws in BGP are constantly being discovered. The problem is so severe that the Department of Justice along with the Department of Defense have recently asked the Federal Communication Commission to take a more active role in securing BGP.[83]

That evening Richard Clarke offered to take us on a private tour of the White House. This was eye opening. We got to see the Oval Office and the Situation Room down in the basement. It surprised me how tiny the room looked, barely enough room for the table and chairs that were in there, let alone any people. Another room that seemed much smaller than I thought it would be was the press room; this is the same room you see on TV, but you usually only see the front where the podium is and not the rest of the room where all the reporters sit. It is a small room. But we all had fun standing behind the podium and taking pictures of ourselves each pretending to be giving a speech while one or two of us stood toward the back and pretended to look like secret service agents.

The next morning we checked all the news websites and were rather dismayed at some of the headlines such as "Hackers Could Crash Internet in 30 Minutes" and "Terrorists Could Add Internet to Hit List." Terrorists? We said nothing about terrorists. How did they come up with that headline? Then that night we got the lead-off joke during Conan O'Brien's monologue.[84]

"This is kinda weird, I found this... talk about something that's a little frightening... I read this in the news yesterday, a group of computer hackers told Congress that hackers are now capable of shutting down the Internet, redirecting commercial flights, and transferring millions of Wall Street dollars around the world. It's weird, yeah, which means, the only thing hackers still aren't capable of doing is losing their virginity." To which there were some uncomfortable laughs from the audience and some boos intermixed with the normal guffaws. "There's a guy with thick black glasses crying right now. In the third row."

His sidekick Andy Richter then interjects, "While he's moving all the money out of your account."

"Yeah right," Conan replies. "I'm completely screwed."

"Yeah."

Conan then pantomimes like he is typing and in a high-pitched voice says, "I'll show that red-haired freak."

Then he looks straight into the camera and in a serious tone he says, "I don't fear nerds."

Then he relaxes, looks over at Andy and says, "That's probably the bravest stand I ever took here on the show." Then again in his serious voice, "I'm sorry, I might be going out on a limb here, but I don't fear the nerds."

There were so many ways they could have gone with this bit, and they went with an overused virginity joke. I stopped watching *Conan* after that.

We also received a mention on the *Rush Limbaugh Show*. Limbaugh called us "long-haired FM types." But there were no longform news stories about the insecurity of US Government computers systems. All the press wanted was to talk about the evil hackers and how they would destroy the world. Our warning message, our call to arms, our rallying cry was drowned out and smothered by the Chicken Littles.

I kind of thought things would just go back to normal at that point, but it did anything but. Press mentions really skyrocketed. A few weeks before our testimony, a piece we had filmed weeks before for *The NewsHour with Jim Lehrer*[85] aired on PBS. In July, the interview we gave to Pamela Ferdinand for the *Improper Bostonian* finally ran. In August, we had an interview with *CNN Sunday Morning*. At the beginning of October, a four-page spread on the

L0pht appeared in the *New York Times Magazine*. Later in October, the *Improper Bostonian* listed "Dr. Mudge" and the L0pht as number forty in their Internet top forty list. Also in October, the piece we had filmed for MTV's *True Life* months before finally aired. There were several other pieces that, even if they weren't full interviews, contained quotes from one or more L0pht members.

Our press mentions were on an almost unstoppable roll. Any journalist who wanted to write anything at all about hackers would come to us either through the L0pht directly or through HNN. Most of these requests we declined, as we either didn't have the time or felt that the outlet in question would not portray our side of the story the way we thought it should be portrayed. A lot of time reporters and their editors already know what they want to say long before they write a story. Then after they write it, they just need a quote or two that upholds their point of view or version of events. As the primary press contact for the L0pht, I think I got pretty good at determining which media requests were interested in telling a neutral, impartial story and which requests were more interested in a quote to support their already-written and sensationally biased angle.

Otherwise things went back to the way they were, just busier with a lot more press. We still struggled to make the L0pht pay for itself. I started working extra hard on the Hacker News Network; we started pushing out more and more modules for Marcus Ranum's new product, Network Flight Recorder, and we started making plans on other ways to generate revenue.

###

During the 1980s the US Army had a unique facility at Fort Irwin in California. Ft. Irwin is approximately one thousand square miles of absolute nothingness in the middle of the California desert about forty miles north of Barstow. Originally used as an anti-aircraft firing range, Ft. Irwin was later transformed into a training facility for armored units. Tanks need a lot of room to turn around in. The US Army has several bases that could be used for training of tank battalions, but what made the National Training Center at Ft. Irwin unique was the permanent installation of an opposing force (OPFOR).

The OPFOR at Ft. Irwin wasn't just a small opposing force designated as the enemy to give the unit undergoing training something to practice shooting at. At Ft. Irwin, the OPFOR were permanently stationed there, giving them an advantage in knowledge of the terrain and other conditions at the training facility. In addition, they wore Soviet-style uniforms; the vehicles they used were mocked up to resemble Russian BMPs and T-72 tanks. They practiced Soviet-style tactics, and some members of the unit even learned Russian to further lend authenticity to the scenario. Various units throughout the Army would rotate through the NTC for training exercises in a fully immersive environment.

When I was stationed at Fort Ord, about three hundred seventy miles North of Ft. Irwin, near the California coast, being rotated through Ft. Irwin and the NTC was considered a privilege. However, as a light infantry unit, the odds of getting sent to an armored training facility were slim. The Army knew the idea of a facility with a permanent OPFOR was a good one. As light infantry units such as the 7th ID and the 10th Mountain Division became more popular, the idea of a similar training center with a dedicated permanent OPFOR but for Infantry units was something that gained support.

By the mid-eighties the Joint Readiness Training Center (JRTC) at Fort Chaffee in Arkansas had begun rotating infantry units through for training like what the NTC at Ft. Irwin was doing for armored units. My biggest memories of Ft. Chaffee were looking at the amazing cloud lighting through the night vision goggles while on guard duty. That and having to get stitches in my finger after getting stabbed by a bayonet trying to open an MRE ("Meal Ready to Eat" prepackaged food ration).

The idea of a permanent opposing force always stuck with me though—an OPFOR that would always think and act like the enemy, that was intimately familiar with the terrain and could really put a training unit through a test as close to a real-world engagement as possible.

Shortly after the L0pht's congressional testimony, I had a brainstorm that the US really needed a NTC for network defense with a permanent cyber OPFOR. This was long before virtualization and containers and constructing even a modest network with a hundred or even a few dozen endpoints would take considerable effort, especially just for a training exercise. I thought the only organization that had the resources and the motivation to pull it off was the government. I wrote up my idea in a medium-length email, including a pitch that the L0pht should play the role of the permanent OPFOR, or at least be training the people who would be the OPFOR, and sent it off to Richard Clarke.

Fast forward twenty-five years later, and cyber ranges for training corporate security teams are all the rage. Virtualization and container technology has made deploying a test network with thousands of virtual endpoints a much simpler exercise. Dozens of companies in the US have such cyber ranges to train corporate defenders and can take things far beyond simple tabletop exercises to fully immersive experiences. IBM, my present employer, has a range like this in its offices in Cambridge, MA. The IBM Cyber Range has a months-long waiting list and allows business to become fully immersed into a cyberattack scenario, including getting interviewed by a news reporter about the recent "breach" their company just suffered. Even colleges such as RIT in upstate New York now have their own cyber range so students can experience the stress involved with facing a real-time cyberattack.

As for my email to Richard Clarke, I don't know if it made any impact inside the government or not. In fact, I don't even know if he read it. Despite not receiving a response, I like to think that the idea had merit and was acted on way back then.

Today, of course, there are various collegiate competitions that are like my original idea, such as the National Collegiate Cyber Defense Competition (CCDC) and the Collegiate Penetration Testing Competition (CPTC), which aim to help train tomorrow's cyber experts by putting them in realistic training scenarios as a competition, both as defenders and attackers.

@stake

Over several weekly meetings we realized that the slow and steady method of building L0pht was just that: slow and steady. A sense of growing impatience settled within the group. There was a lot of money floating around in the late nineties. Between Y2K fixes and the dot-com bubble, many people we knew were becoming very rich very quickly. We were getting lots of press attention and name recognition, and yet we were still just scraping by. We had big plans, huge dreams, and no money to execute them. By this point several of us were drawing some sort of salary from the L0pht but overseeing the finances made me realize just how touchy that situation was. Some months we barely had enough money in our bank account to cover payroll—a fact I tried to keep from Silicosis and Dildog the most since they had both just left cushy actual jobs to come work for L0pht. No need to make them worry they might not get paid.

Mudge, being our natural front man, was tasked with trying to find us some of this money. Every week during our meeting, he would tell us who he had spoken with and discuss a promising lead to another venture capital firm or some other angle he was trying. This tactic resulted in our working with Cambridge Technology Partners and a few other "almost" opportunities that we came real close to signing with but decided not to at the last minute.

Eventually we learned about a small company called @stake that had already been funded by the investment firm Battery Ventures. The company had a few employees, some of whom we already knew. Mudge handled most of the negotiations, but the gist of the agreement as I was led to believe it was that L0pht would keep on being L0pht, just with new offices, a new name, and few new people. Seemed like pretty good deal. We would get paid (and get benefits) to keep on doing what we were doing. Sure, we would lose the L0pht name, but at the time that seemed like a minor concession to be able to hack all day and get paid for it.

I don't know what anyone else's situation was, but for me personally at this point, I was in dire financial straits. I had racked up quite a hefty bill the few short few months I spent at Boston University back in 1990. In addition, I had a decent amount of credit card debt and a couple of defaulted student loans. In fact, I had declared bankruptcy about two years earlier to get out from under the mountain of debt, but Boston University decided that room and board was in fact an educational expense and not dischargeable in a bankruptcy. By this point they were threatening to sue me to recover what to them were a few pennies and to me was a few years' salary. I didn't have any money for a lawyer, let alone anything to pay Boston University with. As a result, I was very motivated to see this deal with @stake proceed, or any deal, actually.

After a few weeks of discussion, we had a meeting over dinner at John Brewer's Tavern on Main Street in Waltham, which was nearby the L0pht. It was a chilly evening in late October, and we were lucky to get a large round table in the back to discuss our options.

Mudge once gave a quote to CNN[86] and may have voiced a similar sentiment at that meeting or earlier: "You can be a garage band for your entire life, and you can be... fantastically talented and have wonderful music, but your music isn't going to make a difference to anybody because nobody is going to hear you." Spoken or not, I think that was a sentiment shared around the table. We really thought what we were doing was in the public good, that we were making the online world a safer place, but we were in danger of no one hearing us.

I didn't mention my financial situation to anyone else, but I did stress that I felt we needed to move forward with this deal. I was impatient. We had been pouring money into the L0pht for seven years now, and I for one was exhausted of what seemed like was not really going anywhere. Our goal had always been to get L0pht to pay for itself, and here was a perfect way for it to do that. I said my piece to the group and then went quiet and ate my burger. Others continued the discussion, weighing the pros and cons. Honestly, I wasn't paying much attention. By the time I was done with my burger, and my few remaining fries had long gone cold, we took a vote. Everyone raised their hands in favor of joining with @stake. It was a unanimous decision.

###

On December 17, 1999, we all went to our lawyer's office, Kotin, Crabtree & Strong in Bowdoin Square in Boston. Battery Ventures had kindly picked up the tab and signed away all the work we had poured into the L0pht over the previous seven years of our lives. To be fair, they compensated us for that work, somewhat. We each received a signing bonus of $12,500, a yearly salary of $92,000 and a retention bonus of approximately $120,000. I say approximately because I'm reading over the original employment agreement now, and the retention bonus part talks about an aggregate pool and then percentages to be paid out and many weird contingencies where it won't be paid, etc. Legalese that's way above my head even now, let alone back then. Honestly, if I was asked to sign this today, I'm not sure I would. I'm sure our lawyer explained it all to us back then and it sounded perfectly fine, but right now I cannot make any sense of this. Regardless, the retention bonus didn't matter in the end because I didn't see a dime of it.

###

The news broke publicly on January 6 with coordinated press articles hitting the *Boston Globe*, Reuters, the Associated Press, MSNBC, and other outlets.[87] The reaction was both congratulatory and sour grapes. We were instantly labeled as sellouts by a sizeable chunk of the hacker community. The business side of things was equally cautious because people did not know what to make of a bunch of hackers suddenly gaining venture capital. Over the next few weeks and months, several companies made statements[88] about how they did not hire hackers at all. While not mentioning @stake directly, this statement was obviously designed to cast doubt on them. I still find it ironic how many companies claim they do not hire hackers at all when many most certainly did; they just didn't necessarily know it.

The RSA Conference in 2000 was nothing like the RSA Conferences of today. The conference was initially formed as a small cryptography conference in 1991 and has since morphed into the most prominent security conference in the world. It was named after the RSA Security company that was named after the founders of the company, Rivest, Shamir, and Adleman. Today the conference is held at the Moscone Center in San Francisco, has over a thousand vendors showcasing their companies, and is attended by over forty thousand people. Back in 2000 the conference was held at the convention center in San Jose and had maybe seventy-five vendors total in the conference hall, with maybe three thousand people attending.

@stake was able to get one of the largest booths at the conference, a triple-sized booth along one of the middle major pathways on the convention floor. By booth I don't mean one of those mega booths with stuff hanging from the ceiling and prefabricated meeting rooms you see at the big security conferences today. A booth for RSA then was maybe a ten-by-ten square separated from the other booths with metal stanchions and drapery curtains, plus a small white cardboard sign printed with the company name in black block letters hanging from the curtain.

@stake held its launch party during the evening at the San Jose Museum of Art. We invited all our hacker friends, many of whom had joined the great migration west out of Boston and had settled in San Francisco, just a short drive south to San Jose. The launch party was an interesting mix of leather jacket and T-shirts with button-down shirts and khakis. Our event was up against the planned entertainment for the conference that evening—a concert by some big-name music star.

At that point I was working closely with our outside PR firm, trying to drum up media interest in our new company. I was less than impressed with the media people we had hired. They showed me their very large spreadsheet of press contacts who they were trying to get to cover our launch and were not having much success. Inside of thirty minutes of just walking around on the show floor, I had secured three print interviews and even convinced the local TV news to stop by the booth and do a quick shoot just as they were leaving. The footage later turned into a two-minute spot on the local news that ended up being more about @stake than the conference.

We knew that @stake was already employing some people that we knew, but we didn't know who everyone was, or at least I didn't, and if I was told, I wasn't paying attention. I didn't find out until a few days before going into the office that one of those people was Garbage Heap (gheap). I wasn't too pleased about that. Gheap was a perfectly fine person, and I had no issues with him personally at all, but knowing that he was now going to be a part of the L0pht upset me. I think possibly because that's how I saw it; we were not joining @stake, these new people were joining the L0pht.

That made the very first day that I walked into the office even more upsetting. On the wall was a large white board with a list of names. There was more than one name on that list I was unhappy with. Not that I had any major problems with them personally. In fact, outside of BBSs and 2600 meetings, I hardly knew them, but I knew them enough to realize that I didn't want them as part of the L0pht. But then it was no longer my call; I no longer had that level of input. Brian Oblivion had always had the final say on who would or would not be in the L0pht, and here we were, more than doubling size overnight with no input from Brian or anyone else. If anyone else was as upset about the situation as I was, it wasn't talked about. I think everyone just accepted it as the way it would be.

The whole situation was a major change that I had not prepared myself for, and I admit I was probably not handling it well. In addition, the existing office just outside Kendall Square in Cambridge was way too small. We were trying to pack about twenty people into a space that could comfortably fit maybe ten, and a big sticking point to me was that there weren't enough chairs. Like there was literally nowhere to sit.

I was still pumping out HNN news every morning and getting articles posted by nine a.m. EST. My ten-minute commute to the L0pht had turned into a thirty-five-minute trek to downtown Cambridge. When I would arrive at the office around quarter to ten, I would find that there were no parking spaces anywhere and ended up having to park on the street several blocks away. Then I would arrive at the office to find nowhere to sit, someone else sitting at my workspace, and people looking at me like, "Why are you late?", not realizing I had been up since five or six a.m. putting the HNN news together. By lunch time I'd be in a foul mood, realize I wasn't getting work done in the office, and head home to finish what I needed to do from there. This being the year 2000, working from home hadn't caught on as much as it has today. It was something you did on the weekends or the late evenings, not during the regular workday when you were usually expected to be in the office. So I am sure there was more than a little animosity building, especially from the new people, regarding my work habits.

Thankfully, about a month later we moved into new offices across the street at 196 Broadway. This was a much larger space, and I no longer had to fight people over my Aeron Chair. I had a nice new Mac PowerBook G3 laptop to work on as well. I still ended up doing a lot of work from home, though. It was easier to roll out of bed and walk over to my Mac Centris 610 and write up the news at six a.m. than it was to drive into the office and try to do it there. I would usually leave in the midafternoon to beat the traffic, but instead of heading home, I would drive straight to the L0pht and keep working on things there. (Despite the VC money and the new offices, we still had time on the lease, so we still maintained the old L0pht space.)

As for the day-to-day work, the merger/buyout/sellout had taken a lot of it away from me. There was no longer any need for someone to pay the electric bill or argue with the ISP or make sure we met payroll. Even providing support for L0phtCrack or running the occasional fdisk command on the main L0pht box was no longer necessary for me to do. More specifically, there was still a need for someone to do all those things, just that the person doing them was no longer me.

Instead, I worked on keeping HNN up to date and maintaining my media contacts so that we could be sure to get some favorable press for @stake. I did several press interviews, some in concert with Ted Julian, the head of marketing and my new boss, about various news items, such as a new virus/worm outbreak for outlets such as the BBC, NHK Nippon News, *CIO* magazine and *Wired*. (Decades later Ted and I would both end up working at IBM.)

With all this additional press came additional scrutiny. Some ingenious reporter finally started adding things up and actually did some investigating. They pulled the LLC incorporation papers of LHI Technologies from the Massachusetts Secretary of State. Those papers had all our real names on them. It did not say which name belonged to which handle, and the reporter never tried to match things up, but he published a story listing all our real names. I panicked a bit when I ran across the story one morning, looking for news for HNN. There was my real name in print. I really thought other reporters would see that and republish it, and that was it. No more hacker handles. But, as luck would have it, no one seemed to notice. The story faded and basically disappeared. I kept tabs on the story and watched it fall further and further down the Google search results until, a few months later, the publication pulled it off its website. Now I don't even remember who it was that published it.

And then there was the time that Mudge got doxed by the White House, and a reporter for the Associated Press tipped us off. Mudge was still doing his various briefings and pieces of trainings for three-letter government agencies even after we got bought by @stake. He had left his full-time government contractor job. He didn't always fill us in on who he was briefing and training, and I suspect his involvement was more than he told us about.

So when the White House held an Internet Security summit briefing, they wanted Mudge to attend. Of course, to get into the White House, your name must be on a list so you can present IDs to the guards. You cannot really put "Mudge" down as the name, so Mudge had to provide his real name. However, during the event, the White House pulled the raw list of names they had provided to the guard shack and provided them to the press as the list of attendees.

I was back in the office at @stake when I got a phone call.

"Hello?"

"Hey SR, this is Ted Bridis from the AP." Ted and I had established a pretty good working relationship over the previous few years, and it was not unusual for him to call me now and then out of the blue.

"Hey, how ya doin?"

"Hey, is Mudge's real name Peiter Zatko?"

That question came out of nowhere and kind of shocked me. I could tell by the way he asked it that he was hoping for a sudden utterance of confirmation, but I held my tongue and replied, "Ummmm...... Why do you ask?"

The White House had passed out the raw attendee list and had forgotten to redact Mudge's real name. It didn't take long for Ted to figure out which name matched with which person and, by process of elimination, determined that the name Peiter Zatko had to belong to Mudge.

I told Ted I would get back to him and hung up and quickly called Mudge. He didn't answer, so I left a message. I called him a couple of more times and maybe even sent him a text, which at the time was a newfangled thing for me, as I had only just gotten my first cell phone a few months before.

Mudge got the message and contacted the powers that be, who quickly took action. They immediately recovered all the attendee lists with the name "Peiter Zatko" from the press and issued new lists with the name "Mudge." Well, it didn't take a genius to figure that one out. By the next day, not only the Associated Press but also the *LA Times* ran stories revealing Mudge's real name.[89] While we thought that was a big deal, we basically ignored it and kept using the handles.

On a Friday at the end of January, @stake had an all-hands off-site meeting at a hotel down the street from the office. As I was to discover over my many jobs at security startups in the coming years, this meeting was standard for a new company. Everyone sits in a circle and expresses their feelings in a come-to-Jesus kumbaya moment to discuss things such as a mission statement and the ethics of the new company. At the time I didn't understand the purpose of it and also didn't understand why I needed to be there. L0pht had been working as a company for a half-dozen years and had done just fine without a mission statement; I didn't see any need for one now.

I tried to discuss this with Mudge beforehand; I tried to explain that if I were there at eight a.m., the scheduled start time for the meeting, there was no way I could get the news posted that morning. I was told they needed me at the meeting. So I copied over the previous day's news and added a header that explained that the news wouldn't be updated until Monday. Then when I got to the meeting, I was almost immediately chastised for not updating the news. I couldn't win. Understandably, this did not put me in the greatest mood to participate in the day's events.

An outside consultant who eventually became @stake's Chief People Officer, which I thought at the time was the corniest made-up title I had ever heard, ran the meeting. I have heard a lot cornier titles since then. There were well over fifty people in the room. I just sat there on the floor because there weren't enough chairs and looked around at all the faces of the people I did not know. All the people who were there were now part of the L0pht, and I barely knew half of them.

As I watched the discussion and debate over the mission statement, I realized that the conversation wasn't organic. Competitive ideas and words were glossed over in favor of what seemed to be a preordained generic statement. Maybe I was imagining things, maybe the ensuing statement did arise from the collective minds of those present, but maybe it had already been prewritten and the discussion shaped to fit the already-created statement. Maybe to make people feel like they had input into the process when they really didn't? I don't know. Either way, I grew increasingly uneasy and agitated as the conversation wore on.

One major bone of contention during that day centered on nepotism. I specifically remember Mudge bringing it up during the company's ethics discussion. I remember thinking, "Is this really that big a deal? Are we really going to have issues with people trying to hire relatives?" Evidently, Mudge thought it was a big deal, because he wouldn't let it go and made sure they wrote it down as one of the core values of the company.

By noon it was over, and they sent everyone home and gave them the rest of the Friday off. I assume part of the reason to have only a half day was to make people feel good about getting time off and partly because they didn't want to buy anyone lunch. I got even more upset about this, especially since I gave up posting the news that morning for what I thought was a useless meeting. In those days, everything was pissing me off.

By the middle of February, Battery Ventures had finally found someone to run the new company. They brought in Chris Darby to be CEO[90]. Darby had no security experience to speak of. He was a former-sales and Biz Dev guy from Digital Equipment Corporation and Nortel Networks, who had most recently been the CEO of a company in North Carolina called Interpath Communications. Interpath billed itself as a super-regional ISP that also supplied fiber optic capacity. Darby had exploded Interpath from basically nothing to over 600 people and $78 million in revenue in just two years. Exactly the stupid growth that VC firms wanted to see and exactly the kind of stupid growth that was fueling the dot-com bubble. Granted, no one really saw it as a bubble at the time, and if they did, no one thought the resulting burst of that bubble would be as bad as it was going to be.

Darby quickly set about establishing his dominance within the company, sending out edicts and moving things around. One of those things was to separate me from the rest of the L0pht. This made some sense. I was busy doing HNN, which they looked at as conducting website maintenance, managing press contacts, and implementing other PR and marketing tasks. They moved me into the marketing department under Ted Julian. I was like, "That's fine, that's what I have been doing, so sure."

The rest of the original L0pht went into "The Lab," a different room on the other side of the office. In fact, the floor pan was such that I seldom even saw Weld, Mudge, Kingpin, Tan, Brian, Silicosis, or Dildog anymore, even though we were working for the same company. If I was lucky, I might run into them in the parking garage and then only for enough time to say hi as we went our separate ways. We didn't even have our weekly meetings to catch up anymore.

One of the major tasks I was assigned while in the marketing department was to come up with a brand redesign and new corporate identity. I thought our current branding was just fine. We had developed this slick animation of a buzz saw from the L0pht logo that cut the old L0pht logo to pieces to reveal the new @stake logo. The new logo was black on gray with red accents. It really popped on a black T-shirt, especially when it had "@stake" on the front and "hacker" on the back. It had no mention of L0pht other than the quarter buzz saw image and our old tagline, "Making the theoretical practical." I thought it was a brilliant use of brand transitioning that kept the enormous brand equity of L0pht and still communicated that this was a new company. Chris Darby disagreed. I suspected his biggest objection was to the word "hacker" since it didn't convey a professional enough image.

I worked with Jess, who was also in the marketing department, and we set about interviewing a half-dozen design firms. This was eye opening for me because, until that point, I had pretty much just slapped together all my websites using raw HTML that I had taught myself. Seeing how the then-new JavaScript, Photoshop graphic slicing, and ASP scripts all became integrated into a website was quite an education. Even in those brief thirty-minute meetings, I could soak up a wealth of knowledge on how the new web would work. More than that, I also learned a lot about branding. While these meetings were almost exclusively sales pitches from each company, they each tried to showcase their best work for previous clients. I could compare and contrast each firm's different styles and takes on what they thought was good for their clients. By the end of that series of meetings, I could find flaws in each company's brand and logo implementations, or at least inconsistencies between one company's approach and another's.

We eventually decided on a company and sent them to work designing a new logo for @stake. They developed a dozen concepts, and Jess and I whittled them down to three strong contenders, any of which I thought would be great. We set up a meeting with Chris Darby and presented the work to him. He spent about two minutes looking at the designs and basically said that none of them were any good. He complained that one of the logo choices had used colors too like FedEx. I said nothing, but I was thinking, "Well, if the colors work for a multi-billion-dollar global corporation, then they are probably pretty good colors." He told us to start over and then abruptly walked out of the room. I only remember thinking, "What an asshole." We spent weeks working on this, got really excited about the designs, and he comes in and shits all over them and leaves in a huff. Not exactly a way to endear your employees to your leadership. Much later I realized it didn't matter what we had presented to him in that first meeting; he was going to shit all over the work no matter what. This was his leadership style—not a very good one, but it's what he did.

So Jess and I started over. We figured if he didn't want the design to look like any others, regardless of how successful it had been for others, and really wanted to strike out into unknown territory, we would give him that. We came up with two really crazy logos and one moderate one, but still sorta crazy (but all three of them still fantastic), and scheduled another meeting. This time he spent more time examining each option and asking the designers questions about why they chose this color or that font. He really seemed interested in the designs, further reinforcing my idea that he threw out the original effort to... hell, I don't know what he thought he was doing other than being an asshole. In the end, he chose the most outlandish crazy logo we had presented him. A fluorescent-orange "@" symbol followed by a white "stake" on a pea-green background in a serif font. Yes, it was as ugly as you can imagine. But that was it. That was the new look of the L0pht.

We had printed several hundred if not more of the old black T-shirts with "@stake" on the front and "hacker" on the back. We had given a few hundred out at the RSA conference but had an enormous amount left over. They ended up getting donated somewhere. For months afterwards you would see homeless people around Boston wearing the old @stake logo T-shirts.

Another thing that evidently didn't fit into the corporate identity makeover of @stake was all the references to hackers. It was labeled "unprofessional." It wasn't until Peter Borbely came on board as Executive Vice President of Worldwide Sales[91] did the whole anti-hacker stance really take shape. Borbley had followed Darby from Interpath and eventually wound back up with him at In-Q-Tel with Dan Geer, which I find a little surprising. Between Darby and Borbely, they eventually made everyone give up their hacker handles and start using their real names, wiping out years of brand equity each of us had built individually. Thankfully that happened long after I left, which is one reason I continued to only go by Space Rogue until years later. L0phtCrack, the company's only actual product, was renamed to LC5. (After @stake was sold to Symantec, L0phtCrack was wrestled away from them and had its name changed back to L0phtCrack. It is still one of the best Windows password-auditing tools available to this day.)

Their thinking being that a professional security company would not sell anything with "crack" in the name. Other projects L0pht had been working on, such as Low Hanging Fruit, a GPS-enabled radar detector that in 2000 had never been done before, had to be renamed to LHF. Hacker News Network at Hackernews.com was another conundrum. It had "hacker" right in the title and at that point was a very well-known and respected media outlet. You couldn't really just shut it down or change its name. One thing I was tasked to do soon after Borbely came on board was to write up a justification for HNN. I thought nothing about it. I figured it was just a normal part of being a real company and would be a way to explain what HNN was all about to people who didn't understand it. So I wrote up a complete business plan for HNN with revenue projections and a three-year plan. I conservatively forecasted one million dollars in revenue from online advertising, T-shirt sales and other income, contingent upon a small amount of investment in web design and other resources from @stake. Considering that the only overhead was partial time from one full-time employee, me, and some Internet bandwidth, I think that was a pretty good return. However, I was told that a million dollars wasn't enough. I was told that the amount of revenue I was forecasting was not worth pursuing since it was not in line with the company's core business of providing security consulting.

At the time there was professional business advice going around in various books, such as Moore's *Crossing the Chasm*, Kawasaki's *Rules for Revolutionaries*, Collins' *Built to Last*, and others, that said that companies should only do one thing. Anything else that was not part of its core business was a distraction and should be cut. Of course, Google would come by a few years later and blow that theory out of the water, but at the time, @stake was wrestling with what it should do. L0pht had a ton of different products and services, some just ideas and some full-blown shipping products with hundreds of existing customers like L0phtCrack and HNN. None of these were central to @stake's core business of providing security services. Some smaller projects where just shelved, others like L0phtCrack were put on life support with just enough resources to service existing customers but no way to improve the product. HNN was also left to starve. But HNN didn't need much to survive; until that point, I had been the only one feeding it, and I continued to do so.

###

At the Black Hat Briefings in 1999, prior to the @stake merger, I met Lori. Lori worked for Secure Computing, one of the first infosec startup companies that had gone public in 1995 and was eventually sold off to McAfee. Lori and I hit it off immediately and ended up hanging out with each other for the entire Black Hat conference. In fact, after Black Hat and DEF CON that year, I went to visit Lori and her son Ricky just outside of Baltimore. I even started updating HNN and doing other L0pht work from her condo. Southwest airlines had a fifty-dollar flight from Nashua, NH to BWI airport that I took advantage of frequently.

By early March @stake was hiring just about everyone it could find. Lori decided she'd had enough of Secure Computing and applied to a position at @stake. She was way more qualified than a lot of the people they had already hired, but she asked me not to pull any strings for her, as she wanted to get the job on her own. I was more than happy to oblige and was more than excited about the prospect of us working at the same company together. She aced the initial phone interview, and they offered to fly her up to Boston for an in-person interview.

The day before the interview, I mentioned to Mudge that Lori would be in town. When he asked what for, I told him that Lori was interviewing at @stake. I had forgotten that Lori had asked me not to saying anything, but I also didn't think that telling Mudge would be a big deal. Mudge didn't say anything to me about it.

The next day I picked her up in the morning at the airport and drove over to the @stake office while she checked her phone's voicemail. She had a message from her recruiter at @stake. When she called him back, he told her, after the plane trip that @stake had paid for, maybe forty-five minutes before the scheduled interview, that it wasn't necessary to come in for the interview after all. What?!

I was absolutely furious. My mind immediately leaped to the fact that I had told Mudge about the interview the day before. And I suddenly remembered his insistence on the no nepotism clause at the offsite all-hands meeting. In my mind, there was only one explanation for what had just happened. And while I was mad enough about that, I was just as furious about how it was handled. You do not call someone forty-five minutes before a scheduled interview, one that you paid for the candidate to travel to, to say thanks but no thanks. They could have at least held the interview anyway and called her the next day to say no thank you.

We were both pretty upset about the whole situation, but it didn't stop her from moving to Boston or from us getting engaged a month later. She eventually found a job at a security startup called Guardent in Waltham while we rented a house in Acton.

In the middle of April 2000, @stake did what was normal for real companies at the time: quarterly reviews. I sat down in a little office with my manager, Ted Julian, and the contractor who had run the offsite all hands who was acting as our head of HR, or Chief People Officer. I was told I was doing exemplary work, that I was an asset to the company, and to keep doing what I was doing. Basically, the best employee review I had ever had with any company. Yet, things would change drastically in just a few short weeks.

On the 12th or the 13th of June 2000, Mudge and Kingpin came out of the Lab and made a beeline for my desk. They wanted to borrow the digital camera I had. I had convinced @stake to pay a few hundred dollars for one a month earlier so that I could take pictures to post on HNN. Granted, compared to those taken from today's "digital camera," the photos back then were the equivalent of using crayons. Looking back, I am sure it was a legitimate request and had no bearing on what would happen a few days later, but in the months and even years that followed, I would dwell on the sudden and direct request for the camera.

On Thursday afternoon that week, just before I was scheduled to leave for the weekend, Ted Julian called me into that little office again. The same one where a few weeks earlier, I was told that my job performance was extraordinary. Only this time he told me just the opposite. He accused me of always coming in late and leaving early and of constantly playing the pinball game they had installed in the office, which annoyed the other employees. (If the pinball game was annoying, why was it there?) Ted then gave me a new project to develop a vulnerability subscription product that @stake could sell to clients.

After meeting with Ted, I was summoned to Peter Borbley's office, where he told me that I disappointed him in my work effort and that I had to "shape up or ship out." Borbley hadn't even been with a company a month, and I had barely interacted with him at all. I remember thinking to myself just how the hell he knew anything about my work output not having been there at all. He then insinuated if I didn't do well on the project Ted had assigned me, that would be it. He didn't have to define what "it" meant.

I was dumbfounded at all of this, coming at me from out of nowhere. I had never received a bad performance review at any job I had held previously, ever. I tried to explain to Ted that I came in late because I was at home working on the news to post to HNN every morning, and I left a little early because of the extra hours that I had been working in the mornings. But he knew all that already. We had talked about it months before. All my protests fell on deaf ears, and I was again told that I needed to develop this subscription service ASAP.

A subscription service, as Ted described it to me in that meeting, was pretty much antithetical to everything that L0pht had stood for. He basically wanted a service that would sell security vulnerabilities to clients. @stake was trying to find a way to monetize what L0pht had always given away for free as a public service. If we found a problem with a piece of software that put someone's data at risk, we always felt it was our duty to let the user know, or at the very least let the vendor know so they could fix the problem. @stake wanted to take this information and, instead of providing a public service, sell the information via a subscription service. Remember, this was in early 2000, long before any serious bug bounty programs existed, and almost all corners of the industry frowned on selling vulnerabilities. But now here I was, in fear for my job, being forced to work on something I absolutely did not believe in. Not to mention that I had absolutely no idea how to build such a product, how it should be structured, or what to charge for it. This was way over my head at the time. All of which I think was probably the point.

I went back to Ted a few times over the next two weeks asking for clarification and guidance but received little assistance. I eventually put together a small business plan for a subscription service that had projected annual revenues of $22 million. Most of it was just guesswork and depended on the research team finding vulnerabilities we could push out to subscribers and the sales team finding clients willing to pay for such a service, which at the time really had an unknown value.

But it wasn't enough. Looking back, developing a subscription service was meant to either piss me off enough to quit or, most likely, fail at so that @stake would have justification to fire me, because that is what they did. Exactly two weeks later on June 29, back into the little room I went with Ted. He told me I had made dramatic improvements in the last two weeks but that it was "too little too late." He asked for my parking pass and ID badge and then escorted me out of the building.

And just like that, I was no longer part of the L0pht. No warning, no goodbyes, no handshakes. Just "can I borrow the camera" and "don't let the door hit you on the ass on the way out." By the time I got home, my L0pht.com and all other associated email accounts had been turned off. No warning, no time to back anything up or migrate what had essentially been a personal account for the previous eight years. This, of course, is standard procedure for any corporate termination, but I had not expected it. Decommissioning the technical assets of a departing employee was my job at previous companies I worked for.

I thought nothing about it. You get a notice, this person doesn't work here anymore, so you disable the email account, turn off network access, and go collect their computer for reimaging. I had never been on the receiving end of it. When you don't know it's coming, it is unbelievably painful.

Getting fired is an amazingly traumatic experience for anyone. I have read that it is one of the top three most stressful events that can happen in someone's life behind moving and ending a relationship. I was hurt, angry, in shock, and probably had a dozen other things going on in my head as well. It is a scar I still carry with me at every job. I almost expect to get fired and escorted out of the office at any moment. I never keep personal effects in my desk or office, I never conduct personal business on the corporate network, I always make sure I have separate copies and access to personal accounts and information, and link nothing to my work email address. I am almost constantly paranoid, and I am constantly trying to second-guess my bosses' innocent actions or statements.

I obviously had to tell Lori when I got home. She was less than pleased with the situation. I wanted to reach out to other people, friends, to commiserate with. I immediately realized that all my real-life friends still worked at @stake. All my online friends seemed so far away and distant, and even if I wanted to reach out to them, I couldn't. All my online access had been turned off. My dial-up worked, but I had nothing to connect to from there. Every other account I had anywhere was tied to the L0pht. I hadn't just been fired from a job, I had been fired from my friends and most of my life. I thought I may as well have been dead.

The next few days I was completely lost. I no longer had any reason to even get out of bed. I didn't have access to HNN, and my routine of waking up at five a.m. to collect the news that I had done every weekday for that last few years was now irrelevant. I learned later that Weld took over the news updates to the site, but the content shrunk dramatically because he didn't have the time to devote to it and it was no longer as hacker focused as I had made it. I learned later that over the next week, traffic dropped off dramatically. Within a few weeks they took the site down. @stake no longer had a product with "hacker" in the name.

The first few weeks after getting fired were rough. I sat in my office at home and just stared at a screen. Sometimes it wasn't even turned on. Eventually I signed up to an email account with a company on the West Coast called Speakeasy.net, I got some web hosting at a company in Pittsburgh called Pair.net (which I still use) and tried to pick up some pieces. The world, both physical and online, seemed alien to me now. I was just sort of floating through it. I didn't know where to go or what to do. For lack of anything else to do and to prevent any further slides down into the abyss that was looming in front of me, I threw together a personal website. I tried to register Spacerogue.com only to find some domain squatter had grabbed it about six months earlier. It felt like someone had rubbed salt in my wounds; everything stung again. (The squatter still has the domain and last I checked he wanted $10K for it.) I ended up using Spacerogue.net to at least have some place online to get my mail and push out a few webpages, some place to hang my electronic hat, so to speak, some place to call home.

I slowly became functional again, and Lori eventually got me an interview with her work's company Guardent. The people there were great, and I worked on starting up what today would be called an open-source threat intelligence service, which was sort of like the Hacker News Network but private and for businesses only. I had no illusions that Guardent was ever going to go anywhere. Just another security startup of the dot-com boom trying to grab a piece of the money pie. Everyone working there knew it, just hoping for that mega buyout or IPO. After the bubble burst, Guardent was sold to Verisign in 2003 for pennies on the dollar. It was a good place to bury my face into a screen and block out the hurt surrounding me.

Getting fired also took a personal toll. Lori and I ended our engagement a few months later. There were other problems with the relationship but being unemployed definitely didn't help.

Having been fired meant I was no longer eligible for the golden handcuff retention bonus that was part of the purchase and sale price of the L0pht, and part of the employment contracts of @stake. At that point things were still raw, and I was wallowing in self-pity and doubt so much that I didn't really care. Fuck all those guys. Lori convinced me I had to fight for it and deserved every penny. She worked through her contacts to find me a great employment lawyer.

I told the lawyer my story. The whole hacker angle fascinated him, and I ended up spending a couple of expensive hours filling him in on the backstory, but I was grateful for the opportunity to talk to someone about it. I finally had an excuse to talk through the entire series of events. In some ways, explaining the situation to my lawyer was cathartic, and in other ways, it just made me more pissed off as I realized the early warning signs I had originally missed. A warning sign like assigning me a gigantic project with no help, knowing that I would fail only to use it as an excuse to fire me. Or another sign when I was pointedly asked to return a crappy $200 camera the day before the fateful day.

I still couldn't understand how I could go from being the golden child during my quarterly review to being untouchable a few weeks later. My lawyer didn't understand it either. Then I learned that someone else had been fired on the same day as me but worked out of the @stake office in Research Triangle Park in North Carolina. After we compared notes, I pieced things together. My coworker at RTP had been recruited out of Interpath by Darby himself, and yet it was Borbely who fired them.

It was obvious what was going on when I stopped and thought about it rationally and put all the pieces together. It was Chris Darby, the Biz Dev ISP CEO they had brought in to run @stake, and his sidekick Peter Borbley, who he brought with him. Just like Darby had asserted his leadership in the brand design meeting by immediately disliking anything presented to him and storming out after two minutes, Borbely was asserting his leadership by firing someone, one person from each office. One person from each office who the other employees most likely thought was un-fireable. Darby himself had asked my coworker from the North Carolina office to follow him over from Interpath. Like myself, this coworker had just received an amazingly positive performance review. Perfect scapegoats for a new leadership team to exert their dominance over the rank and file.

@stake was pretty adamant about not paying me a dime on the contracted retention money built into the initial contract. My argument was that part of the sale price of the L0pht was tied up in the retention bonus and that they fired me without cause, so they still owed me that money. I was even threatening to go to the information security trade press and spill my guts. I had reporters contacting me about once a week asking what happened, why did I leave @stake? I forwarded a couple of these requests to my lawyer to forward on to @ stake, but they wouldn't budge. This dragged on for months. So I was like, "Fine, let's go to court."

At the end of September, two days before my lawyer told me he was going to file paperwork to sue @stake, I couldn't sleep. I kept thinking about the time that L0pht had been sued by Supreme Law Firm and that Brian had been woken up at the crack of dawn and served papers and how scared that made us all feel. I was pretty sure that suing a corporation would be a little different, but I still couldn't get the image out of my mind. So I wrote a brief email to all the former L0pht members that basically said that @stake and I couldn't come to an agreement and that I would file a lawsuit shortly and that we may call them to testify as witnesses. I said in the email that I wanted them to hear it directly from me first, not a stranger knocking on their door at five a.m.

By nine o'clock the next morning, my lawyer was on the phone yelling at me. "What did you do?!", "Never do anything without telling me first!!", "Well, whatever you did, it looks like they want to settle."

I do not know what happened at @stake, but evidently everyone had been told some cockamamie story about my supposed bad attitude, that I was playing pinball all day and otherwise wasn't being a team player and that is why I had been fired. Brian told me years later that he had no idea what was going on until he got that email, and they all confronted Mudge about it. Mudge said something to someone else, prompting the call to my lawyer first thing in the morning the next day.

So my lawyer and I settled for 75 percent of the retention bonus and an agreement that I wouldn't say anything to anyone about what happened or why I was fired. However, my lawyer pointed out that @stake's lawyers wrote the agreement so poorly that there was no penalty clause. In other words, the agreement said I wasn't supposed to talk about what happened, but there was no mention of any penalty if I did talk. My lawyer cautioned me, though, that if I talked, they would probably sue, and then the judge could extract the penalty. In the end I ended up with about 80 grand to me, minus about $25K or so to pay my lawyer, and another big piece to Uncle Sam for taxes. So I got a small chunk of change out of it, but I also lost the $92K-a-year job.

###

Mark Abene, aka Phiber Optic, never had the pleasure of being fired; @stake just refused to hire him at the end of the interview process. Mark was a prolific hacker in the late '80s and early '90s, parading through telephone systems and other networks even before the Internet became ubiquitous. The Secret Service raided him on suspicion of causing an AT&T network outage in '91, and he was arrested a few times on similar charges after that. His last arrest resulted in a sentence of twelve months' imprisonment, three years' probation, and six hundred hours of community service. When he was released in 1995, *Time* magazine called him "the first underground hero of the Information Age, the Robin Hood of cyberspace."[92]

By late summer 2000, Mark was running his own penetration testing business in New York. @stake, desperate for people with any sort of computer security knowledge, attempted to recruit him. Mark probably figured that since they approached him, they must already know about his history. I mean, he was basically a celebrity. How could @stake not know? But they didn't ask, and he didn't volunteer. Besides, this was @stake, a company founded by hackers—not just any hackers, hackers he knew both online and off. Then at the end of the hiring process, @stake abruptly withdrew their offer, sheepishly exclaiming that they had done a background check and discovered his criminal record.

When word got out to the hacker community that the company founded and run by hackers wouldn't hire an actual hacker, charges of hypocrisy, sellouts, and elitism were leveled. In an interview Phiber gave to *Off The Hook*, the radio talk show produced by *2600* magazine, in an episode that aired on September 5, 2000,[93] he said that he didn't "hold the L0pht people personally responsible" but blamed it on the corporate higher-ups.

In September of 2003, Dan Geer, who had come to @stake though MIT and DEC, published a paper titled *CyberInsecurity: The Cost of Monopoly - How the Dominance of Microsoft's Products Poses a*

Risk to Security.[94] Dan was well-known in the security industry even then. He came from a bioinformatics background, with a degree in Biostatistics from Harvard. He co-authored the paper with other very well-known security professionals, including Rebecca Bace, Peter Gutmann, Bruce Schneier, and others. This wasn't a simple blog post; it was a well-researched academic paper published by the Computer and Communications Industry Association.

The twenty-four-page paper argued that Microsoft's dominance of desktop computer operating systems was a threat to national security. The argument was that a homogenized computing environment, much like a monoculture in nature, made it susceptible to outside attacks. In nature's case, a disease could easily infect an entire population. In Microsoft Windows' case, a worm or cyberattack could easily disable large swaths of computing infrastructure. The paper argued for more diversity in computer system hardware and software to make them more resilient to outside forces. This was not a new idea; Peter G. Neumann had said almost the same thing during his US Senate testimony that had preceded the L0pht's two years earlier.

Dan was fired from @stake the day after the report was released.[95]

I heard rumors that Microsoft, then a big customer of @stake, called the company and pressured them to fire Dan. I also heard that Microsoft said nothing to @stake at all, but the company fired him as a sort of preemptive measure to keep their biggest customer happy. By this point I had been gone from @stake for over two years; either way, I could tell that the company hadn't changed much from the time I had been there. If anything, it had gotten worse.

###

Ironically, Microsoft ended up making changes to Windows Vista. They added security measures like memory location randomization; this choice seems to show that they had read the paper and accepted at least some of its findings.

When the dot-com bubble finally burst, it was not kind to security startups, including @stake. In early fall 2004, Symantec ended up purchasing what was left of the company. This included LC5, formerly known as L0phtCrack, and technically HNN despite it having been offline for years at that point. Silicosis was the L0pht member to stay at Symantec the longest. By the time of the Symantec buyout, Mudge, Brian, and I were no longer with the company. Even Darby had left by then, leaving Borbley as President and CEO.

The buyout was not a good thing, according to the rank and file. Messages posted to an @stake alumni mailing list at the time show many of the employees were upset about being cut out of any financial gain from the sale of the company. Posts to the mailing list theorized that only the top executives at the time stood to get any sort of payout from the sale leaving everyone else who contributed to the future of @stake out in the cold. It sounded like exactly how the company had been run the entire time.

Several years later Mudge, Weld, and Dildog were able to regain ownership of LC5, update it, and rerelease it once again as L0phtCrack. Another product that Dildog had started at L0pht, which became SmartRisk Analyzer at @stake, was also wrestled out of the hands of Symantec and eventually became Weld and Dildog's company, Veracode.

Despite all its problems and mismanagement, @stake was a magnet for infosec talent. The concentration of that many smart people, of hackers, in one place has not been easily done anywhere since. The number of people that worked at @stake who went on to further shape the industry itself is mindboggling.

Katie Moussouris almost single-handedly started bug bounties at Microsoft, created the Hack the Pentagon bug bounty, wrote several vulnerability disclosure ISO standards, founded Luta Security, and now advises Fortune 100 companies. Window Snyder has held high-level security positions at Microsoft, Mozilla, Apple, Intel, Fastly, Square, and now runs her own company, Thistle. Dave Litchfield founded NGS software, wrote several books, and, last I checked, is Director of Information Security Assurance for Apple. Dave Aitel co-wrote several security books and founded Immunity Security, where he is still CTO. Andrew Jaquith has held high-level security positions at numerous companies. Royal Hansen went on to Goldman Sachs, Fidelity, American Express, and is now a VP at Google. Dave Goldsmith rose to US CTO of NCC Group, a European security consulting company. Brad Arkin eventually landed at Cisco as the Chief Security and Trust Officer. Jason Chan went on to be the VP of Security for Netflix for over ten years before he retired. Dino A. Dai Zovi founded several security startups and now works as the Head of Security at Cash App.

And of course, those of us from the L0pht. Mudge worked at Google, DARPA, founded the Cyber Independent Testing Laboratory, and advised payment processing firm Stripe. He then took on a senior security role at the social media giant Twitter. He has continued to uphold the original L0pht ideals by blowing the whistle on what he described as "egregious deficiencies, negligence and willful ignorance"[96] concerning security at Twitter.

Weld and Dildog founded Veracode, a company that analyzes software code for security flaws, and brought in Chris Eng, who eventually became their Chief Research Officer. Dildog eventually moved on to work with Dave Litchfield at Apple for a short time and eventually landed at the cloud security provider Lacework. Kingpin starred in the reality TV show *Prototype This*[97] on the Discovery channel, and now runs his own hardware hacking company, Grand Idea Studio. Tan is a high-level security practitioner in the financial services industry, and Silicosis does the same in higher education. I ended up at Trustwave; Tenable; and now IBM's X-Force, their offensive security, incident response, threat intel, and other services arm.

The concentration of raw security talent that worked at @stake is astounding. Other hacking groups of the same era, such as Cult of the Dead Cow, w00w00, r00t, or others, did have an impact and a few of their members went on to careers in information security. There have been other companies and organizations that have had a few smart people that went on to do great things, but almost everyone that encountered @stake, and by proxy the L0pht, has had an amazing impact on such a small industry.

RESURRECTION

After @stake I bounced around in a few low-level tech jobs here and there, mostly hardware repair and desktop support, no longer really having the confidence for anything more extravagant. By the mid-2000s the economy was pretty craptastic, and I once again found myself unemployed. I was getting a fair number of interviews and even second interviews, but no final offers. This scenario occurred about four times in a row, and I finally pieced together what I thought was going on. During the second or sometimes the third interview, I would inevitably get to speak with someone higher in the leadership chain, such as a VP or the CEO. One of the last questions they would always ask me was, "I don't see a college degree listed on your resume, do you have one?" To which I would reply, "I have over a decade of experience in doing (insert job description). In addition I have previously done X and Y and Z, which all correlate directly with what you are looking for." The response was almost always, "Thank you very much for coming in, we will let you know."

After the third or so company that this happened with, I resolved that I should finally get my college degree. After months of trying and burning through all my savings, I was finally able to land a standard desktop support position at a private school in Cambridge. So while I was barely making enough money to cover the mortgage on my tiny condo and still have something left over to eat with, I signed up for my first class at the University of Massachusetts.

I did not know whether I was going to finish even that first class. The memories of my first attempt at higher education at Boston University and high school were still painful, especially regarding finances. I took what I thought should be a somewhat easy class, hoping I had not just wasted seven hundred dollars in tuition. I took College Writing 101 as an in-person evening class; I did not trust myself to do the work for an online class. The class actually turned out to be fun. I got the hard classes out of the way next so that if I ended up failing out or losing my motivation, I wouldn't lose too much money. Algebra I came the next semester. Then Algebra II, Statistics, Discrete Structures, and on and on, doing just one class per semester, as it was all I could afford and all I had time to do. It took me eight years, during which I had three different jobs. By the time I turned forty, I had completed the degree requirements and earned a Bachelor of Science in Information Technology. I could check that box on any job application from then on.

Getting my college degree was a huge part of rebuilding my self-confidence and clawing my way out of the psychological hole from getting fired from @stake, breaking off my engagement, and moving out of my home.

Despite the copious numbers of hackers in and around Boston, there had never really been a hacker convention or security conference in the city. SOURCE in 2008 changed that; it was one of the first conferences to bridge the divide between hackers and professional security types in the area. One of the talks at that inaugural SOURCE conference was a L0pht reunion panel.

I'm not sure why I agreed to do it. The pain of @stake was still very raw for me eight years later, but somehow, I crawled out of my hole for a few hours to sit on the panel. I suspect the draw of seeing old friends from the L0pht and briefly stepping back into the persona of Space Rogue was part of what helped me decide. Most of the former members of the L0pht were there with the notable exception of Stefan and Kingpin, who had moved to the West coast.

But it was more than just the members of the L0pht; many people who I had interacted with from the old days from 2600 meetings or elsewhere were there in the audience. I could hang out and speak with many of them before and after the panel. In addition, the panel was also live-streamed, resulting in a flood of emails afterward. Probably the most important thing to my mental stability that happened at the conference was signing up to this new social media platform called Twitter. Twitter got me back into contact with people I knew from L0pht and my BBS days. People I had only met at cons or maybe through messages on BBSs or forums were now just a tweet away.

Even people I had never met or interacted with but knew of were on Twitter. Twitter played a big part in those early days for me to reconnect with the world that I had shut myself off from. Twitter has changed a lot since 2008; it remained a useful communications tool for some time. Now I find the ads, trolls, misogyny, and other detractions to not be worth the effort.

At some point soon after the SOURCE Boston conference, I made a conscious decision to let it all go. Holding on to all that hate, anger, and bitterness wasn't doing me any good. I started to let it flow off me. Carrying that around for years kept me warm, but it was eating me up. It didn't fall off all at once like an avalanche, but more slowly, like pieces blowing in the wind. I still carry some of that bitterness around with me from those days, but there is less and less, to the point that it is almost no longer noticeable anymore.

In the mid-2000s, the old @stake IT Administrator contacted me out of the blue and says he still has the registration for the Hackernews. com domain and asks me if I want it. I had assumed that the domain had transferred over to Symantec when they bought @stake along with everything else, but somehow this domain fell through the cracks and was still being held by the old admin. He transferred it over to me, no questions asked. I didn't do anything with it other than point it to my WordPress blog at Spacerogue.net, but it felt good to at least have the domain back.

Recently after rereading the purchase and sale agreements for L0pht by @stake, I discovered that the legal documents never actually list HNN as property of L0pht. Everything else, such as L0phtCrack and other products, is specifically called out, but not HNN. I am not a lawyer, but as I read it, HNN was never sold to @stake and therefore could not have been sold to Symantec either. All that time, and they never actually owned it.

Then, out of nowhere in the Summer of 2009, Tan calls me on the phone. I hadn't talked to him at all since the SOURCE Boston panel years before. He tells me we should put the band back together and resurrect HNN. I probably laughed at him; I thought it was a terrible idea. Then he said we should do it as video, and then I knew it was a terrible idea. Neither one of us had any experience working with video at all. We didn't even own any video cameras. At the time I was working off a PowerMac G4 as my main computer, way too slow to realistically process any sort of video. Somehow Tan convinced me to do a pilot episode. I figured okay, at least it will shut him up and I won't have "what if" regrets for not at least trying?

So the next week I started gathering news article and writing a script. It was easy to fall back into the same old habits I had developed a decade earlier. I won't lie, it felt good; it felt really good. I was reading news sites and writing synopses with a purpose again. As I worked on that script that first week, I knew before I even filmed one frame that somehow I was going to make this work.

I ended up borrowing an old, cheap camcorder from my current employer and somehow put together a pilot episode. It really sucked. The video was terrible, and the audio was even worse. But I could see the potential. Tan convinced me to get a green screen off eBay and film in front of that. Lighting was a problem, so I got a halogen work light from Home Depot that threw off a ton of heat and a ton of light. Too much light actually; the first four or five episodes my face was all washed out from being flooded by the halogens. Sound was one of the biggest challenges. People will sit through bad video. If you ever watched MTV through a cable descrambler in the '80s, you know this. However, people will not sit through bad audio.

Editing was a nightmare. Neither Tan nor I had any idea how to use Final Cut Pro, but we muddled our way through it. We never figured out how to smoothly cut from one news story to the next when you only have one camera. Instead Tan had the idea to exaggerate the splice and make it seem like I was doing a Max Headroom impersonation. He threw in some moving parallel lines in the background and the stuttering effect came out well.

Like the original HNN we took a while to find our voice, but it was easy to fall back into the same groove. We focused primarily on hacking as it related to information security; we stayed away from stories about programming or that were purely privacy news items. The original sarcastic humor stayed. Our model, what we were shooting for, was somewhere between *The Daily Show with Jon Stewart*, NPR, and *NBC News with Dan Rather*. I think near the end, we got really close to that.

We developed new segments like "Tool Time" and "Behind the Firewall," and brought back a segment from the old web-based HNN, "Buffer Overflow." Courtnee, an old-school hacker on the West Coast, reached out to us and offered to film an occasional segment that we would write for her. She would send us her clip over the Internet, and we would incorporate it into the show. By the end of our nearly two-year run, we had what I thought was a slick production that was very entertaining.

One of our biggest obstacles was ironically YouTube. YouTube was already the default place to consume online video, but at the time they still had the ten-minute time limit for user-uploaded shows, and their advertising model was not that great. So we hosted our videos on a website called Blip.tv. This site made it hard for people to just randomly find our show and forced us to drive traffic to increase our viewership.

It was a lot of work and I really enjoyed it, but it eventually became too much. Forty to fifty hours a week at my normal paying job and then another thirty to forty hours a week to get the show out every week. Even on weeks I wasn't producing a show like over Christmas and New Year's, I still had to keep an eye on the news because hacking never stops. After about two years, it just became too much, and I had to shut down the show. The ending was abrupt, but it had to be for my sanity.

The resurrection of the Hacker News Network was a big deal to me personally, though. After I got fired from @stake, I was a broken person, and it took me about a decade to climb out of that hole. Working on HNN again was a huge part of restoring my mental health after the prior ten years. As part of collecting news for HNN, I decided to cover the BSides and RSA conferences in San Francisco. I used some of the money HNN had earned selling T-shirts to pay for a plane ticket to the West Coast. I signed up for a media pass with RSA, and despite the conference making a big stink about requiring an ID to get a badge, I somehow got one in the name of Space Rogue without showing any ID. By 2010 RSA had grown from the small sixty-to-eighty company affair held in the San Jose convention center when @stake had launched. It was now a huge multibillion-dollar professional event involving hundreds of companies, tens of thousands of people, and filling both halves of the Moscone convention center in San Francisco.

I had sent some emails to a few companies to request interviews. They were all more than happy to grant a video interview to someone with the name Space Rogue and a video blog with the word "hacker" in the title. One of those companies was Symantec, which had bought @stake, or what was left of it, several years earlier. I found that to be mildly lulzy. I ended up editing that week's episode in my tiny hotel room up on Geary Street, trying to maneuver the small lamps in the room to throw enough light so that shadows wouldn't obscure my face.

I also took my video camera out to Las Vegas and filmed some footage at Black Hat, the professional security conference; DEF CON, the annual hacker convention; and a smaller conference that happens around the same time called BSides Las Vegas. While at DEF CON I ran into Tan, and we hung out for a bit during the conference. I also ran into Mudge. When I first saw him, my first reaction was to turn and walk away, but I forced myself to say hello. This was the first time I had seen him since the SOURCE Boston panel, after which I had resolved to no longer let the anger eat me up. Mudge was pleasant, and we spent some time chitchatting. He came right out and apologized for everything that had happened at @stake. I was shocked to hear that, and I do not know why he decided right then to make a formal apology, but it was a welcome effort on his part.

RESURRECTION

An annual hacker convention that takes place in Washington DC known as ShmooCon invited me to attend and do some filming. Astaro, one of HNN's sponsors, was also sponsoring an RV that was driving from Boston to DC (it later became known as the ShmooBus), in which I was able to hitch a ride. This was in 2010, the year of the "Snowmageddon," or "Snowpocolypse," when over two feet of wet, heavy snow fell across the Eastern seaboard, including Washington DC. Nobody at ShmooCon really cared about the blizzard during the conference, as we were all inside the hotel. Although, supplies of beer and chicken fingers became dangerously low at the hotel bar, and one skylight in the hotel couldn't hold the weight of the snow and crashed to the floor along with an immense pile of snow, landing right in the middle of the lobby. The drive home on Sunday in the RV took hours longer than it should have, although once we got out of downtown and north of Baltimore where they knew how to operate a snowplow, the driving became much easier.

That ShmooCon is where I met Megan. Megan and I really made what I thought was a deep connection. After the conference we furiously emailed each other back and forth, eventually agreeing to meet up in New York City, which was halfway between Boston and her home in Philadelphia. It wasn't long before I was basically commuting to Philadelphia each weekend, driving south immediately after I got off work on Friday and driving back north on Sunday. The next spring I had sold my tiny condo and moved everything to Philadelphia. I found another low-paying job and still pushed out episodes of HNN every week.

It was about this same time I realized that producing an HNN episode every week was extremely stressful, and we still hadn't found

241

any new sponsors. The money was just barely covering the expenses, I was stressed every week, and I just couldn't hold it together any longer. I called Tan, and we talked it over, and in a rather abrupt announcement, I canceled the show. That week, instead of filming a regular news episode, I filmed a monologue thanking the viewers and cutting off the show. Many people thought the ending announcement was some sort of joke or troll and refused to believe it, but I just couldn't do a forty-hour-a-week regular job and another forty or fifty hours a week collecting and filming news and get no return from that effort for years. I was burned out.

In the weeks that followed, I was able to take stock of where I was in my life and what was happening. It was about this time that Megan and I realized that we really weren't meant to be. The breakup was messy as breakups tend to be, but it was better for both of us that it was over.

People still ask me to bring it back, to do HNN again. Maybe I will; I still believe in the idea, and I think the format is viable. Now that self-produced video has exploded and YouTube has made it much easier for self-producers, I think a show like HNN can find an audience and from there find advertisers or at least monetary supporters, perhaps through a Patreon model. However, I think if I ever do it again, I would want to do it the right way. The right way would require more than one or two people doing all the work. I would need a couple of people to write and gather news, someone else to help with the video editing and production, and probably someone to assist with promotion and advertising sales. At the same time, I now have a family to support, so without some sort of large monetary infusion to get things started, I don't see HNN 3.0 happening soon.

HNN had a few great sponsors over the years. One of them was Astaro, which was soon sold to Sophos, and another was Trustwave SpiderLabs. After HNN ended, I was lucky that Trustwave offered me a position and brought me on to help stand up a threat intelligence service like what I had done for Guardent years earlier. The web had changed in the intervening decade, definitely more commercialized but also a lot more integrated into everyday life. As a result, I had grand ideas for what a world-class threat intel system should be able to provide. It would be waaaay more than simple IP reputation and malware signatures, which was what the current threat intel market was largely shaping up to be. It took me a few months to get the system developed and ready for prime time, but I really felt that we were ahead of the curve and were about to define the market. Then, just as we were about to go live with the new service, Trustwave got cold feet and shelved the product. The process of them putting the product on the shelf took several months of them hemming and hawing and dragging their feet, leaving me in limbo in the meantime. While I waited, I moved on and started working on other things.

While this was happening, the person I was working for, Steve Ocepek, left the company. Steve was probably the best boss I have ever had in any job anywhere. He really understands what it takes to motivate people and how to take care of those who work for him. After he left, I got stuck with... well, someone I didn't work very well with. They had me take over the floundering Trustwave podcast since I was evidently an expert at podcasting having previously run HNN. I tried to tell my boss I was burned out on that and didn't really want to do it. I needed the job, so I didn't protest too hard, but I was miserable. Despite that, I still endeavored to push out a quality product. Years later I would still get kudos from people who listened to the Trustwave podcast I produced and found the information it contained valuable.

Thankfully, during this time I ran into a friend at a conference to whom I could express my displeasure over my current situation. He told me, "Let me see what I can do." On Monday when I got home from the conference, I received a call from the CEO of Tenable, Ron Gula, who said, "Hey, come work for me," and I was like, "Sure!"

Tenable was a great company to work for, and Ron Gula was an excellent CEO. The company's flagship product Nessus, a network vulnerability scanner, had a long history with a great reputation. Many security industry luminaries already worked at Tenable, including none other than Marcus Ranum, the former CEO of NFR, which L0pht had contracted with writing modules for Network Flight Recorder years earlier. It was a good feeling to close that circle.

A few years into working for Tenable, my old boss from Trustwave, Steve Ocepek, calls me out of the blue and says, "Hey, come work with me again." I'm not even sure he got to mention what company it was before I said "sure!" The company turned out to be IBM of all places. "Big Blue," the antithetical hacker company if there ever was one. Unbeknownst to me at the time, IBM had changed a lot since the days of the white shirt and blue tie. They had acquired the X-Force brand years before with the acquisition of Internet Security Systems, or ISS, and rejuvenated the brand with the creation of X-Force Red. XFR was just starting out as the offensive security services arm of IBM Security. IBM had offered penetration testing services before, but this would be the first effort by Big Blue to consolidate the service into its own business unit. So far it has been more than successful for both IBM and me. X-Force Red has evolved into just X-Force and now includes incident response and threat intel among other security services.

I remember during my first month or so working at IBM several people reaching out to me through the internal chat programs and email to ask "hey, remember me? I used to go by (handle) and called X BBS in the YYY area code. Welcome to IBM." Evidently, IBM was hiding a ton of hackers within its 380,000 employees who used to surf among the dark alleys of the Internet and BBSs "back in the day." One of those people who reached out to me told me he was in the IRC chat room that I had logged the day the Legion of Underground declared war on China and Iran. Another circle closed.

The mantra of some companies that proudly proclaim "we don't hire hackers" has always fascinated me because my response has always been "how do you know?" Hackers gotta eat, just like everyone else, they gotta work somewhere, they might very well be working for you. I think what they mean to say is "we don't hire criminals," but they mistakenly equate the definition of one with the other.

Another ironic thing about working at IBM was that it is also where Ted Julian ended up. The same Ted Julian who told me "too little, too late" a decade and a half earlier and had collected my employee badge and walked me to the door of @stake. Ted arrived at

IBM through the purchase of Resilient, an incident response platform company. I got to say hello to him at IBM's THiNK conference one year. It was a little awkward, but it closed yet another circle.

After HNN and ending my relationship with Megan, I found myself with a bit of free time. I started hacking on several projects, never really finishing any of them. I checked out the local hackerspace Hive76, which felt a lot like being in the old L0pht but was more nostalgia for me than I'd like. I even tried my hand at online dating.

I met Maureen through OKCupid. She was an hour late for our first date, but I waited outside the restaurant, in the rain for her, and I am glad I did. We more than hit off. I think we both knew that this was something different. It was more than magical. I met her son a few months later, and a few months after that, we were engaged. We got married in June 2014.

Maureen had a large family: four sisters and an uncountable extended family, many of whom she invited to our wedding, along with lifelong friends from college and even high school. I invited the L0pht; despite the estrangement over the years, I still considered them my family. Tan had some medical issues and couldn't make it, and Kingpin had already committed himself to give a talk at a conference. But Dildog, Silicosis, Mudge, Brian, and Weld all showed up. I'm not sure I can describe what it meant to me to have everyone there. Especially since I knew that with the wedding being in Philadelphia, everyone spent more than a token amount of effort to attend. It meant a lot to hangout and be friendly with everyone again during the reception, even if it was only for a few hours. The feeling of us all in that room stayed with me for a long time after.

I rarely blurt out "Hi, I'm a hacker" when I first meet people. Trying to explain to people what I do for work can sometimes be tricky and lead into all sorts of long and sticky conversations, so I usually just say I work in computers. If that isn't enough, I'll say I do internet security or I try to make the internet safe. If whoever is asking keeps pushing, I'll explain that I try to keep bad guys from getting your credit card when you buy something online. When I'm talking with someone I've first met, I almost never use the word "hacker." Why? Because it means so many things to different people, and many people instantly equate "hacker" to criminal. When I use the word "hacker" I also usually have to delve into a long drawn-out explanation about how I'm not one of "those hackers," I'm a good guy hacker. This is usually way more investment into a conversation than I often have energy for, so I just say I work with computers, and for most people, that is more than enough.

This also goes for my wife's family, which includes four sisters, their husbands, dozens of cousins of varying ages, and more. Sure, they know where I work and have a general idea that it has something to do with internet security, but I don't think I ever told them the long-involved story of the L0pht or of testifying to congress or any of that.

In June 2015, Craig Timberg at the *Washington Post* decided to write a major story about the L0pht and our testimony entitled "A

Disaster Foretold - And Ignored: L0pht's warnings about the Internet drew notice but little action."[98] The story ran on the front page, on Tuesday the 23rd of the month. They used a picture of the L0pht testifying in 1998. The picture with Mudge and his long hair, sitting in the center and the rest of us flanked out on each side, and me looking down at the table. A picture we have affectionately come to call "the L0pht Supper" because of its resemblance in style and format to the famous 15th-century mural painting by Leonardo da Vinci.

My brother-in-law who lives in the Washington DC area reads the *Washington Post* every day. According to him, he didn't even notice the front-page picture. It wasn't until he got to page A11 that his mouth dropped open as he realized my face was staring back at him from a half-page photo. The family was a little surprised at my origin story showing up in the *Washington Post* unannounced. My wife's sister was kind enough to have the photo from the paper set into a large frame, which now hangs on my office wall.

In early April 2018, the L0pht members realized, "Holy shit, it's been twenty years!?" At some point a few years earlier, Dildog had been able to re-acquire the L0pht.com domain name from whoever ended up with it and set up our old "resident" email list. Traffic to the list has been sporadic with some of us only checking in occasionally. Occasionally people would accidentally fall off the list as they changed addresses and didn't bother to send an update. No one would even notice for months because of the lack of traffic. It is good to be in contact with people I worked so closely with all those years ago, even if only sporadically. The pain and hurt are still there and will probably never go away entirely, but things are mostly scarred up now, enough that we can talk to each other and occasionally joke about the old days.

The mailing list became the center of how we were going to plan the revisit of our Congressional testimony on the twenty-year anniversary. We thought we might do something in DC, or maybe a panel at DEF CON, or even some other thing to continue our original message and commemorate the initial event.

While we were trying to decide what to do, I submitted a proposal to DEF CON for a panel discussion. I was a little vague about who would moderate and how many of us would show up, because at that point, no one had really committed to the idea. Hell, we were still trying to figure out how to get in contact with everyone as we soon realized that not everyone's email had been kept up to date. In the meantime, Weld tried to get something together for Washington DC. Since it was already late April, scheduling was difficult, but we eventually found May 22 worked for most people.

We couldn't do a full-blown hearing again; instead, with the assistance of the Senate Cybersecurity Caucus, we were able to get four of us in a room. We convinced our old friend Katie Moussouris who had worked with us at @stake to moderate the panel. The format was supposed to be a seven-minute intro by each of us, and then Katie would ask us a few questions and they would stream the whole thing live. I wrote out my statement and timed it to just under seven minutes. I ended up speaking first, and mine was the shortest statement. Weld's, Mudge's and Kingpins' statements were each longer than the one before it, with Kingpin taking up about fifteen minutes, twice the allotted time. I think he might have been subconsciously trying to make up for the lack of speaking he did during the original hearing.

But overall it went well. What we said was well received and, as always, it was good to see old friends from long ago. Weld and I both brought our kids to the hearing, and they had fun playing with each other at the reception afterwards.

A day or two before the panel discussion in Washington DC, we heard from the DEF CON review committee that they had accepted our panel proposal, which is rare. Panels are not generally accepted for DEF CON, and the review board actively frowns upon them. We had recruited Elinor Mills to moderate that panel. She was one of the first reporters at *Wired* to cover the L0pht, and several of us had worked with her on various news stories over the years. Everyone made it to Vegas except Brian and Silicosis. Again, it was fantastic to see everyone in the same room, even if things were still a little awkward, at least for me anyway. The conversation in the green room before the talk quickly devolved into our old banter from twenty years previous as we each pulled up old personal memes and sayings that only made sense to us. It was both a little awkward and familiar at the same time.

The DEF CON conference room was enormous; I think it could probably seat twenty-five thousand people and was about three-quarters full. A lot of our friends and colleagues were sitting right up in the front rows, trying to heckle us and make us laugh. Elinor asked some brilliant questions and kept the conversation on track. And then when it was over, we all just sort of said our goodbyes and went our separate ways.

Our resident emailing list is still working but receives almost no traffic. I'll see someone from the L0pht post a tweet here or there, and occasionally run into Weld or Mudge at a conference now and then. Who knows, maybe on the 25th or even 30th anniversary, they will invite us back to testify at a hearing in DC again. Maybe this time, they will listen.

LEGACY

hack•er | ha-kər noun 1: a person who is inexperienced or unskilled at a particular activity, a tennis hacker 2: an expert at programming and solving problems with a computer 3: a person who illegally gains access to and sometimes tampers with information in a computer system

t is interesting to me that the definitions for the word "hacker" include someone who is unskilled, someone who is an expert, and someone who is a criminal. The etymologist in me wonders how such a dichotomy came about. How in a few short years does a word go from a verb meaning to cut roughly and then change to a noun meaning a computer expert? I've never studied word origins, but I get fascinated by the history of some of them. (Another word with an interesting and hotly debated history is "cyber."[99])

It is definition number three, the one that defines a hacker as a criminal, that bothers me the most. There was a time when the resources needed to explore an interest in high-level computing were difficult to access. Because of computing's rarity and high expense, systems were often closely guarded and access to them was tightly controlled. This restriction forced some people who wanted to learn, who needed to satisfy their hands-on-imperative, who were almost forced through curiosity, to violate some of those physical and virtual controls. For the most part, those barriers to knowledge no longer exist, and most people in the world can now own a high-level computing system for the cost of a good meal.

It wasn't just access to the systems themselves that drove hackers but the lack of easily available information. There was no Siri to instantly answer your queries, no Google where you could look things up almost as quickly, even no Amazon to order an inexpensive book or manual from. Local libraries might have one high-level computing book on the shelves, but a manual for a telephone switching system or computer operating system would likely only be sold to a large company and then only for thousands of dollars. As a result the only way to learn was by doing.

Despite what sensational media headlines would have you believe, hackers are not the bad guys. This idea was a key part of the L0pht's message to the US Senate, and by proxy, to the American public. Most of the great inventors of our time, such as Alexander Graham Bell, Mildred Kenner, and Nichola Tesla, could easily be considered hackers. A large number of people associated with the NASA Apollo 13 moon-landing mission would also be considered hackers. Criminal gangs who are running ransomware campaigns or are stealing credit cards are just that, criminals. They just happen to use a computer instead of a crowbar. They are not hackers, not to me anyway. For the most part, hackers are just curious and want to make the world a better place.

When L0pht started publishing vulnerabilities in products from companies like Microsoft, Oracle, and Novell, it came with quite a bit of fear. We feared what the reaction would be from these giant corporations to that little bit of sunshine. Would they sue us? Would they threaten our Internet provider to cut our website off? Would they threaten our employer into firing us? Would they just call us names and claim our research was irrelevant? And yet despite these risks, we still felt that publishing and alerting the public to the problems we had found was more important than any of these potential reactions.

Through trial and error, suggestions from others, and healthy debate within the community, we arrived at a model that is generally accepted today as the proper way to release vulnerability information. Basically, notify the product maintainer or owner first and allow them time to fix the issue. Only if they refuse to engage with you or unreasonably delay a fix, then, at the researcher's discretion, is full public disclosure considered acceptable.

This process is still under heated debate within the industry. Google has decided that it will give other companies ninety days[100] to patch or otherwise mitigate a vulnerability that it discovers, but even this rather gracious time frame has come under scathing criticism. The argument, of course, is anytime that information about a vulnerability is released, it not only lets people who use the product in question better defend themselves, but it also lets the criminals know where the holes are. A map to all the unlocked doors, if you will. It is obviously not that simple, but there are numerous cases where a vulnerability only begins to be exploited after it has been disclosed. Shortly after Microsoft started rolling out security fixes on the second Tuesday of every month, what came to be known as "Patch Tuesday," the community came up with its own saying: "Patch Tuesday, Exploit Wednesday." Meaning that criminals will reverse engineer the Microsoft patches to find the holes and then race to exploit them before companies and individuals apply the patches. The argument, therefore, is that if you don't disclose the vulnerability or give details about a patch, then the criminals won't know where to attack. This is fanciful thinking.

Once a patch or update is released, even without accompanying vulnerability information, an attacker can examine the new code and find where the vulnerability exists in the existing code. By withholding vulnerability information you are at best forcing the criminal to do more work and possibly delaying their action. Withholding that information also leaves the defender defenseless, blissfully unaware of what holes exist in their systems just waiting for the attacker. While releasing the information may give notice to an attacker it also allows for the defender to prepare for the possibility of an attack.

There have been suggestions over the years to legislate information about vulnerabilities to control the data. The argument is that some of these vulnerabilities may impact national defense or critical infrastructure. The stickler is that the person who works to uncover a vulnerability gets to decide what they do with it. They can choose to notify the product owner and give them a timeframe of remediation, or they can choose not to tell anyone. The researcher can choose to sell the information to the highest bidder, or they can choose what is called "full disclosure" and let everyone know—defenders and attackers alike. History has shown us that legislation in this space seldom goes well and often ages very poorly. We only need to look at previous laws such as the CFAA (Computer Fraud and Abuse Act), the DMCA (Digital Millennium Copyright Act), COPA (Child Online Protection Act), and numerous other laws that have failed to achieve their original promise.

###

In the early days of connecting computers together everyone pretty much trusted everyone else. This level of trust is easily accomplished when the community of connected machines is small and when the entire purpose of connecting machines was to share data; as was the case with the early government research centers and academic institutions that comprised the very early Internet. As the Internet grew by adding corporations, public ISPs, regular individuals, etc. it became more and more difficult to maintain that community but the trust level stayed the same. This was necessary to continue to share data but that openness also led to malicious actors taking advantage of that open trust. This is a problem we are still faced with.

Corporate networks are still all too often 'flat' where everyone has access to all the data. The clerk who works in human resources has access to the data generated by the research department or the administrative assistant that can access payroll data for the entire company. It is not just users but applications and the systems themselves that inherently trust each other and the network design that happily passes traffic from one segment to all the other segments.

The reason this is still done today is because it is easy and it works. If you are under pressure to get your new business up and running it is easy and fast to just connect everything together and let everyone access everything else. It is woefully insecure and full of risk but its quick and it works. Once implemented it is expensive and painful to correct later on.

This problem of trust even crops up in security software. If the product attempts to block or prevent only known attacks or bugs it will, by definition, trust all other traffic and let it through. This was fairly easy when there not many known attacks but as you can imagine today there is almost an unlimited supply of security holes and attack vectors, attempting to block them all is futile. Whereas the opposite approach is much more secure. Block everything and only let the known good stuff through. Known good things are a much smaller finite number. In the past this type of architecture was called Default Deny, today it is more commonly known as Zero Trust.

Zero trust is not a new concept. It has been around for well over a decade and existed before that as a set of loose guidelines and best practices. At its core a zero trust architecture trusts no one, not users, not applications and not systems. Every interaction must be verified and authenticated. When properly implemented zero trust can make it extremely difficult for an attacker to reach their intended target.

One of the biggest issues facing information security today is ransomware, or a piece of malicious software that threatens to do something bad unless you pay a ransom. Ransomware often finds it way inside an organization through email, in what is called phishing. Phishing is essentially a normal looking email that attempts to get the user to click on a bad link or download a bad attachment. Sometimes these emails are very obvious and sometimes it is nearly impossible to tell them apart from a legitimate email.

To combat this email threat companies have employed anti-phishing campaigns in an effort to train users to not click on links. Unfortunately clicking on links is what many users were actually hired to do. Human resources need to open resumes, finance needs to open invoices, users need to collaborate on presentations and spreadsheets. Opening links and attachments is literally part of most employees' jobs. Training employees to be able to tell the difference between a good email and a bad email is a laudable goal but some companies expect, no demand, 100% correct identification. Failure can be met with disciplinary action and even termination in some organizations.

Training employees to recognize the difference between good and bad emails is helpful and can reduce an organizations overall risk but no company will ever achieve 100% detection of phishing emails. Punishing employees who are essentially doing what they have been paid to do, click links, is counterproductive, results in lowered morale, and in the end doesn't protect your network. Employee training is useful but it would be more useful to spend some of that training budget on hardening systems and designing a network that can properly detect a ransomware infestation, isolate the infection before it can spread, and then remediate the affected systems without paying the ransom. This of course has to be done before the infection occurs and is more expensive than simple user training and punishment. This means many organizations take the less expensive and easier road of merely training people not to click links.

In the two and half decades since the L0pht testimony, the level of security awareness in the general population has risen dramatically. There are public service ads on television and streaming services about choosing long passwords, not clicking on strange links, and updating the software on your computer. Banks send you security notices in the mail and in pop-up windows on their websites. Corporations require cyber security education of their employees on a regular basis. While the effectiveness of these messages may be debatable, the fact that they even exist is a testament to the inherent insecurity that still exists in all things.

Is security better now than it was twenty-five years ago? Technology continues to advance and security advances along with it. Today we have nearly ubiquitous two factor authentication, almost universally encrypted website traffic, increased adoption of zero trust, greatly increased user education and awareness, and numerous technological advancements in programing and low-level chip design. We have a new government agency, the Cybersecurity and Infrastructure Security Agency (CISA), that so far has been very effective at coordinating government response and communicating to the nations infrastructure maintainers about all things cyber.

All these advancements haven't stopped the intruders. It has been described as a cat-and-mouse game. Information security implements a new security control, and it works for a short while, and then the criminals figure out how to bypass it. Then the defenders need to develop a new security control and around it goes. Vigilance is paramount. Even with all the advancements we have made over the last two and half decades the criminals are still right there with us matching us step for step.

Buggy—and therefore vulnerable—software continues to be written and released to an unsuspecting public. Adding security to a product, even a product whose main function is security, costs money. Products are optimized for maximum revenue and sales, not for how secure they can be. That optimization can be something as simple as shaving a millimeter of plastic off the case or skimping on the software audit designed to catch flaws, assuming a security audit is even performed in the first place.

That is just products that are created and marketed for sale. Another valuable commodity, our individual personally identifiable information, also has value—great value to the companies that amass large collections of it. Are they taking great care in securing those collections, or is security considered yet another cost that lowers the gross profit of the corporation? Considering the never-ending parade of information leaks from major corporations one really has to wonder just how seriously they take security, regardless of what their press releases say.

Only when and if someone decides to look closely at a product, network, or other system do we know just how secure or insecure it is. If the person who looks and finds an issue has good intentions, if a company decides it is worth fixing, if the fix actually gets applied, then the problem might finally get resolved. If all those "ifs" do not happen, and they often don't, then it only takes one "if" for something bad to happen.

However, even when a company decided to devote time and money to fix a security problem after a problem has been discovered or after a product has shipped, organizations are often unable to apply that fix. When dealing with large networks of thousands of endpoints, applying patches eats up limited resources. Organizations must pick and choose which systems to patch first, leaving some systems without the patch for a window of time, which leaves a window of opportunity left open for the attacker.

Only recently have some companies embraced and even marketed the security posture of their products. While almost every company will say their product is secure and may even announce it on the packaging in bold red letters, only a few have actually done the testing and auditing to back up that claim prior to putting the item on the market. Auditing and testing however is usually a snapshot in time. If the vendor makes a change to the product but fails to rerun the security checks there is no way to know if the item is still as secure as the originally released product. If the consumer installs or uses the product in a slightly different manner from that in which it was tested the auditing and testing may be inconsequential. For most consumers, however, any auditing and testing performed by the vendor is hard to see—the bold red letters might be right there on the tin, but (for now) there is no way to tell what is actually in the package in regards to security.

The US government has stepped in several times to get ahead of the criminals but until recently has seemed to always be playing catch up. The recent creation of CISA has already brought a cohesive voice to the hodgepodge of government agencies that were responsible for the nation's cyber security just a short while ago. There are also efforts being promoted by the Biden administration to apply security labels to consumer devices similar to the Energy Star program. Only time will tell if the current efforts will become fruitful and finally give the good guys the upper hand.

While the L0pht as a hacker collective no longer exists, its legacy lives on. The L0pht set the precedent for how the cyber security industry now releases vulnerability information. The famous hackers that were once L0pht members have gone on to do even more impressive things in the following years. The hackers and consultants who were hired by @stake and indoctrinated into the L0pht way of thinking have now become giants in the industry. All the hackers who were once inspired by reading security information off the L0pht's website or downloaded software from The Whacked Mac Archives or watched the Hacker News Network have changed the world more than the L0pht could have ever done alone. The L0pht's message of bringing security issues to light and getting them fixed still echoes throughout the industry and is more important today than ever. The L0pht's dire warning of a culture increasingly dependent on a fragile Internet made during their testimony twenty-five years ago still holds true; in fact, the fragility of the Internet may be even worse today. Is it too late to listen?

EPILOGUE

"A book is a version of the world. If you do not like it, ignore it; or offer your own version in return."

—SALMAN RUSHDIE

've been reading a lot of historical non-fiction lately. *Hamilton* by Ron Chernow, *The Great Halifax Explosion* by John Bacon, and *The Aroostook War of 1839* by W.E. Campbell, among others. This has been a change of pace from the usual non-fiction works I had been reading such as *Kingpin* by Kevin Poulsen, *Dark Territory* by Fred Kaplan, or *This Machine Kills Secrets* by Andy Greenberg. Having no knowledge or interaction with the topics covered by the former books, I can take them at face value. I put my trust in the authors to tell an accurate story as best as can be told given the available information. The latter group have been too close to home, so to speak, making it easy for me to find flaws or inaccuracies or things I just plain disagree with between the covers.

Of particular interest to me, and something I have thought about a lot while writing this book, has been Joshua Pullen's biography *Joshua Chamberlain: A Hero's Life and Legacy*. If you don't know,

Joshua Chamberlain was the colonel in charge of the 20th Maine Infantry Regiment during the US Civil War and was placed in defense of a small mound of dirt and rocks known as Little Round Top to the far left of the Union Line during the Battle of Gettysburg in 1863. Several regiments from Alabama and Texas bravely (some might say foolishly) attempted to charge up that hill several times until finally, almost out of ammunition and men, Chamberlain decided that the only way to prevent the Confederates from taking the hill and to protect the Union flank was to leave the protection of their defensive position and charge down the hill with fixed bayonets.

I can tell you as a former infantry soldier the thought of being on top of that hill, on a hot July day, repelling wave after wave of rebel soldiers, and then, with no ammunition, being ordered to run down the hill towards the enemy? Absolutely ludicrous.

Regardless, that is what the 20th Maine did. They finally pushed the attacking soldiers off the hill, secured the left flank of the entire Union Army, and by many accounts, allowed the North to win the battle and eventually the war. And despite that, despite the monumental importance of the actions on that hill, that day, and the hundred or more people present in a heighten sense of awareness, no one remembers if Chamberlain gave the order to charge down the hill or not. In the most studied part of the most studied battle in all United States history, no one knows if the command to charge down the hill was uttered by then-Colonel Chamberlain or not.

In the 1993 Hollywood movie *Gettysburg*, Chamberlain is shown carefully maneuvering his troops across the hilltop in preparation, and then Jeff Daniels, who plays a masterful Chamberlain in the movie, lets out a voracious "Charge!", with his saber shining brightly in the sunlight as he holds it overhead. His troops, obeying his command, run down the hill. But actual history does not readily support this Hollywood version of events. Some accounts say Lieutenant Melcher was the one to issue the command, some accounts say no command was given and that the charge was spontaneous. Even Chamberlain himself in later years could not remember if he did or did not issue the fateful command to charge down the hill. In fact, in an address at Gettysburg some fifty years after the war, he said:

> "You see there may be stories, apparently not consistent with each other, yet all of them true in their time and place, and so far as each actor is concerned."[101]

Stories, none of them the same, but all of them true to each person who told them.

Is it really that important that we know every little detail and fact of what occurred in the past, or is it enough to understand the larger actions? That the 20th Maine charged down that hillside on that historic day with few men and almost no ammunition is not in dispute, it happened. Does it really matter who, if anyone, verbalized the order to charge?

Books are funny things. They say anyone can write one, and I guess I am now proof of that. And yet despite books coming from any source, books carry a certain weight. Sure, you can write something in a chat window, send some thoughts via email, or even opine in a five -thousand-word blog post, but once your words have been transferred to a book, it takes on a different amount of significance.

Once transcribed into book form, thoughts and ideas somehow become more permanent, truer. Books become references for others, they become quotes and citations in other books. If I write it down in a book, people somehow give the contents more credence and gravitas than if my words appeared in a message forum, even if they are in fact the same words.

There is no arguing with a book, even if what is in the book is wrong. A book stands alone. Most readers will not seek other sources to corroborate or dispute a book's contents. Books are absolute and once written can take on a certain mythological status, never to be challenged. A reader can write their own challenge to a book if they feel the contents do not conform to their viewpoints but seldom does such a critic achieve the same impact or permanence of the original work. The readers of any book are unlikely to ever see any such challenge, and as time moves forward, this likelihood becomes even more unlikely as the book continues to live on, but the challenge more quickly fades into history.

Yes, there are some who will consume the contents of multiple books on the same subject to somehow arrive at an average truth among the sources. Some will search deeper and look for news articles or other sources of truth to use with the book. They will use citations and cross references to compile an amalgamation of collected thoughts and ideas interspersed with their own to support their thesis, regardless of the alignment of the original sources. However, as history marches on and our digital words fade ever faster, it is the permanence of books alone, and not their challengers or alternate sources, that will continue to thrive.

The literary record of hackers is full of tomes that attempt to act as the historical record for various individuals, groups, and events. Many of these works have received criticisms pointing out the imprecision of the stories that have received a certain amount of permanence by being placed into book form. Katie Hafner's *Cyberpunk* is an early example of a work that was lauded by lay people as a unique look into a concealed world, but for those of us that inhabited that world, we saw it as full of hyperbole and exaggeration. Michelle Slatalla's *Masters of Deception* and Paul Mungo's *Approaching Zero*, having been published in book form and seen as authoritative works despite being criticized, often privately, also have excessive hyperbole and exaggerations.

There have been many books written already that contain parts of the history of the L0pht. Adam Greenberg's *This Machine Kills Secrets* and Joseph Menn's *Cult of the Dead Cow* are two such examples. Considering the L0pht's impact on the events of the time and the public interest, there will probably be more books written that at least touch on the group's significance. Each of these books will have its own truth, and those truths will sometimes align and sometimes will not. In most cases, it is usually about what has not been told than what is.

I felt it was important to add my truth to the pile and hope that its words align to some degree with the other truths already published. Maybe by combining them to the overall average, a single truth might be found. Memories can morph dramatically over twenty-five-some-odd years, and while in the grand scheme of things twenty-five years is but a trifle amount of time, in terms of individual human memory, it is an epoch.

I hope this book has answered some questions about L0pht Heavy Industries and its impact. I also hope that the reader does not take this book as the sole truth; it is but one of many truths, most of which will never be written. If other truths are written, and readers discover disparities or disagreements, the reader should not necessarily conclude that one version is correct, and the other is wrong. As Chamberlain said a hundred and fifty years ago, each story is true to its own actor.

APPENDIX A

Legion of Underground IRC Log

This is a transcript of the press conference held by Legion of Underground to which Space Rogue of the Hacker News Network was invited. This transcript has been edited. Server messages, and comments not relating to the topic, have been removed. No alterations have been made to anyone's statements.

```
Log file opened at: 12/28/98 19:08:31EST

*** Topic for #legions: The Meeting is now in session

*** Topic for #legions set by optiklenz on Monday,
December 28, 1998 20:03:08

#legions: spacerog @rootbot @NeatHack +Big|Feet
+Zyk|on +barby__ +LordPsY +nawk @lothos +t3q
@dethl0k +XeXeN +ShadoWalk @blakcloud @kInGbOnG @
datapleX +optiklenz @sreality +bronc_ @UnixP1mp @
[havoc] +headflux +_rash +m0f0 @dyslexia +elux_
+LordVaXen @DigiEbola +parkay @DataShark

*** End of /NAMES list.

*** Mode is +pmtn

*** Channel created at Monday, December 7, 1998 6:30:08
```

optiklenz: is anyone logging?

DigiEbola: yes

dyslexia: yes

lothos: yeah

optiklenz: ok

optiklenz: at anyrate

DataShark: so am I.

Big|Feet: same here

NeatHack: log is on

[havoc]: shut the fuck up ppl

LordPsY: yup

blakcloud: go on

lothos: ssshhhhhh

optiklenz: today the news reported that two crackers were being sentanced to death

optiklenz: i'll wait for everyone to finish their conversation..

NeatHack: sentanced to death ?? what press any link on that info ?

DataShark: PUT to death.

dethl0k: that

DigiEbola: from what i saw, some guy mailed my ccmail at work, from cnn

optiklenz: Well it's covered by HNN if you want to read an article about it cnn wrote something

DataShark: I heard they were PUT to death.

dethl0k: s cruel

dethl0k: erm

DigiEbola: for 31000 dollars at that.

DigiEbola: china.

LordPsY: ok

optiklenz: What they did is wrong with out a doubt, but it was no more a crime than what our President committed by perjuring himself before the grand jury of the United States of America.

optiklenz: . It does not deserve the death penalty. The death penalty is something that should be heldFor only those who commit the most gruesome crimes that of murder, child rape,

optiklenz: and Being a Benedict Arnold

DataShark: There is a VERY big differance between putting two ppl to death and lying to some ppl.

NeatHack: agree with optik

optiklenz: China's actions has shown superficial, and damaging, and Iraq follows behind.

optiklenz: Iraq has treated human rights issues as poorly as China has.

DigiEbola: look at both of their goverments

optiklenz: A nation made up of starving people While their leader rest in one of his 14 palaces taunting and parading his country men, and above all Involving other countries in his sick escapades.

dyslexia: chine is estimated to have murdered approx 100 million ppl internally since the communists came to power

optiklenz: . The Iraqi military has access to hydrogen bombs. What in the world do they need hydrogen bombs for?

optiklenz: I don't think Something 2+ times the power of an atomic bomb should be operated by anyone for whatever prospect.

NeatHack: ok but what is our realtion with them and thier miss governed govrment ?

optiklenz: i'm getting to that

ShadoWalk: kan the man go on a dialog? please?

DataShark: WMD. they whant other countrys to fear them. same as the US.

NeatHack: koll

[havoc]: human rights!

optiklenz: We need to carry out what the government won't, and can't do.

NeatHack: optiklenz I agree.. We need to carry out what the government won't, and can't do.

lothos: i agree optik

DigiEbola: burn them.

kInGbOnG: preach on brother optik

optiklenz: The government has made threats over China's current human rights standing. They're cutting trade deals or they have in the past.

APPENDIX A

optiklenz: Is it good enough?

DataShark: no.

optiklenz: to put it simply.. no it's not

DataShark: it is fucking sad

NeatHack: no

optiklenz: China doesn't give a fuck if we trade with them or not.

NeatHack: right

DataShark: erm..

optiklenz: They dont but we sure do

DigiEbola: thats the way we are.

optiklenz: We get most of our imports from china in the first place. Look at the tag of Your shirt or any one of your household appliances and tell me differently

NeatHack: cuase is shipper to produce their and ship to here...

NeatHack: that is one point.

LordPsY: sure its cheaper when children make ur shirts

optiklenz: What is a threat with out some sort of whacked out maneuver to accommodate It, and bring intimidation The Chinese are all to familiar with "intimidation"

ShadoWalk: ok optik.. so what are we going to do about it?

lothos: optik

lothos: my shirt was made in mexico

lothos: heh

optiklenz: The Chinese kill people when they want their point heard and when it Comes down to it we all ultimately do that with out as much as the pull Of a trigger or the push of a button. The U.S cant say they've dealt a Fair hand either

optiklenz: There are enough problems in Washington as it is now.

zortin8r: shit

zortin8r: the meeting star?

DigiEbola: not to jump ahead, but can anyone be extrodited for screwing with them?

optiklenz: When half the government officials perform on a pants down agenda

dyslexia: wit the trial of the person who is accused of trying to start a democratic party

dyslexia: Digi, there is no extradition agreement between the US and china for computer crime

optiklenz: some action has to be taken by an outside group

NeatHack: outside group? like

optiklenz: not the FBI, the NSA (donut shortage? Not on your life)

optiklenz: and no not the fucken A Team

optiklenz: I'm sure they know who we are.

DigiEbola: well, if we are so hip to trade with them, they could pressure.

optiklenz: and if some compliance is not met I'm sure they'll know on a first hand basis. I know what some of you are thinking at the moment "has optik gone mad?! is optik on another one of his week long drinking spree's?!" Answer: "No"

DataShark: well (playing the devils advocate) what GOOD can come of some intravention buy a group already involved.. what about getting some other ppl involved.. maybe the l0pht or HDF..

optiklenz: other people have been involved

zortin8r: someone bring me up-to-date what are we talking about?

optiklenz: look at the cdc, and the hongkong blondes..

optiklenz: zort you know the routine

optiklenz: pick up a log on your way out

zortin8r: k..

DataShark: the cDc no offence will not get involved.. (will they)?

bronc_: cDc + HKB = 0

DataShark: thats what I figured.

optiklenz: At anyrate I'm damn serious if we don't act against our nations rights policies, and the

nations of others we may not have the right to do
so as time progresses. Many years ago our Countries
four fathers wrote, "Governments are instituted
among Men, Deriving their powers from the consent of
the governed; That whenever any Form of Government
becomes destructive of these ends it is the "Right
of The "People" to alter or to abolish it, and to
institute new Gove

DataShark: werd.. (no offense:))

optiklenz: THEY GOVERN WHAT WE PUT IN OUR MOUTHS!

optiklenz: ! DAMMIT LETS NOT LET THEM DO THE SAME
TO WHAT COMES OUT OF OUR MOUTHS!

DataShark: optiklenz: are you saying we should act
agenst the US govnt?

DFalcon: hey bola

DigiEbola: i do not like the fact that somewhere
in this world, someone can be put to death for
something we do freely.

LordPsY: he

optiklenz: I bring up Popular Sovereignty this Is
the basis that government can exist and function
only with the consent Of the governed (well guess
what. That's us). It is the people who holdpower it
is the people who are sovereign!

DataShark: I agree with lerfty.

optiklenz: Data> and if we do nothing it makes
things better?

DigiEbola: it is about power, and who can wield it.

DataShark: I did not say that.

ShadoWalk: optiklenz:.. so we act against who?

DataShark: I cannot as a person sit idly by and watch someone be persicuted for somthing that in reality IS NOT A CRIME

ShadoWalk: or whom

optiklenz: It is certainly seem'd like what you were insinuating

DigiEbola: we as a country are not going to shake up china, because we want their shit

optiklenz: it rather

NeatHack: optiklenz you know I done the war in lebanon and I saw political people going up and going down... I know in my opinion when $$$ come to play it is hard to stand but you can stand with nice understanding .... I lived the situation for year POLICATAL WAR AND REAL WAR ...

optiklenz: I'm very aware of that

zortin8r: 8

zortin8r: ack

NeatHack: when u can stop the $$$ game you win

DataShark: so what can we do? do we openly protest? do we *laff* write our congressmen?

DigiEbola: and that does what?

DigiEbola: show me a straight congressman

[havoc]: true.

DigiEbola: ill take you to hell to ice skate.

NeatHack: ture

DataShark: heh

ShadoWalk: i think i know where he's goin with this.. i'm just waitin to see if i'm right

[havoc]: mass hack.

optiklenz: I say this to you LoU members.It is our right our duty, and our justice to pull through with a strike against Iraqi data systems to do so we not only aid the people of those countries, but we bring light to the subject at hand to nations everywhere. So I ask you this if you are with me then we must act now, and we must act fierce. We develop the hardware, and software they Utilize. We code the security tools that they use we can just as easily disassemble

DigiEbola: name the target.

blakcloud: i cant say much about this cuz im not inthe states but personally i dont think it is right what is going on over there and that it should stop... i dunno...

ShadoWalk: he said it

optiklenz: They've been fucking shit up for years well guess what? It's our turn.

DataShark: WERD!

ShadoWalk: optik.. lemme get a modem and i'm in

NeatHack with you optik

[havoc]: damn straight.

DataShark: optiklenz: lets kick some ass.

dyslexia: ppl, the bottom line issue is human rights, that is something we all must fight for

optiklenz: One serve deserves another, and I plan on playing to win. If one official looks at things, and thinks to himself what he stands for is wrong, and things do need to change then we not only dominate the war, but we've already won the war. Even if things stay the same if we could bring the awareness to people who are otherwise dense in cameraperson with their actions then we're that much closer

kInGbOnG: wh00p!

DigiEbola: we have fought for it in that past.

optiklenz: Yeah but we are giving it a new twist

optiklenz: our idea of war is blowing shit up

NeatHack: optik what about our gov how they will act toward this ???

optiklenz: nothing good ever came out of killing someone

NeatHack: talking canada and US giv

[havoc]: information warfare!

optiklenz: we have nothing to do with the u.s government

ShadoWalk: so we take down iraq's databases

optiklenz: thats the plan

LordPsY: hmmm

_defiant: haxor iraqxor?

NeatHack: I know ... but when u do stuff to iraq they will take it as US attacking iraq

DigiEbola: rm / -Rf and dont look back?

LordPsY: Thats a big thing

optiklenz: We have the right, and power not to kill, but to speak out, and with our actions cripple an otherwise already broken enconomy. With the trigger they use to kill innocent people I use the same trigger to shut them down, and not only denounce one man, but the entire communist government of china, and fascist rule of Iraq.

ShadoWalk: and therefor erase all their amassed knowladge of biochemical warfare.. and deliver a message at the sdame time

dyslexia: optik, you have considered that if we become pain enuff to iraq or china, they may choose direct intervention with ourselves as the targets

lothos: iraq == .iq i think

DigiEbola: yah

DigiEbola: they are not beyond hitmen.

optiklenz: Dyslexia> yes

dyslexia: beyond, that is their only recourse

NeatHack: ok optik imagine we are able to shut all IRAQ system what will affect the ECOnomy ,, ?? or the political GAmE ... or the Shit War ??

rootbot: [sreality] rootbot! rootbot! gimme sum! gimme sum, sh1zz!

DataShark: erm.

NeatHack: how the damage will affect them ?

DigiEbola: how good can a iraqi admin be?

optiklenz: haha

optiklenz: Thats what Im saying

ShadoWalk: bet i could take him..heh

[havoc]: so optik

optiklenz: We need to make it clear that killing people (innocent lives) is not the only resolve.

DataShark: keep in mind we HAVE troops over there (the US) I have friends there. lets walk lightly and carry and BIG FUCKING STICK if we do this.

[havoc]: the plan for an attack.

spacerog: Are you going to operate under the LoU name or form a new group?

dyslexia: Digi, most of the arab countries and israel have much experience at dealing with hostile attacks, both politacally, physical and data wise

DigiEbola: their systems are reputably old

optiklenz: Data> that's the plan

[havoc]: should we hop over to europe somewhere and launch ? or from within the us

datapleX: lothos!

datapleX: bah

DigiEbola: dys

datapleX: oh

DigiEbola: true

ShadoWalk: so optik.. are we going to wait until this rash thing is over?

NeatHack: Well guy I think you are missing the TARGET here... buy shutting couple of server of ALL the net in iraq they will not understand I think ?

DigiEbola: they use propoganda like wild fire

XeXeN: yes

ShadoWalk: so as not to piss off all the other muslim nations?

NeatHack: U must affact them at ecomiy level

NeatHack: or political level

dyslexia: neathack, the unfortunate reality of economic sanctions etc are lost on the leaders, they dont suffer, only the people do

DigiEbola: it would be nice if we had loyal iraqi hackers

DigiEbola: working for us

ShadoWalk: i saw we take out every military database we kan find.. rm / -rf it

NeatHack: that is true dysl

NeatHack: then how to affect them ?

lothos: spacerogue brings up a good point

lothos: do we do this as LoU or what?

dyslexia: bring them to the attention of the world, simply as otik says

bronc_: sheesh..

NeatHack: that is an idea that can affect the, u see. .ShadoWalk> i saw we take out every military database we kan find.. rm / -rf it

dyslexia: optik at least

Big|Feet: hrm.. on the defcon mailing list a while back someone brought up the idea "why not attack their systems" and it was argued that they don't have much connection to the net (if any) so what systems are you attacking?

DataShark: what is iraqi's top level?

DigiEbola: well, you know nobody likes a smart ass, and as soon as one of us walks thru one of their servers and posts, they are going to be PISSED.

lothos: .iq i believe

dyslexia: heh, they will have links allright, but the majority will be through sympathetic arab countries in the case of iraq

_defiant: SOMEONE EXPLAIN TO ME WHATS GOING ON

_defiant: heh

DigiEbola: defiant

DigiEbola: we are going to war.

ShadoWalk: shyt

DigiEbola: heh.

DataShark: DO we do this as LoU or what?

LordPsY: hehe

DataShark: DO we do this as LoU or what?

LordPsY: ah hes back

DigiEbola: i want china.

optiklenz: no

optiklenz: we dont do this as anyone

LordPsY: so

DataShark: anonymous?

optiklenz: no names will be left no handles or affiliations

optiklenz: the chinese embassy has us under investigation

DataShark: what a supprise.

ShadoWalk: whooooooohoooooooo

datapleX: heh

ShadoWalk: lets get rowdy

_defiant: werd

[havoc]: information warfare at its best.

_defiant: heh

NeatHack: _defiant :the Big image is :optik come up with the idea to attack iraq and china since they are soing shit with them population....

datapleX: uhm...that is really messin' w/ some shit

_defiant: NeatHack: didn't everyone say that before heh

DigiEbola: oh great

dyslexia: ppl, action against governments who ignore the rights of and pretty much enslave their ppl is good in my book, buts it's not just limited to iraq and china

NeatHack: and we kind agreed what we are trying to figure out what damage can be cuased ...

DigiEbola: some ninja fucker is going to hunt us all down

ShadoWalk: 6.4 gigz of kiq azz

datapleX: heh

optiklenz: one thing I want everyone to know is that we only operate if we can do so without risk

_defiant: ok, lets talk about something in a public chan, then try and be anonomous

_defiant: makes sense

optiklenz: as i said i have no problem working with a client on his network while blasting on chinese communist

NeatHack: make sence...

DigiEbola: defiant, nothing on irc is anonymous

_defiant: Digi: i was pointing out the irony in it

DigiEbola: _defiant: yes yes

dyslexia: heh, indeed digi, that is true

optiklenz: but I would not want to indulge any member into something that would end up ruining his/her life

zortin8r: its not like irc is encrypted or anthing..

DataShark: HAHA

optiklenz: If we attack Chinese systems the attacks need to originate from china. Same goes for Iraqi networks.

DigiEbola: well, efnet has services specially for the purpose of watching

optiklenz: heh

ShadoWalk: optiklenz: i may be a bit lame.. but i learn hella quik and i'll do it reguardless of consequences

NeatHack: and how u do so originate the attack from china ??

zortin8r: has anyone here _ever_ encountered and Iraqi network? cause i have never seen one before..

NeatHack: u mean physicaly in china ?

optiklenz: do the damage from a chinese network

spacerog: I assume that HNN was mailed because you wanted this publiciced, yes?

Big|Feet: [optiklenz]: i never even knew iraq had access to the net.. what systems to you plan go nailing so to speak

optiklenz: spacerog it's your call

optiklenz: Big> iraqi has networks

DigiEbola: everyone has networks

optiklenz: just because a majority are internal does not mean they are sasfe

d4hp: herm ...

optiklenz: safe rather

Big|Feet: yes

DataShark: optiklenz: do we REALLY want alot of attention draw to this before we do some damage?

zortin8r: i think me and BigFeet are feeling the same thing here.. where the hell are the iraqi networks?

spacerog: opti: cool

Big|Feet: like i was saying before
_defiant hides and had nothing to do with it ;)

dyslexia: optik, for access to iraq we will likely need to look in sympathetic arab nations

Big|Feet: the public is not allowed access to the internet in iraq

DigiEbola: Big|Feet: not so

optiklenz: yeah

DigiEbola: Big|Feet: there are a few

blakcloud: very few

optiklenz: whatever we can do to keep sadaam from going on the net for his daily dose of kiddy porn

DigiEbola: matter of fact

Big|Feet: probly.. but censored

DigiEbola: during the bombings, there was some on

datapleX: heh

NeatHack agree with that optik

NeatHack: roflllll daily dose of kiddy porn

Big|Feet: hrm.. saddam's pron stash

DataShark: haha

DigiEbola: hmm, ya know, if we upload a shitload of kiddie pr0n to his servers

datapleX: hahaha

dyslexia: thats whta they are hiding from the arms inspectors, lol

zortin8r: haha

DataShark: ok..

DigiEbola: i guess the government will have to arrest him

ShadoWalk: heh

_defiant: optik: i agree with it all again, but like, i don't want to get arrested again

DigiEbola: yah, my new years resolution is that i dont have to mess with any kind of law enforcement this year

[havoc]: cover your ass and the chances of you getting caught are reduced.

optiklenz: If they want to fight we stand steadfast with what we believe in, and are ready To strap on our armor and take defense. LoU was established over 7 years ago As a research team, and we also called ourselves mercenaries. "We are ready to Commence, and take partition in electronic warfare if ever requested . The attack will go on for one Week. The time will be extended if needed . If anyone disagrees on the actions We are about to take let me know why. I

DigiEbola: you hit a server, you better root it

_defiant: havoc: i was arrested for something i never did before, make no sense

optiklenz: hshs

optiklenz: def> yeah that happens a lot around here

_defiant: optiklenz: i'm still down with it as long as we cause no wars etc

DigiEbola: lets tear them a new electronic asshole.

optiklenz: it's common to hair "what network? computer? huh whats that?" over here at the office

optiklenz: s/hair/hear

sreality: #1.. I doubt iraq actually has military databases

optiklenz: geez maybe i am drunk and just dont know it yet

[havoc]: :)

Big|Feet: they have to have something

zortin8r: if iraq does have military databases and networks, how do we go about finding them?

_defiant: DataShark: hah, no, they were serious about it

DigiEbola: if it wears a turban, and crawls in sand, root it.

sreality: well

_defiant: it was like

_defiant: YOUR UDNER ARREST

sreality: best thing to start with

_defiant: heh

DataShark: ohhh I have one question.. can some teach me howto hack? Im running into truble when it says to press the any key...

sreality: is the iraq tld

sreality: scan the shizz outa that

_defiant: and some police woman was frisking me

optiklenz: this is just recreation

optiklenz: heh

sreality: then hand probe the boxes

sreality: there cant be many

DigiEbola: DataShark: i removed the any key long
time ago....

DataShark: DAMNIT lerfty.

headflux is idle, automatically dead [bX(l/on p/off)]

optiklenz: never once have they sent a chick down here

optiklenz: basterds.

sreality: then goto any nations that surround iraq

Big|Feet: what any any chinese governet buildings in
the us i bet they have some info

DataShark: optiklenz: haha

_defiant: optiklenz: yeah, ccu guy and 2 chicks

Big|Feet: or iraq or that matter

sreality: hey.

sreality: umm you forgot something

d4hp: tee hee

sreality: the iraq databases are gonna be in their
language

sreality: and umm

DataShark: sreality: HAHAH oops..

sreality: none of use has charater support for that

optiklenz: sreality> thats what altavista
translator's for

optiklenz: heh

sreality: so how are we gonna know what that is

Big|Feet: altavista

d4hp: yeh ..

Big|Feet: hehehe

ShadoWalk: oh yea.. i learn hella quik

d4hp: ok there bud

optiklenz: haha

sreality: the altavista translater doesnt do middle-eastern languages

ShadoWalk: ok zort..heh

_defiant: zortin8r: YOU TELL HIM HEH

NeatHack: sreality> so how are we gonna know what that is NO PROBLEM

datapleX: uhm...me to. I would like to try to get into LoU at this time to.

sreality: becuz those languages are like

NeatHack: I SPEAK ARABIC

DataShark: sreality: heh well that is somein we will havta work on..

sreality: scribbles

d4hp: Im from Iraq

DigiEbola: optiklenz: how would you like this done?

hunting parties or completely independent?

spacerog: Any objections with using the LoU name in a story for HNN? If I say "A bunch of hackers declared war..." no one will listen.

DataShark: anyone speek raganise?

NeatHack: sreality> so how are we gonna know what that is I am orginaly LEbanon

sreality: BLAHDALKHDAKHJD DIAHIASHIDHA OJIEIAUIDE MBDOMADIJWE!

sreality: hahaa

optiklenz: ok will if anyone has any objections they have until 8:00 pm pst

d4hp: as a matter of fact, Im from the iraq military

NeatHack u have a BIG arabic resource.,. GUYS ..

DataShark: IM in.

DigiEbola: data says he is in.

sreality: its a semi good idea

d4hp: boooo!

sreality: but it has some faults

DigiEbola: so thats 2 ppl, and a shitload of terminals

blakcloud: hehe

DFalcon: what ya guys talking about ?

t3q: datapleX: w3rd.

sreality: #1.. we need FIRST OFF some iraqie translators

DigiEbola: we also have osu here, so we can work anonymously

datapleX: werd

sreality: #2.. we need to probe the shit outa all middle-eastern countries

NeatHack: DAM read what I said sreality> #1.. we need FIRST OFF some iraqie translators

DigiEbola: i want lists

optiklenz: ok well

[havoc]: if we are going to do this with a serious mind, we need to gather together and find specific targets, and take them out.. in a team effort. *zortin8r* wow.

optiklenz: I'll be going through possible targets

DigiEbola: if its buried in the sand, i will set up a mail somewhere for it to be sent to

sreality: NeatHack: so like what, your gonna translate it all, lebanon is partially french speaking too

[havoc]: this ballz out attack wont work without a plan.

LordPsY: #3 We should get some more infos bout the Iraqi networks

NeatHack: sreality don;lt worry I will handle this part

bronc_: so we are going at attack Iraqi networks?

NeatHack: translation is ON ME>..

optiklenz: havoc> yeah this was just to see if we should go through with something

DataShark: NeatHack: ok.. you deal with the translater and the char set..

optiklenz: I'm not playing cat and mouse here so if we go in we go in prepared without risk

ShadoWalk: i'm following dtatplex

optiklenz: or we all go back to our jobs and coding

sreality: grr

DigiEbola: all i know is, one character i understand of the iraqi alphabet is #

Big|Feet: i should would like to see the whole plan .. should be beautiful

NeatHack: I cna have window in arabic linux I do not know ??

dethl0k: jobs and coding ;p

sreality: its not safe to rely on ONE person

DigiEbola: if i see a #, its all good.

[havoc]: we need to make a key'd channel just for this purpose. so we can concentrate on the attacks.

dethl0k: j/k

sreality: we need two

sreality: what if theres alot of shit to translate

d4hp: tee hee

datapleX: _defiant: I was told to bring it up at the meeting...

d4hp: erm..

d4hp: like...

NeatHack: I can have resource .. sreality

optiklenz: As of now I have not been in contact with any of the HKB members

NeatHack: well let us not put this as WALL

_defiant: not a bad idea, we should also talk to cDc to see if theres anything we can do more "legal" together

optiklenz: but I've talked to a few before

lothos: we have #!LoU

DigiEbola: well, it would be nice to have some help

sreality: fuckg

sreality: okay

sreality: #1

sreality: anyone whos not a meber

sreality: err member

optiklenz: bronc> i'll email you something I got from a supposed "HKB" member

sreality: should get the fuck outa here

sreality: grr

DataShark: optiklenz: cc that to me..

bronc_: o i h

optiklenz: i dont plan on taking long with this attack

_defiant: optiklenz: sort fucking legions.org out as well i can't get ssh to login

bronc_: I was told this by a reporter

spacerog: Ok, I'm gone. Thanks for the info. I should have a story up tomorrow morning

bronc_: dunno if it was true

optiklenz: defiant> what version are you using?

spacerog: If anyone has anything to ad send me mail at contact@hackernews.com

DigiEbola: i lub j00 spacerog

DataShark: spacerog: later.

optiklenz: talk to you later space..

Log file closed at: 12/28/98 19:53:08EST

APPENDIX B

L0pht Senate Testimony

Transcribed from the YouTube video:

Hackers Testifying at the United States Senate, May 19, 1998 (L0pht Heavy Industries)

https://www.youtube.com/watch?v=VVJldn_MmMYz

Senator Thompson: … If you gentlemen would come forward. We're joined today by the seven members of the L0pht hacker think-tank in Cambridge, Massachusetts. Due to the sensitivity of the work done at the L0pht, they'll be using their hacker names of Mudge, Weld, Brian Oblivion, Kingpin, Space Rogue, Tan, and Stefan Von Neumann. Gentlemen …

Off Camera: I thought you were the Kingpin?

(Laughter)

Senator Thompson: I ah, I hope my grandkids don't ask me who my witnesses were today, and say … Space Rogue …

But we do, we do understand your — and do appreciate your being with us. Do you, ah, May I ask your name?

Mudge: I'm Mudge

Senator: Mudge, would you like to make a statement?

Mudge: Yes, I would. Thank you very much for having us here. We think this is hopefully a very great step forward and are thrilled that the government in general is, is starting to approach the hacker community, we think it's a tremendous asset that the hackers bring to the table here, an understanding! Emm! My handle is Mudge, and I and the six individuals seated before you, which we run down the line: Brian Oblivion, this is John Tan, Kingpin, Weld Pond, Space Rogue, and Stefan Von Neumann. ... We make up the hacker group known as the L0pht. And for the last four years, the seven of us has been touted as just about everything, from the Hacker Conglomerate, the Hacker Think Tank, the hangout place for the top US hackers, network security experts, and the Consumer Watch Group. In reality, all we really are, is just Curious. For, well over the past decade, the seven of us have independently learned and worked in the fields of satellites communication, cryptography, operating systems' design and implementation, computer network security, electronics, and telecommunications.

To other learning process, we've made few waves with some large companies such as Microsoft, IBM, Novell, and Sun Microsystems. At the same time, the top hackers, and the top legitimate cryptographers, and computer security professionals pay us visits when they are in town, just to see what we're currently working on... so we kind of figured we must be doing something right.

I'd like to take the opportunity to let the various members talk about few of their various projects, their current projects, and what they are going to be working on the future. Umm! Weld?

Senator Thompson: And if you got the testimony this morning … if there are any points, in the process, that you want to make, very briefly, with regard to some of the previous questions or testimonies, feel free to do that also.

Mudge: Definitely will.

Weld Pond: Huh! Good morning, my name is Weld Pond, I'm a hacker, programmer, thirteen-years' experience, working as a software developer, in the soft commercial software industry. My college training is as a computer engineer. At the L0pht I specialize in writing software programs for exploiting computer network security and operating systems security. My current projects include finding vulnerabilities in Microsoft Windows, anti-security. I am actively working on L0phtCrack, a program that we've created to exploit the weaknesses in Windows, and to use anti-password security. We just use cryptography to secure the passwords, but we have found vulnerabilities in their implementation. These programs have been extremely well received by the military government and corporate security groups, who use it to test their own passwords for weaknesses. Ehm! Prior to the release of this program, security experts claim to have taken thousands of years to uncover Windows anti-password, our program can do it in days and sometimes, some cases, hours.

As a licensed amateur radio operator, I also enjoy radio communications. Future project plan is collaborating with the L0pht hardware people to create secure public wireless networks, something we're very interested in.

Kingpin: Good morning! My name is Kingpin, I am the youngest member of the L0pht and one of the electrical engineers and hardware hackers. Some of the L0pht members concentrate on software programming, I work with hardware design and implementation of electronic circuits. My interests include embedded system design, surveillance and counter-surveillance tools, and wireless data transmissions. My current research project involves experimentation with the monitoring and eavesdropping of stray electromagnetic fields from computer terminals, otherwise known as TEMPEST Monitoring. Using low-cost electronic equipment, one can capture the contents of computer screens from more than 200 km away, possibly gaining passwords and other sensitive information. The phenomenon of TEMPEST monitoring has been known to the industry for decades, but there's not much unclassified information available on how to both capture the omissions, and also protect oneself from becoming an eavesdropping victim. My research will not only help me learn about the monitoring technology, it'll enable me to educate others to help them protect their computer systems from prying eyes.

John Tan: My name is John Tan, at twenty-eight, I've been involved with computers, telecommunications and security for fourteen years now, the last it of which have been spent in the financial services industry. My involvement with the L0pht is primarily been nondescript but I have achieved some notoriety in terms of documentation of some of the existing problems of Novell Netware, and a compilation of manually created PalmPilot document library. Recently, I have consulted for various manufacturing financial services and management-consulting firms regarding information securing policy, and how to establish a corporate security effort. I will continue in the future to pursue an understanding of the rest to the information age and communicate those findings to the government, the industry, and the media to provide a clear consistent message of where we are and where we need to go.

Space Rogue: Good morning! I am Space Rogue, although my background contains no formal computer training, I amassed a great deal of knowledge in the area of computer security, and the use of technology applications in the area of physical security. Currently, I am working on assessing the vulnerabilities in various proximity detection devices such as those used by EZ Pass, —, and controlled assess cards. In conjunction with Stefan Von Neumann, seated here today, and others of the hacking community, — seeking vulnerabilities in Apple's share IP by Apple computers. I wish to take this opportunity to thank members of this community for inviting us here today.

Brian Oblivion: My pen name is Brian Oblivion. My focus currently is microprocessor system design, satellite communications equipment, wireless communications architecture, and systems administration. Over the past few years, I've conducted research on cellular networks, exploring the encrypted the data channels and the protocols explored — bypassed hardware-based 9 cryptographic, authentication used to track call expenses. Recently, I'm researching various digital coding methodologies involving both dedicated hardware and software analysis via digital signal processor. This will result in the exposing of claimed secure wireless messaging and communications systems and thus increasing the requirement of a more secure communications infrastructure. As an amateur radio operator, I am exploring authentication methods for amateur radio data networks. Technology developed in this area arena will be applied to commercial wireless networking products, protocols, and equipment that we utilize not only authentication but encryption of the radio channel as well. The L0pht for me provides the much-needed avenue for the dissemination of the present state of insecurity of various consumer-networking products. If it wasn't for groups such as ours and other motivated individuals in the security community, the state of awareness we have today would be years behind. Thank you!

Stefan Von Neumann: My name is Stefan Von Neumann, I have been working with the L0pht since 1993, focusing primarily on high-power electronics, flaws in data networks, and increasing convergence of power distribution and data distribution. My professional background includes supporting users on common computing products and networks which gives me first-hand experience with how relatively unaware of computing risks most users are. Even worst for software publishers, Internet providers and utility companies are tight-lipped about flaws or risks inherent in products and services that touch the daily lives of most Americans. For example, in many areas, the country, including Boston-area, electric utility companies are using radio transmissions and/or powerlines to transmit data, meter data, from customers locations. The same utility companies are also using such data transmissions for controlling their power systems. Even public water companies are using radio transmissions for controlling our water systems. In the same way that the so-called phantom controller was able to impersonate an airport control tower and issue instructions to a pilot, one could impersonate a legitimate utility company and disrupt water or electric service. Another example is Internet data sent over cable television systems. Most customers of these services are not aware of the potential for another user to watch their "private" communications across the cable TV network, and worse, the users are not aware of the possibility that an improperly configured computer could make available their data without their knowledge. I would personally like to see the same type of independent review process that should exist for software companies extended to utility companies and Internet service providers. Finally, customers and end users should be made aware of the risks. Thank you for having us here!

Mudge: I am one of the network system — at the L0pht, basically I am the person who breaks into the systems and undermines the network security, and that's what I do with my day job ... companies like that. Some of my previous projects were L0phtCrack, along with Weld Pond in which we developed a tool for showing administrators and users the insecurities in Microsoft passwords. I've released several security advisories on various pieces of commercial software, which has prompted vendor patches, which means they improved the software after we pointed out to them. Unfortunately, many times they would not improve the software until we actually went public with the findings, companies do indeed want to ignore problems as long as possible, it's cheaper for them. Recently, I conducted training courses at NASA's geo-propulsion lab to try and raise their level of awareness as to the vulnerabilities, especially with the name-brand recognition. In the very near future, I'll be conducting training courses over the NSA. Shortly after that, the L0pht will be releasing a white paper on new cryptographic weaknesses that I along with one other top United States cryptographers have found in a very prominent commercial operating system which remain nameless.

If you're looking for computer security, then the Internet is not the place to be. If you think that you're an exception to the norm to have a secure setup to communicate over the Internet, you're probably mistaken. Furthermore, if you feel that the government is giving you access to the enabling technology, you need to combat this problem, you're wrong yet again. The foundation of the Internet is over twenty years old at this point, and while the technology still works, it's being asked to perform tasks that was never intended to via secure fashions, nonetheless. How can we be expected to protect the system and the network when either of the seven individuals seated before you can tear down the foundation that the network was built upon, let alone the systems that are sitting on top of it. So even if computer systems and other peripherals on the network were secure, the problem still moves.

Can the systems be secured? Well in many cases, they actually can be, for instance, the problem with the enemy air-traffic controllers could be remedied by incorporating relatively trivial an inexpensive cryptographically secure authentication. The same would hold true for MDC 4800, which is a protocol most commonly used by mobile police data terminals to remotely pull and update records. Personal paging protocols? Yeah! Everybody has little personal pager now day, such as —, which the White House communications agency uses to coordinate movement of the president, would also benefit from this relatively trivial modification. Why don't strong authentication properties exist in these protocols? Most likely the same reason that simple security mechanisms are missing from all of the software or almost all the software sold corporations and agencies today, it's cheaper and it's easier for companies to sell in secure software. There's no liability attached to the manufactures and there's no policing done to stop companies from selling and secure software under the guise of secure.

In an industry where "time to market" matters, who wants or cares to add security or even thoroughly test the product? Now, you should, you, the government consumer, should carry or want software products to include security authentication mechanisms, and I think you do. You should incur the companies to include this in their products and hold them liable when the products fail. There are parts to the situation that the government can directly help. Lived in the constraints on cryptographic export would encourage companies to more readily include authentication encryption in the products, the Cellular Telecommunications Protection Act is an example legislation that is in place right now that hinders consumer watch groups such as ourselves, I'm just perpetuating the insecurity status quo that's out there.

In conclusion, hopefully you having us here is not a fluke and hopefully we've not offended in anyway, but this might be the beginning of an ongoing dialogue between the government and hacker groups such as ourselves. Perhaps the information from such meetings will end up becoming an enabling mechanism for future change that will help organizations of all sizes, not just large government organizations. We encourage you to read the written testimony, and we are more than happy to answer any questions in as much detail where technical detail or non-technical detail as you see fit and expel to clarify upon any concerns. Thank you very much.

Senator Thompson: Thank you very much. And you've not offended any of us, and just the contrary, I think it's probably appropriate the gentleman such as yourself are the ones who want to come forward and demonstrate that the emperor has no clothes. So we appreciate your coming here, especially, I love the fact that the Washington Post describes you as rock stars on the computer hacking elite. So we appreciate you're being with us here today. I am informed that, you think that within thirty minutes, the seven of you could make the internet unusable for the entire nation, is that correct?

Mudge: That's correct. Actually, one of us with just a few packets. We've told a few agencies about this, it's kinda funny because we think that this is something that the various government agency should be actively going after, we know that the Department of Defense at very large, investigation into what's known as denial-of-service attacks against the infrastructure. In our various day jobs we contributed a large portion of the information to that actual investigation. Much to our chagrin, the learning from it were instantly classified which we were giving them largely public information. It is very trivial with the whole protocols to segregate and separate the different major long-haul providers, which would then be the national access points, the metropolitan area, either section, AT&T can talk, MCI can talk too, PSI Net can talk too, alternate et cetera, et cetera, and keep it down that way as long as we really wanted to. It would definitely take a few days for people to figure out what was going on.

Senator Thompson: You state that, with regard to commerce over the Internet, which is a rapidly growing as we all know, that the Internet was not designed for it. What you mean by that?

Mudge: The internet was designed out of the Defense Department Advanced Research Project agency to simply have computers talk to each other. This was a very laudable act; a very laudable goal and I think they succeeded fantastically. This was largely an academic environment with some government research organizations, it drew up, it flourished, it struck everybody by surprise and now big businesses saying let's jump on board and make some money off of this. Well! you know this this is kinda like, you've be driven in Boston, you know the streets are tremendously designed in a wonderful fashion because they follow the cars around and laid the pavement down. I mean, you can get it to work, but it can be really painful and that's the stage we're in right now.

Senator Thompson: You say that you've been working with the; some governmental agencies with regards to some of these problems, and of course with commercial and traditional. It occurs to me in listening to you and listening to our prior witness that there doesn't seem to be an inducement for industry to do much about this at this stage the game, is what you're saying essentially isn't?

Mudge: Mmm!

Senator: And I hope that there are some more forward-looking people as some of these industries that we've had in times past. You can look at the mobile industry or the tobacco industry and a number of industries. We've kept our heads in the sand — executives about problems on the horizon and, uh, this is going to be something as much as we dislike lawsuits and there's too many of them in this country, this is clearly going to be something that is going to hit somebody big-time, one these days before long and hopefully it won't take economic disaster you know, the calls and all that. But you can see it on the rise in, can't you? I mean they're gonna have to come to terms with the fact that their ability to do something about this is out there and they're turning their backs on the way to make their systems more secure than not doing and we're gonna be clearly having to answer for that. You say that the Internet and commute computer security is almost nonexistent, could you elaborate on that a moment? What more do you mean literally?

Mudge: There are many aspects that make that up. The operating system says, we just heard testimony from Dr. Neumann, very correctly they aren't incorporating any sort of real security mechanisms, there is a lack of education, there's a lack of understanding as to what the problems are out there, there are no mechanisms for places to keep abreast of current findings. I mean, the security rail network security in particular is very rapidly changing so it's kind of difficult. It's not like with the cars, What's the analogy? Somebody give the recall, they send you a letter if your Ford Explorer is going to have a very serious problem. The number of operating systems out there, they aren't sending people letters, they're saying you have to do your own due diligence and come to us and find out what we've made publicly available or what we've decided to alert you to, at the same time keep in mind that if we don't alert you to it, we save a lot of money and we save our top engineers times by not having to throw them at the product where they can add new bells and whistles and to whatever …

Space Rogue: The analogy is … the Volkswagen Beetle just got recalled; evidently, they found three cars that had a problem, three. They didn't cause any serious deaths or injuries, but they just found three potential problems in the vehicles. They sent out eighty-five hundred letters to every purchaser of the vehicle in United States. If there's a software company that has three hack attempts against with three successful hack attempts against its particular piece of software or operating system, they're not gonna go call every single one of their people that just spent a lot of money to buy their software, telling them, hey! There's a problem and we need to call back our software so we could fix it … right now it doesn't happen.

Weld Pond: Some other problems that are found are reported to the manufacturers, and they don't even make a fix publicly available. They work on the fix internally and if you have the same problem and you come to them and you say, you know, I'm getting broken into someone's attacking my system in this way. They'll say, okay! We have this behind-the-scenes fix that you can apply to your system, but we haven't even made it publicly available yet and until the problem mushrooms up and enough people complain about it, then they'll come out with the public fix, but if it's behind-the-scenes people that are contacting the manufacturer, we've seen that they don't really come public and even tell the other users of this system that the problem exists and here's the fix for it.

Mudge: This is one of the main problems with the computer emergency response team.

Brian Oblivion: In the industry where the systems administrators claim that the software provided them isn't shipped in a secure manner, the industry says that they shouldn't be responsible for that, and I'm not quite sure because I'm not a lawyer even in nearly skilled in political matters, but I don't know if there's any legislation that can could fix the liability problem, I don't know, but I know that this is one of the issues out there.

Kingpin: I just want to add one thing to that, in the point of liability, the car manufactures will be and are held liable if something goes wrong in a product. If something goes wrong in one of the ten thousand cars, and it explodes, they will be held liable. If something breaks in the software, the companies aren't held liable and they feel, why? You know why, did they have to tell people when they are not responsible?

Weld Pond: Just another, — analogy which we've found which sort of makes sense is some; Kryptonite makes bicycle locks, and they say our lock is so good if your bike gets stolen, it's a $30–$40 locket, if your bike gets stolen will pay up to a thousand dollars to replace your bicycle. So, basically, they're saying our security works, and we'd stand behind it, software vendors do not stand behind their security. They say, well if it's broken, then the problems maybe we will fix it, but if you lose thousands of dollars, say you have an e-commerce site up on the Internet, your whole business is built around their software, which they've told you is secure they've told the only bad at all these great features and you can run your business on our software and then your business fails because of their ... they caused your business to fail essentially if it's e-commerce, your site's down, you're not making money, they say sorry!

Mudge: One of the things about the Kryptonite locks is, they're not unbreakable and they're not un-pickable, and the company knows that, but they've raised the bar. They've raised enough that the ankle biters, the novices, you know, will go to the next bike that's on lock. The same thing with car alarms, you get a discount on your insurance for doing or performing due diligence. You just raise the bar and you get a get away from the noise level.

Senator Thompson: Thank you very much. I have one more question, and all the other members have questions. Part of what you're trying to do is demonstrate something that you feel like the American people need to know, and that's part of our job also and I'm curious … if a foreign government was able to assemble a group of gentlemen such as yourself, and paid them large amounts of money and got them in here or hired him here to wreak as much havoc on this government as they could in terms of infrastructure, the governmental operations, whatever! How much damage can they do?

Mudge: We've had some of your aides come to talk to us to source us out at the beginning, and I think they were relatively impressed with what we've managed to put together without any funding whatsoever. Brian, do you want to talk about some of the satellite communications or let alone just taking us down from the financial aspects. There are so many different ways that havoc could be wrecked.

Brian Oblivion: Regarding satellite communications, you could, if you're highly paid enough, you could assemble jamming gear to temporarily knockout uplinks, you could the take an area, I'm sure you're aware of like the — guns and the EMP blasts and typical informational warfare, it's more on the physical level rather than just the information security where you would be able to disable equipment by generating high-energy pulse, and disable the clock which controls everything in the computer system to malfunction ...

Senator Thompson: What would be the effect of that?

Brian Oblivion: ... It would be like, well! It depends on equipment. It would be ... You could do it to a telephone switch or, generally, national access points for the Internet or in unshielded buildings, sometimes they're in just regular commercial buildings without any type of electromagnetic protection.

Senator Thompson: What would be the effect of that? How would we feel that?

Brian Oblivion: You would feel that by an instant disruption of Internet service on that point including ...

Senator Thompson: What's another area?

Mudge: I'll let Kingpin talk about TEMPEST ... Some of the areas that you could, should worry about, our new phone systems are down, the electricity is gone and your financial markets? We recently had a very close call on the financial markets. The disruption of services is a wonderful way of messing people up. And in addition, by disrupting service in certain patterns you can force people to take other routes. Let's say that I have taken over MCI's networks, which would not be a tremendously difficult thing to do, I mean, most people can get access to the metropolitan area — in the national access points, physical access even. So, I can watch everything that goes through this major backbone providers transitory networks, but I can't watch Sprint.

Well! What am I gonna do? I'll disrupt Sprint service so that everybody routes through me, now I can learn everything you're doing, I can watch your movements, I can stop your movements, I can issue requests on your behalf. You'd be surprised how much stuff is tied to the general networks now.

Space Rogue: I think if a nation-state funded a group of people to attack the United States electronically, the number of systems that can be disrupted or compromised is so great that it would probably wreak a lot of havoc in the country. Whether or not the country can recover from that in inadequate period of time or defend against it is a good question. But there's definitely some potential there for her abuse.

Kingpin: Mentioned in my initial statement about TEMPEST monitoring, which would allow outsiders or insiders to receive emissions from computer terminals. One can see the screens of people's ... the can read the email safe off the screen or maybe if they're accessing some confidential system or looking up some kind of criminal records or something like that. And the outside or inside or intruder could then become familiar with the system and access it in a different way.

Mudge: What would you do to them with the mobile data terminal stuff?

Kingpin: With the mobile data terminal, the same type of thing can happen. You can either intercept the dated via just wireless transmissions or you can monitor the terminals with TEMPEST technology, and by just monitoring the transmissions you can view what the police are transmitting and receiving about criminals or internal government agencies are or something …

Senator Glenn: Thanks much gentlemen. I think I had, — names here, but I think I had the pleasure of talking to a couple of you gentlemen some twenty-four years ago in a different venue and that was a fascinating conversation and this fascinating this morning. I'm not quite clear now, does the L0pht do this on a business basis now too? Or you just amateurs that get together doing this … because it says in your testimony here, "Space — what you do is to have fun, pushing the envelope, examining security systems, providing full disclosure to all those in the security industry our findings." Is this strictly an amateur group or you are available for hire from people who wanted to avail themselves of your expertise?

Mudge: We've been a strictly amateur group for a long time, it's a very monetarily taxing for us so …

Senator Glenn: You all have day jobs

Mudge: We all have day jobs and this all comes out of our pockets, for all the equipment that we try and salvage together and the different projects we want to learn about. We do one, the purse strings become very tight, go out there and take consulting jobs or/and do different consulting works. Quite unhappy that you can't help a lot of people out, unfortunately, a lot of people are scared to come talk to us, we have to end up beating people over the head publicly in order to get them to even fix their problems, which doesn't endear with them tremendously.

Senator Glenn: Let me expand the area of vulnerability just a little bit here and get your comments on this. A sink of communications satellites here and talking about that, can you get into the command structure, the command signals that look to position those satellites, could you relocate them and foul up the whole system not by destroying them or by fouling up the computers necessary but take him out their positions.

Brian Oblivion: Actually, companies like COMSAT and other — telemetry command control systems are using authentication for their command structure, which is what we would recommend to other more commercial, or actually just the other areas of wireless telemetry in control. That would increase the bar of the state of security of radio-controlled to entry system.

Senator Glenn: How about the GPS system? Is it vulnerable also? The global positioning system, we're going to be relying a lot more on that, we're relying on that for some weapons systems are used to be highly classified, now there's been lot of writings about them. We're using that to tremendously increased degree these days for our military and for commercial aviation, everything else. I have a little Magellan handheld I use model airplane flying back and forth and it's great.

Space Rogue: The problem with GPS is very weak signal, it's very easy to jam that signal. As a matter of fact, there was an incident few months ago in Upstate New York where a test was being conducted by the Air Force. The test unbeknownst to the Air Force personnel was interfering with the GPS signals of two aircraft landing in New Jersey, luckily it was during the daytime and the aircraft was trying to rely on GPS signals to land, but they lost their GPS so they went on and man-landed that way.

Senator Glenn: — to get into the GPS system and actually relocate some of those satellites slightly, which would throw off up a large and screw up all the information that you're getting, is that possible?

Brian Oblivion: Traditionally the military has been very good about authentication methods on telemetry, and command and control systems. So, I think you'd be more your worried about setting up, you know, 2.6 gigahertz Jammer rather than somebody actually moving the satellites round or colliding them in a manner ...

Senator Glenn: ... easier to jam it than relocate it.

Dr. Neumann: On August 21, I believe it is 1999, a lot of the receivers' sale, they have a year 2000 type problem, where they run out of bits and it resets to January 1980, just thought I would toss that one in.

Senator Glenn: Don't be flying that day if I want to be going where I'm supposed to be going is what you're telling me, I'll check that one out. How about could you get in and transfer Federal Reserve funds to someplace?

Mudge: Just about everything is possible, it depends on how much money wanna throw at it, time and effort. From the amount of time and effort and the money, which is nonexistent for us, and the fact that we know we like not being in jail, we'd say, no, we wouldn't do that if we really wanted to and really had to, yes! Because if you make it easy enough for yourself or somebody else to use it, you make it vulnerable.

Senator Glenn: I look at you guys as the white hats in this whole thing. Yeah! I think your motivations as far as I know is excellent, I think you wanna be considered that way. But let's say we have a bunch of bad guys now, can you with your expertise, trackback and find out who the bad guys if they are trying to foul up GPS for federal reserve or something else, can you track that back and locate the people that are not of good will?

Mudge: Backtracking, reverse hacking is a relatively tricky area. Based upon the route to the antiquated protocols that you're dealing with, there's not a tremendous amount of information as to where things came from, just that they came. It's kinda like, you know, giving confession to a priest, you have this big blind in between you and you're just hoping and trusting that the person is actually there listening to you and that they can do anything about it you.

Space Rogue: ... no return address and nothing inside, you receive something but there's no way to know where it came from.

Senator Glenn: Okay! That's what I'm afraid of. Mr. Neumann is still here and I think his answer when I asked, is a secure system possible? That could not be hacked, I think his answer was he didn't think so. Do you gentlemen agree with that? Do you think a system can be designed that would be foolproof that we could use for defense and for key elements such as the northeast grid or our financial, the Federal Reserve or whatever is it possible to design a foolproof system?

Space Rogue: I don't think it's possible to design a foolproof system, but I don't think that should be the goal. The goal should be to make it very difficult to get in. The more difficult you make it, the less risk you assume from someone, foreign nation state or teenage kid, from breaking into that system. So that the goal is to raise the bar and then have a plan to reconstitute after that fact if it does happen.

Senator Glenn: Mr. Neumann, I think maybe you're in power distribution, I think you said so. Can you blow a computer? Can you overpower it? Can you put enough material in it and just blow it? You don't need to worry about getting the material up for fouling up and just put it in and blow up the computer. Can you do that?

Stefan Von Neumann: Not so much an issue of blowing a computer, destroying it over powerline, there's high-energy radio frequency, there's EMP they can do that from means other than a powerline. Maybe more of a concern would be interruption of power. We were in the course of one of our investigations, able to use a power interruption that was nothing to do with us, it happened to be — but to our benefit. A power interruption that was and deliberate could be.

Other Member: I want to think so much of overpowering, so many high-power electric currents coming in, I was thinking of getting in and fouling up circuits in such a way that will dump its programming and things like that, can you do that?

Stefan Von Neumann: Yes! Mudge care talk about buffer overflow?

Mudge: I think what, maybe they're talking a bit more about bit shifting in. There's been a tremendous amount of improvement in actual analysis of cryptographic protocols by bombarding with X-rays to actually flip bits inside. The trick is to be able to control this little black box and watch the information you're sending in and the information that you getting out from it. As you change it — even if you don't necessarily know what you're changing, precisely. Buffer overflows are extremely common coding problem. Many of the problems that are out there, that contribute to this lack of security are extremely simple, buffer overflows are spotable in source code by a first-year college computer programmer, by people without any sort of college computer programming skills. The notion of race conditions where there's a certain amount of time between what I tell you, something in between what you tell another senator that I could go in and change that information, so Senator Lieberman believes that you said something else. These are all very straightforward problems, they weren't addressed because computers really came out of a tremendous amount of fun and joy in research and exploration, they didn't think about the commercial ramifications and aspects. Probably didn't answer the question at all there.

Senator Glenn: You may want to run for public office one day. — Blew my whole train of thought ... I know what it was. Little just a while ago Mr. Neumann was here about would it be possible to set up a whole different system for defense, for intelligence matters, for a CIA, for NSA, for people doing very highly classified work that we don't want out. Would there be an advantage to us funding and setting up a whole separate system and how long would it be invulnerable if we did such a thing? Is it worth the effort to be very expensive to do it? How would we … Would it be worth doing?

Mudge: One of the things that was said earlier was, there are no easy answers, maybe not any answers at all. But what I believe is there are answers, they're just quite painful. Yes! I think that is one of the ways to do it. Several the agencies within the government currently do that. It is very expensive. If you had extremely sensitive information, you do not trust it with other networks that are less sensitive, that are less trusted. The actual computer systems can be made to be relatively secure, the physical hardware in it becomes very costly, it's cost-benefit … the analysis that you end up doing here. The software can be improved upon, the software doesn't have to be fantastic. One of the things that strikes me is there's a tremendous amount up interest in the year 2000 problem and every time I hear it, I have to sit back, and I chuckle to myself because we're worried about the year 2000 when the systems crash but they're crashing left and right right now and nobody cares. The systems, you can work with them right now. They do crash, I mean, how many times has somebody in here run Windows and had to reboot it or a Macintosh? I mean, left and right they still work. If you put them in a secluded room, put a guy with a gun next to it and don't let it talk to other systems its relatively secure.

Senator Glenn: I'm not quite sure what we'd do if we required the computer industry to do something. You say there are no incentives for the industry to do much, I'm not quite sure what they do, this is like some people may want to buy the equivalent of a Model T Ford, or buy a tiny car, other where people want to buy more security and so they buy a great bigger ... Lot of people going to — now because they are bigger and heavier show less fatalities in an accident, things like that. You can have different levels that people want to go. How would you go about the computer industry? What would you require them to do that would make this program better or would it just be making government agencies and people know that if they're gonna go to certain types of information or banks or the federal, whatever, that they have to buy a computer that is upgraded to a certain level and we should be much more cognizant of these security levels when you purchase a secure a computer than ever before, that's kind of like the — statement but you know what I'm driving at, I think. How do we regulate this? I'm not sure we could.

Weld Pond: Actually in the industry now, Microsoft sort of does the Model T in another car. For example, they have windows which this so the Model T that's for your individual user at home, and they have Windows NT, which is a more secure system. The problem is, it's just more secure doesn't mean it is really good enough for doing what you to say is a secure system that's good enough. And the problem is they, you know, we get back to we have no liability in the ... to say our, you know, it doesn't work, sorry we'll fix in the next release. They don't have any way of telling you, the customer, or no one really does, that I know of ... what they did to make this system secure. You can't say show me your security architecture, show me the development process that went through and looked for the problems and show me that the system is secure. No one's doing that, no one's really selling a commercial product that does that, that can assure you the buyer that you are buying the Cadillac with the bulletproof glass. So no one's really selling that and no one's really assuring anyone, that, that's true.

Space Rogue: ... Microsoft is just saying trust us, and there's really no way to test the product to find if in fact it is secure by the end user or the consumer. So, unlike the Cadillac with the bulletproof glass, you can go up and you can look at the glass to see how thick it is. You can't do that with software.

Senator Glenn: My time is running up, we don't have lights here. Just one more question here. What seem to me, maybe all of our concern and maybe this overstate, our concern about whether people get in, have access or can manipulate the system and transfers something to another spot or something maybe this isn't our biggest danger maybe it's, Stefan's thing over here, when you just get anyone to do harm to our country or just get in fact blow the computer or do the transfers as you said about by X-ray or whatever it is, and you've dialed up the whole thing irretrievably, rather than going in and trying to manipulate the system, is that, should our biggest worry be in this area? It would seem to me that, that might be something that'd be easier to protect against than all this getting in and fouling up some specific software program. Is that? Or am I over-optimistic?

Stefan Von Neumann: It's much simpler for someone to perform a deniable service than it is to change the data and insert their own or to, to manipulate …

Other Member: — You'd know it when it happens, that's for sure?

Stefan Von Neumann: Yes! Much less expensive to do that kind of damage and much simpler. Easier to prevent against? Perhaps and perhaps more straightforward in the short term to harden the major network access points, to the extent of military facility. TEMPEST making more TEMPEST-proof facilities.

Senator Glenn: Or X-ray-proof shielings, something like that.

Stefan Von Neumann: Yeah! Maybe simpler in the short term.

Kingpin: There is documentation on that. And it is possible to shut down the sheens with the high energy. Protecting against it has been done, it is done, and it's fairly simple. You can basically include something in a giant metal box, which will prevent the, you know, the outside. Or if, I don't know if that's done a lot inside the government, some military computers need to be TEMPEST proof.

Brian Oblivion: Think I was just going to say that the box needs to be grounded.

Kingpin: Yes! They should be grounded. Thank you.

John Tan: One of the things I think is coming out here is, got to do with the … it's not just the encryption, the strong encryption, it's not just the Network or the operating system. It's all these things have to be applied across the board in order for one person to actually have enough responsibility. To be able to tackle the problems themselves, they have to be in an environment where there are others, not only in their own industry but in other industries that are trying to raise that bar so as a whole the security goes up.

Senator Lieberman: Thanks, Mr. Chairman. Thanks to all of you. Senator Thompson indicated that somebody referred to your group as rock stars of the new computer age. It's probably not what you came to hear, but I think you're performing an act of very good citizenship, and I appreciate it. I'd compare you, I hope you don't mind I'm not gonna call you rock stars, I'd compare you more to Rachel Carson, who's sounded some real warnings about what environmental pollution was doing to the environment and in the defense context you may be modern-day Paul Reveres, except in this case it's not the British coming. We all know who's coming, that's the problem. Yeah! Well, the chairman's question before was — I mean you are obviously very bright and very creative and work at this, but if there's anything we have learned to the modern age, is that you don't, you cannot, particularly in this age, particularly because the computers where knowledge and information travel so quickly, just as you have been able to do this at L0pht. There could be, there're people all around the world who are able to do this, and they may not be good citizens. They may be up for higher to people who don't wish to swirl. So I appreciate what you doing and I must say in this regard, it may be the appropriate metaphor here, not Chernobyl but unfortunately Oklahoma City, where if we looked at it we would've understood as some did that there was real vulnerability. But we didn't do anything about it, and I think that's what you're telling us, and I hope we can continue to work with you to try to raise our guard. I think the other thing you've helped me to understand is that there is no such thing that's absolute secure, nothing, no system is foolproof. I think what you said is that the aim here should be to make it more difficult to break the system, to infiltrate it. — There never has been absolute security, I suppose it's just that the consequence of insecurity in an age in which we're also reliant on computers, are more consequential, they're more massive, they are more widespread. Let me ask you a couple of questions following up on that thing of accepting that there's no, no system is foolproof. You've said here in your testimony that, given thirty minutes, you might be able to render the Internet unusable, not forever obviously but for some period of time. What can we do, what can the system do, what can the government do, what can private do, what can folks do to try to protect against that?

Mudge: The one method of doing that, that we were referencing, there are several, there are dozens of them actually, but this is a good example; you can prevent and you can stop that particular attack from happening however, the nature of the Internet and the companies that are providing the long haul backbone connections of it is to move the information as quickly as possible across that because that's money. Every packet, millions of packets go by a second is worth a little bit of money if you even stop to look at the packets, you have to send slightly less than your maximum capacity might be, in which case your competitor, now has an edge on you because they can offer faster more efficient service. So in order to protect yourself you very slightly I know one millisecond per packet, degrade service but that definitely cascades into a noticeable financial hit which the companies aren't willing to take, so they remain vulnerable.

Senator Lieberman: Let me just compare things and go to you Stefan Von Neumann. You talked about your work in utility systems. Let me ask you just to compare, for instance today — said who talked about said ten or fifteen years ago somebody wanted to do damage to utilities system could cut wires, could if they were more aggressive, blow up a power station, substation. So compere that, the effects, something more primitive like that from somebody with hostile intent to the possibilities that you envision in the new world.

Stefan Von Neumann: It could be more well times or more specific of an impact, I mean, where the detonation of an explosive in a substation could take down entire grid, where specific computer control of an area, you may be able to interrupt only one customer service say if there was commercial entity that was a target. That one commercial entity or that one government building could become the denied of electric service, or water service, or whatever this utility service was that was going to benefit the attacker.

Off Camera: Computer service?

… Yes! Exactly. So, in the past where it simply was destruction it might not have had the specific focus on the attack point but now it allows that.

Space Rogue: I think another issue is, if somebody goes out and cuts the line of a place, we send in the repairman to fix the line and we're all set, you blow up a building, we rebuild it. If we attack the computer systems, how do we reconstitute from that? There are no plans in place right now to recover from that.

Stefan Von Neumann: And there may be no way to anticipate the follow-up. If there's an attack, a physical attack, an explosion against or a line cutting then there can be increased security in that area on those same facility so the same thing wouldn't happen again. If it's a computer issue, I mean the attacker could be sufficiently skilled that they could simply change their methods slightly and go around any defense that's put up in the place of the first tech.

Senator Lieberman: And the ability to find the attacker would be compromised and will be harder to find the attacker.

Stefan Von Neumann: Simply because the nature of the Internet as it is with the no authentication, no proof of where you are, or who you are.

Space Rogue: In your line cutting analogy, the guy who snips the wire, maybe somebody saw him and we can track him through witness. If he comes in over the Internet and attacks the computer systems, you don't know where it came from and nobody saw him.

Senator Lieberman: Final question. Somebody used a VW example and it's an interesting one, you know as you said, three cars show some signs of the impact of the — the effect, the recall eighty-five-hundred of the new beetles that they sold in the US. And as you should correctly, so as I know, the three indications of hacking into a system and nobody is under obligation to do it. I haven't a looked at this in a while, but the automobile companies, the recalls are not motivated simply by, let use the term here "good citizenship," there's law and there is the fear of liability. So, this is complicated area, and as Dr. Neumann said, we have to be real careful not to jump too quickly without thinking about it, but is there a way in which we should be setting some standards here? I mean for instance, very simplistic standard would be to require our systems operators or service providers or manufacturers to give public notice over instances of hacking, successful hacking into their system.

Mudge: Or this public notice of vulnerabilities that they found their system, this is definitely a double-edged sword because when you give the information out, other people can figure out how to exploit it. However, if you don't give the information out, the people out there can't protect themselves; I think we've tried it, the route where we have kept the information secret, the computer emergency response team at Carnegie Mellon does that I think, and I know a whole bunch of people in the commuter industry agree with me on this that they've become more detrimental than beneficial by a long shot, couple words of encouragement from right behind me. Full disclosure is very important and you have to educate people. Education is one of the largest things that's really missing out of this. If I'm an administrator and there's a problem in what I have to control but the companies don't let me know about it, I can't be expected to fix it. Even if the companies don't have a fix themselves, if I know of the problem, I might be able to put other things in place in front of it so I can catch it, I might have a different setup. Not everybody has the exact same setup...

Weld Pond: You might disconnect your system from the network.

Mudge: Yeah! I might say, hey! That's really bad I need to get off of there right now. But I'd be able to do that.

Stefan Von Neumann: I'd go one further, not only to point out the flaws but also to point out the inner workings this may be rehashing some of the well-known but the unix environment being around for many years being public being able to be examined has mostly fixes on quite well-known Microsoft Windows NT, all their code is completely hidden from public eyes, they don't release it. Has as been said, a black box to the public even if even if an end user wanted to go and look inside the internals of say, Windows NT, they're not allowed to, it's illegal, according to the software licensing put forth by Microsoft, to disassemble to try and reverse engineering that kind of a limitation is just putting the brakes on investigation of the flaws.

Senator Lieberman: Good comparison to close. I wanna thank you again. This is another classic example of what we find very often, who undecided as lawmakers which is that we see a problem we want to make it better weak kind of play law, but this isn't an area of very developed expertise, which most of us don't have. So, we rely, we often rely on science and on the people who have more expertise and then try to make the best judgment we can. I, in thinking I really want, I know you've already, you to go your day jobs and night vocations. But to the extent that you find time, I really ask you request you think about what the government, we as lawmakers, if anything, I mean, it maybe that you want to come back and say you're only going to mess it up here. What we might do through law to deal with some of the, to protect ourselves from some of the vulnerabilities that you've identified. Thanks very much.

Senator Thompson: Thank you very much for being here with us today. I like that Senator Lieberman thinks that you are performing a valuable service to your country and we appreciate that, and want you to continue to help us. I think the liability question is a very good one, I wonder for example whether or not it's a matter of laws, whether or not there are already laws under the common law, under state laws, the law of —, law of negligence and fraud, Uniform Commercial Code and all those things. The first time some big company has been compromised because of this, that it may fix itself because it'll be a massive lawsuit and everybody will wonder why we didn't address this in the beginning, but the fascinating issues and, you know, you've pointed out that our computer security is virtually a nonexistent and how easy it is to obtain sensitive information and shutdown liable governmental operations and we going to have to do something about it, it is that simple.

ENDNOTES

1. Jen Ellis and Trey Ford were then employees of the internet security company Rapid7 and were doing a lot of important policy work. They had organized this training session for Hill staffers.

2. https://en.wikipedia.org/wiki/Osborne_1

3. Of course, now, thirty-five-plus years later, I want nothing more than to go back.
   https://www.azquotes.com/quote/795209

4. Jason Scott has attempted to compile a listing of every BBS that has ever existed.
   http://bbslist.textfiles.com/support/introduction.html

5. Only recently did I make the connection between IMF and the Impossible Mission Force, the independent espionage agency from the *Mission Impossible* TV and movie franchise.

6. Katie Hafner, *Cyberpunk: Outlaws and Hackers on The Computer Frontier* (Simon & Schuster, 1991).

7. Vernor Vinge, *True Names* (Dell Publishing, 1981).
   https://en.wikipedia.org/wiki/True_Names

8. https://en.wikipedia.org/wiki/Operation_Sundevil

9. https://en.wikipedia.org/wiki/Computer_Fraud_and_Abuse_Act

10. https://en.wikipedia.org/wiki/Electronic_Communications_Privacy_Act

11. https://en.wikipedia.org/wiki/Stored_Communications_Act

12. https://en.wikipedia.org/wiki/Enhanced_9-1-1

13. https://en.wikipedia.org/wiki/Steve_Jackson_Games#Raid_by_
the_Secret_Service

14. *Computer Underground Digest*, Volume 4, Issue 57, November
11, 1992.
https://www.2600.com/secret/pc/pc-cud.html

15. William Gibson, *Count Zero* (Victor Gollancz Ltd, 1986).

16. Steven Levy, Hackers: Heroes of the Computer Revolution
(Doubleday, 1984).

17. https://w1mx.mit.edu/flea-at-mit/

18. Hyper Text Markup Language, the format of basic web pages.

19. File Transfer Protocol, a method of transferring files from one
computer to the other via the Internet.

20. Window Snyder and Frank Swiderski, *Threat Modeling*
(Microsoft Press, 2004).

21. Annaliza Savage, "Unauthorized Access," December 1, 1994.
https://archive.org/details/UnauthorizedAccess

22. TBS, "CyberMania '94," November 5, 1994.
https://www.youtube.com/watch?v=Af9M8llS9JA

23. CollegeHumor, "Bleep Bloop: Cybermania '94," June 12, 2013.
https://www.youtube.com/watch?v=ggqjjoZov7s

24. Net Café, 1996.
https://www.youtube.com/watch?v=xP0tPxAgInY

25. New England Cable News, March 20, 1997.
    https://youtu.be/P5j7chCzzPA?t=464

26. I didn't know it at the time, but evidently, this was borrowed
    from Steve Jobs, who said it in an interview in 1985. David Sheff,
    "Playboy Interview: Steven Jobs," *Playboy*, February 1985, 59.
    https://allaboutstevejobs.com/verbatim/interviews/playboy_1985

27. *Wired*, "The L0pht," August 1996, 42.

28. New England Cable News, March 20, 1997.
    https://www.youtube.com/watch?v=69eQ6S6Ev1M

29. "The NewsHour with Jim Lehrer," May 8, 1998, NewsHour
    Productions, American Archive of Public Broadcasting (WGBH
    and the Library of Congress), Boston, MA and Washington DC,
    accessed January 3, 2020.
    http://americanarchive.org/catalog/cpb-aacip_507-x639z9185k

30. New England Cable News.
    https://www.youtube.com/watch?v=69eQ6S6Ev1M

31. A digital datalink system for transmission of short, relatively
    simple messages between aircraft and ground stations via radio
    or satellite.

32. HOPE 2000, "MTV - How did it happen," July 14, 2000.
    https://www.youtube.com/watch?v=cu1p4my0Ag8

33. https://en.wikipedia.org/wiki/Class-4_telephone_switch

34. Filter Fresh Coffee Advisory, January 14, 1997.
    https://web.archive.org/web/20200225165435/https://
    dl.packetstormsecurity.net/unix-humor/telnet.coffe.machine.html

35. https://en.wikipedia.org/wiki/Netcat

36. Kris Holt, "Microsoft is merging its Windows and hardware teams," Engadget, Associated Press, February 6, 2020. https://www.engadget.com/2020/02/05/microsoft-windows-hardware-panos-panay-office-teams/

37. Jerod Pore, "Cyberpunk Technical Journal," *Wired*, January 1, 1994. https://web.archive.org/web/20161220214113/https://www.wired.com/1994/01/cyberpunk-technical-journal/

38. *2600 Magazine* Vol 13, 1996, 49. https://books.google.com/books?id=ciE9AQAAIAAJ&pg=PA49&q=Whacked+Mac+Archives

39. Kevin Collier, "More Men Accuse Proto-Hacker "Cap'n Crunch" Of Inappropriate Sexual Contact," *BuzzFeed*, December 8, 2017. https://www.buzzfeednews.com/article/kevincollier/more-men-accuse-proto-hacker-capn-crunch-of-inappropriate

40. Beyond HOPE, "The L0pht (Complete)" August 9, 1997. https://www.youtube.com/watch?v=IHhniy9zPoQ

41. Matthew W. Granade, "Blast Kills One, Downs Power In Cambridge" *Harvard Crimson*, August 8, 1997. https://www.thecrimson.com/article/1997/8/8/blast-kills-one-downs-power-in/

42. Kelly Jackson Higgins, "Who Invented the Firewall?," *Dark Reading*, January 15, 2008. https://www.darkreading.com/who-invented-the-firewall/d/d-id/1129238

43. Nate King, "How security market needs transformed Network

Flight Recorder," *TechTarget*, Jul7 27, 2017.
https://searchsecurity.techtarget.com/feature/How-security-
market-needs-transformed-Network-Flight-Recorder

44. Y Combinator, May 28, 2018.
https://news.ycombinator.com/item?id=17170095

45. Dildog, Twitter.
https://web.archive.org/web/20211118153934/https://twitter.
com/dildog/status/1438588719074881540

46. "NFR and L0pht to Deliver Improved IDS," *InfoSec News*,
March 2, 1999.
https://web.archive.org/web/20070510014025/http://www.
infosecnews.org/hypermail/9903/1502.html

47. Ellen Messemer, "Check Point to acquire NFR Security,"
Network World, December 19, 2006.
https://www.networkworld.com/article/2302247/check-point-
to-acquire-nfr-security.html

48. http://supremelaw.org

49. [L0pht Advisory] "MacOS - FWB passwords easily bypassed"
BugTraq, October 30, 1998.
https://seclists.org/bugtraq/1998/Oct/235

50. Hobbit, "CIFS: Common Insecurities Fail Scrutiny," January 1997.
http://www.cs.miami.edu/home/burt/learning/Csc524.031/
workbook/cifs.pdf

51. A one-way mathematical function used to map data of an
arbitrary size to a bit array of a fixed size. Hashing a password
should result in a string of characters that should be impossible

to convert back to the original password.

52. A random value inserted into a hashing algorithm to make attacks such as brute forcing or the use of rainbow tables infeasible.

53. Jeremy Allison, "Windows NT password hash retrieval," Insecure.org, March 22, 1997. https://insecure.org/sploits/WinNT.passwordhashes. deobfuscation.html

54. Larry Lange, "'Hack' punches hole in Microsoft NT security," *EE Times*, March 31, 1997. https://web.archive.org/web/19981201072421/http://techweb. cmp.com/eet/news/97/947news/hack.html

55. Andy Greenberg, "He Perfected a Password Hacking Tool - Then The Russians Came Calling," *Wired*, November 11, 2009. https://web.archive.org/web/20190713095310/https://www. wired.com/story/how-mimikatz-became-go-to-hacker-tool/

56. https://en.wikipedia.org/wiki/Petya_(malware)

57. Jonathan Wilkins, "ANNOUNCE : NTCrack v1.0," BugTraq, March 27, 1997. https://seclists.org/bugtraq/1997/Mar/99

58. "Microsoft's Response to the EE Times Article on Windows NT Security," Microsoft.com, April 1, 1997. http://www.microsoft.com/security/eetimes2.htm

59. "L0pht Advisory: release of L0phtCrack for NT," BugTraq, April 11, 1997. https://seclists.org/bugtraq/1997/Apr/27

60. Larry Lange, "Enhancements to Windows NT 'hack' could cause more problems," *EE Times*, captured December 6, 1998. https://web.archive.org/web/19981206114812/http://pubs. cmpnet.com/eet/news/97/948news/enhance.html

61. Larry Lange, "Hackers keep the heat on Windows NT security," captured December 5, 1998. https://web.archive.org/web/19981205132055/http://pubs. cmpnet.com:80/eet/news/97/950news/hackers.html

62. Larry Lange, "Microsoft Opens Dialogue With NT Hackers," *EE Times*, Jul7 15, 1997. https://web.archive.org/web/20200207172327/https://www. blackhat.com/media/bh-usa-97/black-hat-eetimes-3.html

63. Larry Lange, "The Rise of the Underground Engineer," *EE Times*, September 22, 1997. https://web.archive.org/web/20200207172320/https://www. blackhat.com/media/bh-usa-97/blackhat-eetimes.html

64. Hobbit, "CIFS: Common Insecurities Fail Scrutiny," January 1997. http://www.cs.miami.edu/home/burt/learning/Csc524.031/ workbook/cifs.pdf

65. Bill Gates, "Trustworthy Computing," *Wired*, January 15, 2002. https://web.archive.org/web/20200107080951/https://www. wired.com/2002/01/bill-gates-trustworthy-computing/

66. Pond Weld, "00 Passwords 2015 Keynote 1: Chris Wysopal," December 15, 2015. https://youtu.be/1wh3z2KYJcM

67. Dan Goodin, "Seminal password tool rises from Symantec ashes,"

May 27, 2009.
https://www.theregister.com/2009/05/27/l0phtcrack_returns/

68. Rene Millman, "New version of L0phtCrack makes cracking Windows passwords easier than ever," September 1, 2016. https://web.archive.org/web/20170608230628/https://www. scmagazineuk.com/new-version-of-l0phtcrack-makes-cracking-windows-passwords-easier-than-ever/article/530687/

69. Terahash, "Terahash Acquires L0phtCrack," April 21, 2020. https://web.archive.org/web/20200421191549/https://terahash. com/news/terahash-acquires-l0phtcrack.htm

70. "Changes for L0phtCrack," July 1, 2021. https://web.archive.org/web/20210923170826/https:// l0phtcrack.gitlab.io/

71. Eduard Kovacs, "Password Auditing Tool L0phtCrack Released as Open Source," October 18, 2021. https://web.archive.org/web/20211019171506/https://www. securityweek.com/password-auditing-tool-l0phtcrack-released-open-source

72. FBI, "Solar Sunrise: Dawn of a New Threat," 1999. https://archive.org/details/Solar_Sunrise_Dawn_Of_A_New_Threat_NIPC_1999_Tape

73. Reuters, "China: We're Only Human," October 26, 1998. https://www.wired.com/1998/10/china-were-only-human/

74. Niall McKay, "Crackers Attack China on Rights," Wired.com, October 27, 1998. https://www.wired.com/1998/10/crackers-attack-china-on-rights/

75. James Glave, "Crackers: We Control Your TVs," Wired.com, July 20, 1998. https://web.archive.org/web/19981207022013/https://www.wired.com/news/news/technology/story/13838.html

76. Niall McKay, "China: The Great Firewall," Wired.com, December 1, 1998. https://www.wired.com/1998/12/china-the-great-firewall/

77. BBC News, "China sentences bank hackers to death," December 29, 1998. https://web.archive.org/web/20130823064341/http://news.bbc.co.uk/2/hi/asia-pacific/244202.stm

78. Mary Lisbeth D'Amico, "Hackers spar over cyber war on Iraq, China," CNN 199.01.13 http://www.cnn.com/TECH/computing/9901/13/cyberwar.idg/

79. Chris Stokel-Walker and Dan Milmo, "'It's the right thing to do': the 300,000 volunteer hackers coming together to fight Russia," *Guardian*, March 15, 2022. https://www.theguardian.com/world/2022/mar/15/volunteer-hackers-fight-russia

80. Space Rogue, "Hackers and Media Hype: Big Hacks That Never Really Happened," August 27, 2012. https://www.youtube.com/watch?v=gCqSH_0AXuY

81. U.S. Senate, Computer Security in the Federal Government and the Private Sector: Hearings Before the Subcommittee on Oversight of Government Management of the Committee on Governmental Affairs, United States Senate, Ninety-Eighth Congress, First Session, S. Hrg. ;98-440 iv, 504 p. (Washington: U.S. G.P.O., 1983)

https://books.google.com/books?id=udt_2nGyANIC&pg=
PA22&source=gbs_toc_r&cad=3#v=onepage&q&f=false

82. Emmanuel Goldstein.
http://groups.csail.mit.edu/mac/classes/6.805/assorted-short-
pieces/goldstein-markey.html

83. Diana Goovaerts "DoD, DoJ press FCC for industry-wide BGP
security standard," Fierce Telecom September 16, 2022.
https://www.fiercetelecom.com/telecom/dod-doj-press-fcc-
industry-wide-bgp-security-standard

84. *Late Night with Conan O'Brien*, May 20, 1998.
https://www.youtube.com/watch?v=qS6UoJu3lbg

85. *The NewsHour with Jim Lehrer,* August 5, 1998, NewsHour
Productions, American Archive of Public Broadcasting (WGBH
and the Library of Congress), Boston, MA and Washington,
DC, accessed January 3, 2020.
http://americanarchive.org/catalog/cpb-aacip_507-x639z9185k

86. Internet Security Firm Promotes Safe E-Commerce, CNN
February 9, 2000.
https://web.archive.org/web/20200207002313/http://edition.
cnn.com/TRANSCRIPTS/0002/09/tod.01.html

87. Brian Fonseca "Odd coupling links hackers with security firm,"
InfoWorld, January 7, 2000.
https://web.archive.org/web/20041116162703/http://www.
infoworld.com/articles/ic/xml/00/01/07/000107icstake.html

88. Space Rogue, "Hackers need not apply," Space Rogue Blog,

December 11, 2009.

https://www.spacerogue.net/wordpress/?p=191

89. Rob Rosenburger, "White House reveals Mudge's true identity," March 1, 2000

http://web.archive.org/web/20110521015841/http://vmyths. com/column/1/2000/3/1/

90. "@stake Names CEO to Lead Rapidly Growing Internet Security Services Firm," @stake, February 14, 2000.

https://web.archive.org/web/20000819004151/http://www. atstake.com/events_news/press_releases/ceo.html

91. "@stake Announces Appointment of Chief Financial Officer, Chief People Officer and Executive Vice President of Worldwide Sales," @stake, May 10, 2000.

https://web.archive.org/web/20000819004140/http://www. atstake.com/events_news/press_releases/execs.html

92. Joshua Quittner, "Hacker Homecoming," *Time Magazine*, January 25,1995. https://web.archive.org/web/20071013173246/ http://www.time.com/time/magazine/article/0,9171,982254,00.html

93. Mark Abene, "Off The Hook," September 5, 2000.

https://archive.org/details/wbai-2600-off-the-hook-2000-09-05

94. Dan Geer, *"CyberInsecurity: The Cost of Monopoly,"* September 23, 2003.

https://www.schneier.com/essays/archives/2003/09/ cyberinsecurity_the.html

95. Dan Verton, "Fired @stake CTO Says Microsoft Critique Was

'Business as Usual'," October 3, 2003.
https://ithealthcare.computerworld.com/article/2572299/fired--
stake-cto-says-microsoft-critique-was--business-as-usual-.html

96. https://www.msn.com/en-us/money/companies/twitter-is-
facing-a-truly-grave-threat-e2-80-94from-a-man-called-e2-80-
9cmudge-e2-80-9d/ar-AA110YSa

97. IMDB.com, November 23, 2019.
https://www.imdb.com/name/nm2706174/

98. Craig Timberg, "A Disaster Foretold – And Ignored,"
Washington Post, July 22, 2015.
https://www.washingtonpost.com/sf/business/2015/06/22/net-
of-insecurity-part-3/

99. https://www.spacerogue.net/wordpress/?p=655

100. https://about.google/intl/ALL_us/appsecurity/

101. Joshua Lawrence Chamberlain, "Chamberlain's Address for the
20th Maine Monument at Gettysburg," American Battlefield
Trust, October 3, 1889.
https://www.battlefields.org/learn/primary-sources/
chamberlains-address-20th-maine-monument-gettysburg

ABOUT THE AUTHOR

With over two decades of experience, Space Rogue (Cris Thomas) has testified before the U.S. Senate Committee on Homeland Security and Governmental Affairs, and has been interviewed by Wired, CNBC and even MTV. He created the wildly popular websites the Whacked Mac Archives and Cyber Squirrel 1. He produced the weekly podcast SpiderLabs Radio, and the critically acclaimed weekly news video program the Hacker News Network. His writing has appeared in Network Computing, New Statesman, The Hill, and the Christian Science Monitor. He has spoken at security conferences such as Def Con, Blackhat, and Shmoocon. Space Rogue currently works as the Global Lead of Policy and Special Initiatives for the legendary IBM X-Force.

Printed in Great Britain
by Amazon

18811144R00208